To:

George Wray

Best wishes —

Remember Coeur De Lene —

Frank Blair —

LET'S BE FRANK ABOUT IT

By FRANK BLAIR
with Jack Smith

DOUBLEDAY & COMPANY, INC.
GARDEN CITY, NEW YORK
1979

ISBN: 0-385-11493-1
Library of Congress Catalog Card Number 76-53411

Dedicated to Lil
and all who helped
me make my way
in a career fraught with pitfalls

INTRODUCTION
By Lowell Thomas

WHEN FRANK BLAIR asked whether someday would I do an Introduction to the book he was writing, I of course said I would do so. After all, Frank has been one of the outstanding personalities of this electronic radio-TV era. Is there anyone who didn't hear him on the popular NBC "Today" show? Even so, when his manuscript was sent to me, I suppose my subconscious thought was, well, here we go again. In other words, I was all set to read a chapter or two and then write an "Intro." However, when I read Frank Blair's first page, I was lured on to the second and then the third, and soon found myself swept along by his intimate personal story.

I'm sure Frank and a host of my other colleagues are constantly asked the question by young people: "How can I get started in the communications world?" If the number of times and the way this question is put to me are any indications of young people's goals and interests today, there are many thousands who will be especially interested in Frank Blair's autobiography in which he tells *how to*—and in detail.

As for me, I've never been able to give a satisfactory answer vi

to those who put the question to me. I didn't start out with any desire to become a news commentator or have anything to do with radio. (At the time the term "newscaster" hadn't been invented.) I was sort of lassoed and pushed into it without knowing what it was all about. The story of this is in the first volume of my own autobiography *Good Evening Everybody.* Once I did arrive on the air, over a period of nearly half a century I had one sponsor for sixteen years and another for twenty.

Frank on the other hand, has had a far wider variety of experience—as an announcer, a station manager, a newsman, an executive in nearly every department, and he has had scores of sponsors. He knows the game from every standpoint— knows it better than anyone I have encountered.

So Frank Blair's story should be read by all the hundreds of thousands who would like to get into this exciting field that offers fame and fortune. Furthermore, he tells about it in a way that will hold and fascinate not only those who would like to emulate him but also the endless millions who have followed him over the years, and to whom he is almost a part of the family.

Doing Introductions to books written by friends has been one of my hobbies. The first one I ever did probably has been read by more people than anything ever to emerge from my typewriter, this in spite of the fact that I am listed as the author of fifty-five books (including worldwide best sellers, such as *With Lawrence in Arabia, Count Luckner the Sea Devil, The First World Flight,* and so on). That first Introduction was for Dale Carnegie's *How to Win Friends and Influence People,* which we are told has had wider distribution than any book except the Bible. So I hope Frank Blair's superbly told personal story will ultimately reach as many readers as Dale Carnegie's *How to Win Friends* . . .

THE ALARM CLOCK went off at four-thirty that wintry morning, and while I struggled to get my eyes open, Lil reached over and touched my arm, the warm, familiar touch of love.

"Wake up, hon," she said. "It's your day."

I kissed her, and she slipped into her dressing gown and went off to the kitchen to start the coffee.

I got out of bed and stepped over to the window. Our apartment was on the nineteenth floor of Plaza 400, a forty-two-story residential building off Sutton Place. Below me, the city spread out in a myriad of blinking lights. I heard a siren scream. The town looked beautiful—but menacing. Few people would willingly venture alone onto those deserted streets at that hour. That was New York, my town for nearly a quarter of a century, a place of excitement and glamor and lately of danger. For me, though, much of the excitement had gone and the glamor had worn off. Once it had titillated my ego to be at the center of things, reporting the news to millions, interviewing the great men and women of the time, rubbing shoulders with the stars. Now I was glad to be getting away.

As I had every morning for so many years, I listened to an all-news radio station while I showered and shaved and gulped my coffee Lil made for me. My transistor went with me from room to room. The news still had its fascination for me but on that day—March 14, 1975—there was a quality of sameness about it that I had become more and more aware of over the past several years. Secretary of State Kissinger had arrived in Israel with a new set of Egyptian peace proposals, the United States had resumed its airlift to Phnom Penh, and President Ford was calling for tax cuts. Hearing it all on station WINS, I had a feeling of *déjà vu* and I wondered if I had lost whatever spark I once had.

But I still could not switch off that transistor. After forty years in newscasting, I still had the urge to hear what story would come next. I was addicted to the news, and of course I had an important, practical need to hear it, anyway. I did not want to arrive at 30 Rockefeller Plaza that morning without having a jump on the job—without knowing at least the high point of the news stories I would have to deal with. Preliminary homework was much in order. My last day would be rough in the best of circumstances; however eager I was to break away, I could not do my last newscast and say good-bye to old friends on the air without feeling a surge of sentiment, which would have to be controlled. I knew it would be a farewell show for me. I did not know the elements of it, but there were sure to be some tugs at the heart strings.

I finished the coffee, and Lil walked me to the door. She kissed me good-bye. In another hour or so, she would join me in the studio. So would a considerable number of our progeny —twenty-one of them, at last count: seven children—husbands and wives—and ten grandchildren. Only our oldest son, Mike, and his three children had been unable to make it. The rest had converged on New York from places around the country. NBC limousines would be plying from hotel to hotel in mid-Manhattan to pick them up and deliver them to 30 Rock to watch the old man's last show. Old Man? Hell! At sixty I had a good many productive years left. Lowell

Thomas, my old friend and mentor, was still going off on skiing holidays in his eighties. There was still so much I wanted to do and could do once I got off the Manhattan merry-go-round.

As I stepped out of the elevator into the main lobby at Plaza 400, the lobster-shift doorman was dozing at the main reception desk, with a copy of the *Daily News* in his hand. Doorman? No. Security guard. The reception desk was a modern version of a sentry box. "Visitors Must Be Announced," the sign said. If they refused, no doubt they would be wrestled to the floor. The tenants of our luxury building, as the management proudly called it, were carefully guarded from the thieves and thugs and rapists of New York, although all of us knew that an occasional armed stranger might slip through the security net. Every apartment door had its sophisticated lock, or locks. Was this what we had worked so hard to get?

"Good morning, Mr. Blair," the doorman said, rousing from his nap. "Your limo is here."

"Morning. And thanks."

Every morning, a big, shiny chauffeur-driven Cadillac picked me up at the door of Plaza 400 and delivered me to the Fiftieth Street entrance of the RCA Building, the only one of four entrances that was kept open through the night—open and well guarded. The limousine was a luxury I enjoyed, but I did not delude myself that NBC provided it out of the goodness of its corporate heart. There was a safety factor involved for the "Today" show. If I chanced to oversleep—God forbid!—and failed to appear at the apartment-house door at the appointed hour, the chauffeur would be right there and he could rout me out; I would still be able to make it to the studio in time for the show.

I stepped out into the cold. A chill March wind hit me.

The chauffeur climbed out of the limousine and held the door.

"Morning, Mr. Błair."

"Morning, Red."

We drove away. The street lights glowed along Second Avenue and the big Cadillac glided noiselessly. The sidewalks were deserted. Traffic was minimal. There were a few taxis abroad, some of the cabbies cruising, some speeding toward the warmth of some all-night coffee shop.

We drew up at the Fiftieth Street entrance of the RCA Building. I thanked the driver, greeted the security guard, and stepped inside, and so began the last day of my twenty-three years on the "Today" show.

The headquarters of NBC News—the newsroom—is an enormous, brightly lighted room the size of an auditorium, with rows of desks for writers and editors. It is certainly one of the few newsrooms in the world with wall-to-wall carpeting. At five in the morning, most of the desks there are unoccupied and the telephones are silent. When I arrived that morning, only a duty manager and the "Today" news staff were at work. My news editor and writers had been there since midnight, and by midnight another news editor had already put in an eight-hour shift, planning and organizing the film coverage that would be brought in from around the country and, by satellite, from around the world. Altogether, by five in the morning, the "Today" news staff had dedicated thirty man-hours of editorial time to the newscasts that would originate in Studio 3K during two hours of the "Today" program. Film and tape had been selected and edited, still pictures had been chosen and captioned, our graphic artists had worked up the maps and charts I would need, and the script for the seven-o'clock newscast had been written and edited, although late bulletins might be inserted. In earlier years, I had written some of the material myself, but as television became more complex and the demands upon me increased, that had become impossible.

I went over the seven-o'clock script (the scripts for the newscasts at seven-thirty, eight, and eight-thirty were still in the mill). I untangled a slightly tortured sentence that I thought might be hard for the viewers to understand, and then I looked up and nodded to News Editor Tom Furey to signify that all seemed in order and I had no questions. As usual, the staff had done a good job. I liked the choice of news and the way it had been handled. It was crisp and straightforward.

"Good luck!" Furey said.

I thanked him.

"And Frank," he said, smiling, "try not to blow it!"

The writers laughed. All four of them—Tom Maccabe, Nick Allen, Denny Dalton and Dale Curran—were old friends and drinking companions of mine. They wished me well.

Tom, I thought, had been teasing to cover up some emotions of his own. We had worked together a long time. He was one of the best.

I picked up the script and walked out of the newsroom for the last time. I made my way down the long, carpeted corridor lined with color photographs of NBC newsmen and newswomen. A few years earlier, the picture of me had suddenly vanished from those walls, and when I noticed the disappearance I wondered for a moment if someone in the executive suite had been trying to tell me something. Apparently, though, the photograph had been stolen by a tourist on an NBC guided tour. A replacement photo had been hung in its stead. Now I wondered how long it would take the brass to order it taken down.

I made my way to makeup. The makeup room at NBC looked like a two-chair barber shop. It was on the third floor, near Studio 3K. Our makeup woman, Barbara Armstrong, greeted me with a smile. I sat down and she did my face again, as she had done on so many mornings over so many years. In the beginning, I thought, I must have been an easy job for her—a few dabs with the powder puffs to take away the sheen, and that was that. But as the years passed she had had to spend more and more time on me, hiding the lines of age. Makeup had always been a bore for me. Once or twice after the show I had been too tired to get the stuff off. It had looked fine, I guess, on camera, but it must have looked weird as I stood at the bar in Hurley's, the neighborhood watering hole where I had wasted so many hours and days of my life.

I said good-bye to Barbara and went out toward Studio 3K, along the crowded corridor that was always cluttered with props for "The Doctors," the soap opera produced in the studio adjoining ours. I made slow progress, because so many people—technicians, cleaning women, Gloria (the woman who kept our coffee urn filled)—so many stopped me to wish me well. I thought to myself, as I often had in the past, that these were people I liked better than some of the stars.

In 3K, where I had done so many thousands of newscasts, I shook hands with the producers and directors and the rest of the cast—Barbara Walters, Jim Hartz, Gene Shalit, and the newscaster NBC had chosen to replace me, Lew Wood, a tall, slim, handsome man who, ironically, only a few years earlier had been let go by the same company that had now hired him for one of the choice news spots in network television. Lew had been well received as the anchorman on the local evening news program on NBC's flagship station,

WNBC-TV, in New York. He had done a good reporting job in Vietnam, and he had been well liked on network radio. But a local news director, (his name, significantly, now long forgotten) had called him in one day and announced that he had no future at the National Broadcasting Company. Lew had made a living for a few years doing commercials, and now he was back at the top. Such was television!

I sat down at the "Today" news desk for the last time. Out on the floor of the studio, under the high-powered lamps shining down from almost every square foot of the ceiling, four cameras were in position and already projecting our images onto the monitors in the control room. Two of the cameras were operated by young women—another sign, I thought, of the changing times. Both of them were top-notch camerapersons.

Associate director Sid Vassal's voice droned out over the studio out speakers:

"Five minutes."

That meant five minutes to air time. I lowered my eyes to my script. I had already gone over it twice, line by line, and if a new story had been slipped in without my knowledge—well, more than thirty years had passed since I first taught myself to sight-read out loud. But still, with all the emotions I felt that morning, a bit more study could only help.

By now, Lil and the children and grandchildren would be arriving in the Green Room, where guests of the show were entertained. Any who had already settled in would be watching me, I thought, on the monitor there.

Our stage manager, Jim Straka, began the final countdown, using the fingers of his upheld hand—five, four, three, two— and then he cued Barbara and the show began. The "Today" sunrise flashed on screens in homes and motel rooms all through the eastern section of the United States. The familiar words rang out:

"Good morning! This is 'Today'! It's Friday, March the fourteenth, and here are the headlines. . . ."

Barbara's voice sounded strong. She seemed confident. Yes, the lady had arrived. She was now our cohost. Ironically, until Frank McGee's death only a year earlier, Executive Producer Stuart Schulberg had not allowed her to read the heads. The judgment had been that she lacked authority and her slight lisp would affect the dignity of the news. Now Barbara led the show.

She told the viewers that this would be a farewell show for Blair, all two hours of it.

"I must warn you," she said, "that we feel a little choked, so if we suddenly say silly things, or laugh hysterically for no reason, it's just a desperate effort to keep from crying out loud."

Barbara's emotion seemed sincere. I had helped her a lot when she had first joined the "Today" staff as a writer. I had promoted one or two of her first on-camera assignments. She had been camera-shy and badly lacking in self-confidence. Now she was a changed woman, needing no help, and if she lacked confidence (sometimes I suspected that she still did) she concealed it admirably. Now she was tough and hard and brash and sometimes even cocky. But perhaps she had had to be. She had fought her own way to the top. There had been a succession of what we used to call " 'Today' girls" before her. Their role had been limited to doing light features and exchanging chitchat with the host and second banana of the show. Barbara, however, had gone from fashion features to interviewing some of the most important figures of our age, including Richard Nixon when he was in the White House. The times had been right for her, of course. The women's-lib movement had gained strength and it had suddenly been in the interests of the networks to give women a break. But Barbara could not have made it without talent and ability and some very, very hard work.

As she went ahead with the opening of the farewell show, Gene Shalit interrupted:

"Whoever has the handkerchief concession in the studio this morning will clean up."

JIM HARTZ: "As usual, Frank will be the coolest one on the show."

If only Jim knew!

Jim introduced me and I began the news.

I don't think there was a quake in my voice, but I assure you my mind wandered during the commercial break midway in that last newscast. The news of Gerry Ford reminded me of the White House and I began thinking of all the time I myself had spent there and of all the Presidents I had known in the past. I remembered introducing Franklin D. Roosevelt to the radio audiences when he gave his Fireside Chats. I remembered covering FDR's news conferences at some of the great moments in history. There were times when I had actually run three blocks through the streets of Washington, from the White House to the studios of Mutual News, to get some of those big news breaks on the 11 A.M. hourly newscast. I recalled dining with Harry Truman and Bess in Kansas. I remembered rushing out to Colorado to cover Dwight Eisenhower after his heart attack, and for a moment, I felt again the sadness and torment that came over me as I reported John F. Kennedy's assassination and funeral. I recalled the way I had inadvertently labeled President Lyndon Johnson as a Republican in a broadcast to millions (Should I have apologized? I never did), and I remembered how grateful I had been for the big favor that Richard and Pat Nixon had done for me before he won the presidency and fell into disgrace.

Sitting there under the lights in 3K, waiting for Jim Straka to cue me to resume the broadcast, I looked over the last stories in my last news script, and thought of some of the big stories I had reported in the past—the outbreak of World War II, the Cold War, Korea, the McCarthy hearings, space, Vietnam, Watergate. The list seemed endless. I had reported a big chunk of history, but now I was approaching my last story. I thought of the people who had been with me on "Today" when some of the great news stories of the past were breaking on our air: John Chancellor, who had been too much of a trench-coat reporter, too serious and dedicated a journalist to be a successful host on a morning show like "Today"; and Edwin Newman, the erudite and versatile Ed who had been called in to replace me as the "Today" newscaster when I served for a time as the show's "second banana." I thought of Dave Garroway, surely one of the greatest showmen of modern times, and of Jack Lescoulie, a man of fine talent who had been kept in Dave's shadow; I remembered Joe Garagiola and his wit, and Hugh Downs, who had started his career as a fifty-dollar-a-week radio announcer (ten times what I had once earned for the same job!) and wound up as one of TV's top personalities. All of them had been good friends, as had most of our " 'Today' girls." I thought of Lee Meriwether, now a TV and movie actress, and Estelle Parsons, now one of the Oscar-winning greats . . . Maureen O'Sullivan, a Hollywood star who just couldn't hack it on live TV, and, of course, Helen O'Connell, who had first captured my heart long years before when I had introduced Jimmy Dorsey's Orchestra to a network radio audience from the stage of the Earle Theater in Washington. Helen—doll-like and lovely—and Bob Eberle had been Jimmy's singing stars.

Sometimes I had thought Lil might be just slightly jealous of Helen. Lil had insisted otherwise. She had told our friends she was proud when other women appeared attracted to her man. Lil had always been confident of my love, and rightly so, and the three of us—Helen and Lil and I—have been firm friends for more than a quarter of a century. There had been many, many " 'Today' girls," but none like Helen.

While I sat there dreaming in 3K, Jim Straka caught my attention and began his last countdown for me. The commercial was ending. I began the last minutes of a career in news that had spanned more than forty years. The first news I had broadcast in 1935 had been news of the Great Depression. Oddly, the final story in my last news script was about Detroit auto workers who had exhausted their unemployment insurance benefits.

I signed off. So far, so good, I thought. There was a lump in my throat, but until that moment, at least, I felt I had justified Jim Hartz's prediction that I would be "the coolest one" on the set.

Then the hard part began. The first of the tributes came up —Bob Hope, on tape, wisecracking that I had been the only man on the block who went to bed before his own kids. Memories of the early days flashed through my mind: driving through snowstorms to get to the studio in the early-morning darkness when I lived in the suburbs, the first struggles to keep the show alive, the boost the ratings got when a chimpanzee joined the cast, the crowds watching from the streets when we produced the program behind the huge windows of the RCA Exhibition Hall, all the great people I had worked with over twenty-three years, men and women struggling for fame and fortune and often achieving both. Most of them had been kindly, earthy people, and many had helped me over the humps. I felt the lump. I wondered how I could get through another hour and forty-five minutes of nostalgia.

The routine called for me to do a second, highly abbreviated newscast at seven-thirty that morning, but I had long since decided that I would not in fact do it. I could make it, of course. The discipline and training of forty years would not desert me. But it would be a strain, and I felt it would be good for the show and a nice gesture to Lew Wood if I turned the job over to him.

When seven-thirty came, I beckoned Lew to my side and introduced him as the new kid on the block. I handed him the script and stepped away.

I choked up badly through the rest of that program. There were times when my eyes grew misty. But I loved all the nice things that were said about me—the tributes from Chancellor and Newman and Lescoulie and Estelle Parsons, who were with us, live, and taped segments from Garroway, Hope, Hugh Downs, former Secretary of State Dean Rusk, Julian Goodman, the NBC Board Chairman (I used to sleep on the couch in Julian's office in the old days when he was our news director in Washington), and from General Mark Clark, the World War II hero who appointed me to the Board of Advisers to The Citadel, the military college of South Carolina. Rusk especially flattered me: He said he had been listening to my newscasts for twenty-three years and had never yet been able to discern my personal political views.

Lil joined me in front of the cameras near the end of the show. Barbara questioned her a bit about our lives together. And then—a surprise to me—Jim Hartz read a message of good wishes from the President, Gerald Ford. I could see the pride in Lil's eyes.

She and I had come a long way together, the daughter of a Parris Island civil servant and the son of a telegrapher from Charleston. It had been a rocky road at times. We had had our heartaches. But there had been good times, too. There had been a lot of joy and happiness.

We were holding hands as the show ended and our children and grandchildren swarmed onto the set—our family, along with the men and women I had worked with, producers, directors, editors, writers, engineers, lighting men, production assistants, secretaries—the whole lot of them—each one moving toward us to shake hands and say good-bye, all of them singing "Auld Lang Syne."

Lil's eyes were misty, and so were mine.

In the last moments, my discipline cracked. My face began working, and I felt the hot tears flooding my eyes. I was relieved when the TV screens faded to black.

We left the studio for the last time, and a few days later we moved out of Plaza 400 and back to the low country of South Carolina, where my story began.

II

MOTHER USED TO TELL ME I was found under a cabbage leaf in Mama Pinckney's garden. The miracle of birth was not something that young parents attempted to explain to a child in those faraway years. I reached the age of puberty before I first began to doubt the cabbage-leaf theory of my genesis.

Mama Pinckney was my mother's adoptive mother. She was a great hulk of a woman with a heart as great as her girth, a heart that overflowed with love and compassion. As a young woman she lived in the sleepy little village of Yemassee, South Carolina. Her husband, William Nicholas Pinckney, ran the dispensary (state liquor store) there. The Pinckneys were Catholics, and as such they were very much in a minority in the South Carolina low country, but despite what was considered her religious aberration, Mama was adored in her village, by blacks as well as whites, because of her warmth and persistent acts of charity.

The Pinckneys' friendships reached across religious barriers. Their good friends, the J. E. Moores, who lived in the neighboring town of Walterboro, South Carolina, were Methodists. Young Moore was a civil engineer there.

On a spring day at the turn of the century, word came to Mama Pinckney that her friend Marybelle Holcombe Moore had died in Walterboro, leaving a sickly, seven-month-old daughter who was nearly blind and not expected to live. The Pinckneys hitched up their horse and buggy and rode the twenty miles over the rutted, dirt road to Walterboro to offer help and sympathy to J. E. Moore. They returned with his baby. Mama enveloped the child with love, nursed her to health, and finally adopted her, giving her the name Hannah Moore Pinckney.

While Hannah Moore Pinckney was growing up in Yemassee, a boy named Francis Samuel Blair was growing up in Minneapolis, Minnesota, and studying Morse code telegraphy, which fascinated him as the major means of fast, long-distance communication.

Higher education in those times was limited to the prosperous few, and Francis' parents were not prosperous. His father was a grain elevator manager. At the age of seventeen Francis left home. He got employment as a railroad telegrapher and began a migration that took him steadily southward. He moved from town to town, always toward the South, as he found jobs telegraphing for the railroads. In time, he wound up in Yemassee, a railroad junction, and went to work for the Atlantic Coast Line. At Yemassee, he met, courted, and married Hannah Pinckney.

I was born in Yemassee on May 30, 1915. Mama Pinckney delivered me in a bedroom of the Pinckney house under the light of oil lamps. That house was on a dirt road where horses and buggies were commonplace and a motor car was a rarity.

I was three months old when we moved to Walterboro, and I was two years old when we moved again, this time to Charleston. World War I had broken out, and Dad had enlisted in the Navy as a telegrapher. He was stationed at the headquarters of the Sixth Naval District in Charleston, and the Pinckneys had settled in Charleston, too. Mama had opened a boardinghouse at 314 King Street, and for a time we lived there. We were paying guests. We stayed on after the war ended and Dad went back to his job with the railroad.

To Charlestonians, Dad was a damn Yankee, but one with definitely redeeming qualities. After all, he had married into the Pinckney family, whose name was steeped in the history of the South. Dad was a quiet, soft-spoken, and hard-working man, well-groomed, well-manicured (he manicured himself almost every day with a penknife), and he was free of bad habits; he had given up cigarettes for Beechnut gum, and he limited his drinking to a glass of Virginia Dare at holiday time. He had a lithe athletic body, his muscles hardened by years of bicycling to and from his job. He was of above-average height. He towered over my mother.

Mother was an attractive woman with a girlish figure and hip-length brown hair that she brushed diligently every day. She was meticulous about her dress and appearance. She had a fresh complexion and lustrous brown eyes which, however, were excessively weak, as they had been from birth.

Mother had been reared in the Roman Catholic faith, and like Mama Pinckney she was devout. But unlike Mama, who was as open as a full-blooming rose in the sun, Mother concealed her emotions and hid the warmth she felt for her family and friends. She rarely smiled. When this southern lass looked up at Francis Blair and spoke her mind, it was in a voice of unchallenged authority. Mother made most of the major decisions in our family, and most of the minor ones as well. Her word was law, and it was rarely open to appeal.

She was a stern disciplinarian. I know now what she was trying to do. I was an only child and she had an abiding fear of "spoiling" me. I know her view that a child who goes without discipline is unprepared for life. But of course no small boy could possibly appreciate such thoughts, and when my father suggested one spring evening on Mama's piazza that I might go along to work with him one day—it sounded like a thrilling adventure—I was sure Mother's reply would be a decisive "No."

Instead she said "Yes," and for me the answer opened the door to one of those little childhood experiences that at first glance seem commonplace and unimportant but help to shape one's life.

Dad put me on the crossbar of his bicycle and pedaled me to the place where he worked as a telegrapher, a railroad tower about five miles out of Charleston.

Dad's tower was known to local railroadmen as Southern Connection. It was where Southern Railroad and ACL trains bound for Charleston's Union Station were diverted to the terminal tracks, and where the "through" trains for Florida were switched onto the main line through Yemassee.

There at Southern Connection I saw sights and heard sounds that could only be wondrous to a small boy.

I saw great steam locomotives huffing and puffing. I saw passenger trains coming around the bend, speeding past the tower and roaring on to grow steadily smaller and finally disappear in the distance. Sometimes there were passengers on the porches of the rear observation cars, and sometimes the passengers thought to wave to a wide-eyed child as the train sped by.

Dad allowed me the ultimate thrill: He allowed me to stand on the platform alongside the tracks. To thwart any impulse I might have to get dangerously close to the edge, he told me that speeding trains created a suction that could sweep me under the wheels. As the trains passed, I grabbed a doorknob and held fast.

It was an afternoon of unbelievable excitement, and I suppose it made my mind receptive and impressionable.

Inside the tower I stood at Dad's side while he copied a message in Morse code. The dots and dashes told him the *Carolina Special* was due and should be switched to Track No. 4. He stepped over to one hand-operated lever, which rose out of the floor taller than I.

"Want to help?" he asked.

I stood in front of him, grasped the big iron lever, and pulled hard, while Dad braced a leg against an adjoining lever and pulled from above me. Slowly, the lever came forward. The semaphore signal outside the tower changed its angle to indicate "Approach with Caution," and the track switch interlocked into position. In a few minutes the *Carolina Special* approached, slowed down, and switched over to Track No. 4.

As the train disappeared, a thought popped into my head: If my father had gotten his message wrong, if we had pulled the wrong lever, the train would have been on the wrong track. There might even have been a head-on collision. Dad's job suddenly seemed wondrously glamorous and important to me.

I think this was my first lesson in the importance of accuracy in communications.

In the spring of 1920, Dad got railroad passes for my mother and me to travel to Walterboro. This, of course, was to be a thrill. I loved trains. We were to visit my grandfather, J. E. Moore, and my mother's sister, Atalie, and her husband, Oscar Marvin, and their son Donald, who was younger than I.

Mother packed sandwiches and fried chicken in a shoebox for the train trip and made sure I was appropriately attired. I was made to wear my good blue suit with the celluloid collar that scratched my neck, white knee-length socks, and my good Buster Brown shoes. My Buster Brown haircut was carefully trimmed.

Once aboard, I sat upright in the red-upholstered seat with my nose flattened against the window. Occasionally, cinders got in my eyes, and Mother performed some deft ophthalmological surgery with her white linen handkerchief.

Man or boy, one could stare out of a train window at the swamps and scrub pine of South Carolina only just so long before getting bored. As I began to squirm, the news butcher —the man who traveled the trains selling newspapers, magazines, novelties, and candy—came by our seat.

Mother examined his wares and ordered a glass pistol filled with candies for me.

"That'll be fifteen cents, ma'am," he said.

Mother was shocked. She told the news butcher it was sinful to charge so much for a toy and a few candies. But she fished around in her purse and found a nickel and a dime.

"Now, Francis," she said, "save some of the candies for your cousin Donald."

The fidgets got me when the candies were low, all but the few I was obliged to save for Donald. But I had a pistol, and there were a number of likely targets in adjoining seats— pretty little girls with curls, restless small boys in sailor suits, harried mothers looking flustered and sweaty, and fat men dozing behind their newspapers.

In my imagination, I beaned them all, one by one, shouting "bang" as each imaginary bullet exploded out of the barrel.

Then the conductor came through. He stopped at our seat and patted my head.

"What a nice little boy," he said.

I developed an instant dislike for railroad conductors.

But having called me nice when I was being a brat he smiled amiably and said:

"Frank Blair's little boy, isn't it?"

My attitude softened, and I felt proud that my father was so widely known.

The conductor's immediate mission was to bellow out:

"Next stop, Greenpond! Change trains for Walterboro!"

Greenpond consisted of a railroad station and a country store. A two-coach train was waiting on a spur line, the engine puffing out smoke, as we pulled in.

We climbed into the front coach and found it nearly empty. Only four other passengers were aboard.

As a railroad car it was a museum piece. Oil lanterns hung from the ceiling. A pot-bellied stove stood at the far end. The windows had been left open, and the seats smelled of smoke and dust. They were spattered with cinders.

Mother opened the shoebox and we had lunch. There was just the possibility, she said, that Aunt Atalie would offer us nothing until dinnertime. But when we finished eating she did away with the box and all evidence that we had had our chicken and sandwiches. She wanted to be sure Aunt Atalie would not sense her concern.

As the train chugged into Walterboro there was a grinding screech and a lurch that nearly threw me out of my seat.

Only Great-aunt Lillie and her husband, John, who was the mayor of Walterboro, were at the station waiting for us. Aunt Lillie was J. E. Moore's sister-in-law, my deceased grandmother's sister. She was a buxom woman in a low-waisted dress. Her husband was natty in a seersucker suit and straw hat. He was clean-shaven and erect, and he looked like the pictures I had seen of the President, Warren G. Harding.

The greeting we got was effusive. In fact, I learned to dread being greeted by Great-aunt Lillie. As I said, she was a buxom woman. She grabbed me and crushed me between her ballooning bosoms and I nearly smothered. She smelled of talcum powder.

Walterboro was a placid town of white clapboard stores and houses and rutted dirt roads. It had come alive, I think, because the train was in—an event. Buggies rattled along the streets, some of the horsemen waving long whips. The automobile had yet to work its metamorphosis on Walterboro's way of life. Only a scattered few cars were in sight. One was parked at the station. This was Great-uncle John's. It was a deluxe Model T Ford Touring Car, complete with an automatic starter and isinglass curtains which, however, were not raised this day. The weather was too warm.

Aunt Lillie got into the car first. She entered from the starboard side and slid her ample frame under the steering wheel. Even then I had heard of Henry Ford, who to my mind was a genius, and I wondered how he could have overlooked putting a door on the side next to the driver's seat.

Aunt Lillie drove. Great-uncle John had never learned to drive. He preferred horses. He was proud of his Model T, but I don't think he had quite come to trust it. He sat erect beside his wife and stared straight ahead in kind of regal dignity.

As Aunt Lillie steered us through the streets of Walterboro she occasionally sounded the Klaxon: "Ah—oo-guh! . . . Ah —oo-guh!" She sounded it when there were no buggies in her way. I don't think her intent was to give warnings. I think it was to call attention to the approach of His Honor the mayor.

Uncle John served as mayor of Walterboro for forty years. He died in office, and in his will he left money for a statue of himself to be erected in the town park. It stands there still, proud but moldy.

Aunt Lillie drove to Aunt Atalie's house on the outskirts of town, the last house before a sign that read:

YOU ARE LEAVING WALTERBORO
COUNTY SEAT OF COLLETON COUNTY
COME AGAIN
John D. Glover, Mayor
Yemassee: 22 miles

Aunt Atalie's house was alongside scores of acres of rich farmland that my grandfather owned. There was a long piazza lined with rocking chairs, the backs and seats of cowhide. A picket fence separated the grounds from the dirt road. There was a spacious yard but it had no grass—just black earth. At one side of the house there was a barn and behind it a grape arbor.

An old man sat on the piazza. He was dozing when the Model T chugged up. He looked like the Colonel Sanders of today—long hair that was almost white, a neatly trimmed goatee, a mustache, aristocratic features. His mustache was lightly stained with tobacco juice.

The Model T backfired, and the old man awoke with a start.

"Atalie, they're here!" he shouted through the screen door.

He got up, spat a stream of tobacco juice over the bannister, and hurried to meet us just as Aunt Atalie, her husband, and their small son Donald burst through the door.

In the babble of greetings the old man reached down, lifted me up, and clasped me to his chest.

"I'm your grandpa, son," he said. "Captain J. E. Moore, Spanish-American War."

. It sounded important. Grandpa generally referred to himself that way. Months passed before I discovered, to my surprise, that "Captain" and "Spanish-American War" were not part of his name.

My grandfather put me down, and Donald and I stood staring at each other. I felt uncomfortable and somehow belligerent. I was in a suit with a starched collar; Donald was in overalls and he was barefoot.

I wanted more of my candy pills, but I knew this was not to be. I held out the glass pistol to Donald.

"Want some?"

He accepted and we declared an unspoken truce, and later that afternoon Mother permitted me to wear overalls and go barefoot, after I had soaked my feet in cold water so I wouldn't catch cold.

"Son," Grandpa said, as we sat together rocking on the piazza, "what do you want to be when you grow up?"

"A railroad engineer, sir."

"Pah!" The old man stopped rocking. He spewed tobacco juice into the front yard. He turned to me and said:

"No, sir, not my grandson. No, sir. You're going to West Point and be a military man, like your grandpa."

The next day as I rode my pinto pony (a yellow broomstick with a string for a harness) hard by Grandpa's piazza, a stream of tobacco juice shot out over the bannister and landed on my head.

It was unintentional, of course, but it was a perfect shot. The old man couldn't have done better with a Norden. He leaped out of his rocker, leaned over the bannister, and half whispered:

"Son, son! Come here quickly. Grandpa's sorry. It was an accident. Come here quickly."

I did, of course, and he wiped my hair with his handkerchief, mumbling, "Lord, help us! Don't tell your mother!"

He gave me a penny.

"Now go get a jawbreaker," he said.

A jawbreaker was one of those huge balls of hard candy that would last a small boy's mouth all day.

Grandpa invited me into what he called his "quarters." His quarters consisted of a room off the piazza. It was lined with guns, a place where he stored his memorabilia of the Spanish-American War, including his faded uniform. He showed me his fishing tackle, and I am sure my eyes widened in admiration. Grandpa seemed to have hundreds of dollars' worth of tackle, a child's delight. I had fished occasionally with my father in the streams around Charleston, using my bamboo pole, and it was a pastime I dearly loved. Grandpa told me that one day soon he and I would go fishing and perhaps I could use his favorite fishing pole. The prospect filled me with excitement.

Well, we never did get to go fishing together. Captain J. E. Moore, Spanish-American War, was a doting grandfather, but in the remaining days of our visit he was preoccupied with other things.

On our next visit, with my father accompanying us, Grandpa summoned me to his quarters again.

"Son," he said, "I want you to have a present—anything your little heart desires."

His speech seemed slower than normal, and more deliberate.

"I'd really like some fishing tackle, Grandpa," I said.

He struggled to his feet, threw open the door of the closet where his treasures of tackle were stored, and told me to help myself.

"Take what you want," he said. "Take it all, boy! Take it all!"

My heart thumped.

I took out a fine pole, beautiful reels, shiny spinners, marvelous lures, when my father appeared unexpectedly and collared me.

"Take it back, Francis," he said. "All of it."

The joy drained out of my life.

Dad explained that Grandpa was ill.

I think I had known that all along. Somehow I knew Grandpa had been drinking.

Captain J. E. Moore, Spanish-American War, a grand and lovable old man, spent many of his last days alone in his "quarters," sometimes with a bottle, reliving what he considered the glories of a war fought nearly a quarter of a century before.

On a summer evening soon after my last visit to Walterboro, my father cycled home early from his job. He arrived at dusk as Mother and I sat in the porch swing on our piazza. There was a set look on his face, and despite my years I sensed that something was wrong.

"Got a message from the agent at Walterboro," he told Mother. "J.E. passed away this afternoon."

My hand went to my hair, and I felt to see if there was still tobacco juice there.

III

It seems to me that almost everything I experienced in my childhood helped to prepare me for a career in television.

Today's children spend twenty-five hours a week watching the idiot box. The children of my generation used their time to dream, to imagine, to experience life firsthand rather than vicariously. In the process I think we got an earlier and possibly stronger start in developing skills and creative powers.

Boredom is a feeling I cannot remember experiencing in my childhood.

My place for dreaming was a cluttered yard down behind Mama's boardinghouse. Even after Mother, Dad, and I had moved to a home of our own, Mom's house and the yard behind it lured me constantly, after school and on Saturdays and through many of the long, sultry days of the Charleston summers.

There was a grocery store on the ground floor below Mama's. This was a store that Charleston was proud of. It was an "automated grocery store," innovative and futuristic in its concept. In other stores there were aproned clerks to fetch the grocery items one by one from the shelves as the ladies read down their lists. In the automated shop, the ladies plucked the groceries from the shelves themselves and took them past a checkout counter. The store was a forerunner of the modern supermarket. As such it was a busy place, and it spewed empty crates and boxes and barrels into the yard behind it. The yard was accessible to us via an outdoor stairway, and the crates and boxes and barrels became the stuff of our dreams.

My companions in wonderland were Cousin Ranny and our Uncle Nick, my mother's adoptive brother who was seven years older than Ranny and I.

Nick was talented with a penknife. He could carve a dagger or a pistol out of the end of a wooden grocery box. He could turn broomsticks into swords or rifles. We were fully armed for our imaginary exploits. We were well horsed, too. We fashioned our steeds out of pickle barrels: A horse's head was crudely carved in wood and nailed upright at one end, a rope attached served as the reins, and another board nailed across the barrel became a saddle. The barrels, of course, rolled from side to side and forward and back, to give us the feeling of galloping at great speed. We supplied the sound effects: "Bickety-bick, bickety-bickety-bick," as our horses sped across the plains of the Wild West, "bang-bang" as we exchanged shots with the villains racing ahead.

We lived out our dreams. The pickle barrels could become many things—motorcycles, for example, on which we, as intrepid policemen, could give chase to evil men with our soprano sirens screaming, or caves in which we could hide from marauding Indians.

What dreams we lived out there behind Mama's boardinghouse often depended on what motion picture had been playing the previous Saturday at the Majestic Theater, two blocks away. Hoot Gibson and Tom Mix inspired us to live the lives of cowboys, but sometimes we fought in World War I.

Indeed, my most fanciful creation, the product of patient work that absorbed and delighted me, was an airplane. In a strange way it was an augury of some of the days that were still to come for me as a flier in World War II.

The plane I flew in childhood was made from a packing case, the sides of which became wings. It had a fuselage covered with rotting canvas, a joystick made of a chopped-off broomstick, and rudder pedals fashioned from tin cans. The instrument panel was drawn in crayon.

It was stationary, of course, mounted on two barrels only a couple of feet off the ground, but as I sat in it, it flew. It flew at incredible speeds and soared to awesome heights. At times it became a fighter plane, and when it did I often shot Germany's Red Baron out of the skies. The Red Baron was a devilishly clever flier, but hardly a match for me. He shot me down only once in all the times we met in mortal combat. When my plane took that fatal hit and burst into flames, I smiled across the skies and waved a friendly farewell to the Red Baron. Then the barrels turned over because of my bodily gyrations, and I crashed and sprained my wrist.

Mother announced at supper one evening that Francis was going to learn to play the violin. I was seven years old at the time, and my reaction was mixed. I liked the idea of getting music out of an instrument. But practicing every day? And the violin? I would have preferred the drums, or at least the saxophone. But Mother liked the violin, and in our house her word was law.

She and Dad bought a violin, which I am sure they could ill afford, and I became a student of Mrs. Ida Bailey, a widow who taught music to supplement her income. Mrs. Bailey and I had an instant personality conflict. The rasps and squeaks that came from my violin jangled her nerves. Nevertheless, I put in my time in daily practice sessions in front of my bedroom window, sometimes stealing envious glances at the sandlot ball games under way on the vacant lot across the street. Mother listened from another room, often while entertaining friends at bridge.

There had been a young Hungarian boy in Budapest a few years earlier who practiced his violin in not dissimilar circumstances, in a room adjoining his father's dental surgery. Practice bored him as much as it did me, and he had a parent who monitored from a distance, too—in his case his father, who listened while drilling teeth. That boy was more resourceful than I. He beat the problem of boredom. He memorized the music, then read fiction while practicing. He learned to play with one part of his mind while reading with another, and it all helped him to develop not only a great talent but also an almost unbelievable musical memory. He could memorize entire orchestral scores. The boy was Eugene Ormandy, who became conductor of the Philadelphia Orchestra and one of the musical greats of our time. Well, I myself went on to become the leader of Curly Blair and His Charlestonians, but that is another story.

My violin lessons with Mrs. Bailey came to an abrupt end one summer day when Mother, mercifully, decided it was too hot for me to practice. But when autumn came, I actually began to miss the violin. I told Mother and Dad I wanted to study again, but this time under Professor G. Theodore Wichman, who had organized and conducted the Charleston Philharmonic Orchestra. Professor Wichman took private pupils. He charged one dollar a lesson.

He came to have a strong influence on my life. He looked like the Ichabod Crane of my imagination. He was tall, thin, gangly, and bespectacled, and he was a strict disciplinarian. He had no inhibitions about rapping his violin bow across my knuckles when I hit a sour note, and he had an uncanny perception: he always knew when I had skipped practicing.

When I had, he showed no tolerance. But I liked him and admired him, and under his tutelage I learned to read music and even to make some tolerable sounds come out of that violin. In fact, in my high-school years, I was to become a professional musician. A professional? Well, at least a semiprofessional. In a way it was music that would get me started in broadcasting.

IV

In 1925 the Order of Railroad Telegraphers struck the Atlantic Coast Line Railroad. Among other things, the telegraphers were rebelling against the seven-day week. They were demanding the dignity of one day off out of every seven. Some of the union members went on working, doing double shifts. But Dad joined the strike. He was a man of principle, he said, and he could never be a scab.

Dad was known all through the South as a first-class telegrapher. He was never out of work for more than a few days at a time. Soon after the strike began, he was offered a job with the Postal Telegraph Company in Augusta, Georgia, whose relay office was on the top floor of the *Herald* Building. He accepted, and we moved forthwith to Augusta. I was transferred to the fifth grade of an Augusta school.

It was in Augusta that I got my first steady job. I sold the Augusta *Herald* on the city streets. I would go to the newspaper office and buy ten papers at two cents each and peddle them for five cents each. Thirty cents a day seemed a good deal to me. I became aware that I could actually earn good money. In time, I began getting up in the early morning and selling the morning paper as well, the Augusta *Chronicle*. Then I began selling the Sunday paper from a vantage point outside our church after Mass. I had a good business going.

And I had become aware without really thinking about it that there was money to be made in news.

In time Dad arranged a transfer to the Postal Telegraph Company office in Charleston and then, once there, he changed jobs again. He went to work for the Western Union handling commodity quotations and press copy for the *News and Courier* and the Charleston *Evening Post*. Sometimes, to earn extra money, he also covered baseball and football games, telegraphing play-by-play reports and lead stories from the press box. Often he took me to the games with him.

I bicycled to his office at Western Union's East Bay Street relay station one summer afternoon and found him taking a message in Morse. I was familiar with Morse code. Dad had taught me Morse about the time Mother was teaching me the alphabet. I knew that the dots and dashes he was translating that afternoon were spelling out a long message that was neither personal nor concerned with business.

When the signoff came Dad pushed his eyeshade to the top of his forehead and turned to me.

"That was a press message," he said. "Very important."

Dad showed me the dispatch he had typed to pass off to the Charleston *News and Courier*. I do remember I was enthralled. Here were the words of a reporter telling the people of Charleston about a news event in a far-distant community. It seemed to me there was a romance and importance about his job, the job of informing people.

The next day I got a copy of the morning paper and went back to Dad's office. I found the carbon of the original dispatch and compared it line by line with the story as it appeared in print. It had been changed! The editor had omitted entire paragraphs. I was outraged. The editor had not only despoiled my father's meticulous work, I also felt he had changed the reporter's meaning.

I began dropping in at the Western Union office regularly after that and comparing the carbons of the original press dispatches with the version finally printed in the paper. I think this was what first awakened my interest in news.

Later my absorption in the news was so intense that, in order to stay on the news job with the "Today" show, I gave up extra income of more than two hundred thousand dollars a year.

It was about this time that two things began to have their first real impact on my life: religion and the theater.

Many of the kids in my age group in our neighborhood were of Catholic families and most of us were altar boys. The mystery of the Mass enthralled us.

Almost all our activities came to center around the Sacred Heart Church. There were altar boy outings and church picnics, and there was the parish hall with its basketball court and a well-equipped stage.

When Father John Hughes announced that James E. DeRain, a parishioner who had written published music, would organize and stage a minstrel show with an all-juvenile cast, I determined to try out as an end man. The minstrel show was an accepted form of entertainment in those days. Like jazz and the blues and folk music, minstrels were part of our heritage. Eddie Cantor and Al Jolson in their black-face routines were the big stars of the day. Minstrel shows would not be accepted now. An end man's impersonation of an old southern black as a bumbling inferior would not be tolerated. But in the social and intellectual climate of Charleston and much of the rest of the nation in the middle twenties, few whites realized that a minstrel show was demeaning to an entire race.

When we went to the parish hall at Sacred Heart for the

minstrel tryouts, I really wanted to put cork on my face and tell silly jokes. Instead, each of us was asked to sing a song.

When my time came I was petrified. My knees buckled, my voice trembled. When I tried to sing the only song I knew, "I Wonder What's Become of Sally," I sounded like Alfalfa in an "Our Gang" comedy.

That was my first experience of stage fright, and thank God, my last. It taught me to have sympathy for some of the public figures I would work with later in life—men and women whose eyes would glaze and whose hands would shake in the moments before air time.

But in spite of my unprofessional performance I was taken into the cast of the All-star Juvenile Minstrels as a "sweet singer." Mr. DeRain gave me a real tear-jerker of a song entitled, "That's What God Made Mothers For!" It was a sentimental ballad, Mr. DeRain said. It most assuredly was. Let's see if I can recall the words.

I dreamed I saw my dear old mother kissing me good-bye.
And though her heart was breaking,
And a tear shown in her eye, she whispered,
"Boy, don't let our parting grieve you anymore,
But just remember this is what God made all mothers for!
To watch over you when a baby—to sing you to sleep with her song,
To try to be near you to comfort and cheer you,
To teach you the right from the wrong,
To do all she can to make you a man and over a million things more,
To sigh for you, cry for you, yes, even die for you,
THAT'S WHAT GOD MADE MOTHERS FOR!"

There were weeks of rehearsals, and then opening night was upon us. We were too excited to be nervous.

Our costumes were outlandish. Charlie Ravenel, the interlocutor, wore a full-dress suit of white sateen. The sweet singers wore blue jackets with white duck trousers and red bow ties. The end men wore exaggerated costumes with red jackets, checkered pants, and yellow bow ties that were so wide they stretched almost from shoulder to shoulder. We wore white gloves. It was the first time some of us had ever worn long pants.

The show was a success. Each of us got to do an encore. Perhaps this was because the audience was biased in our favor. It consisted largely of our fond parents and doting aunts and uncles.

Nevertheless, our fame spread. We were invited to perform at other parish halls and, as the All-star Boy Scout Minstrels, we even played on the big stage of the Academy of Music Theater to raise money for the Scout Council.

My singing career ended abruptly, however.

Dad had given me a new catcher's mitt and I was playing catcher in a sandlot ball game on the field across from our house on Race Street. Wallace Whetsell was the pitcher, and Wallace threw a mean fast ball. One of his pitches got past my new mitt and hit me smack in the *vox humana*.

The next day my voice changed from Alfalfa falsetto to a sort of rasping baritone. And I was never again able to sing, "That's What God Made Mothers For!"

Charleston of my boyhood was a city of warmth and camaraderie where children played unmolested in the alleys and on vacant lots, where businessmen in straw hats and ladies in long skirts walked unhurried along narrow, winding streets, and where black women from the neighboring islands sold beautiful flowers on the post office steps. Great freighters and ships of the Navy steamed in and out of busy Charleston Harbor, past the Battery and Fort Sumter, plying between distant and glamorous ports. Merchant seamen and uniformed sailors idled on the sidewalks, watching pretty girls. The Citadel, the military college founded in 1842, commanded Marion Square in the center of the city. White church steeples dominated the horizon. The Dock Street Theater, one of the oldest in America, stood silent and darkened, a theatrical ghost of the past.

Charleston was a city where blacks lived in decaying neighborhoods and black children attended rigidly segregated schools. I had only a passing interest in the old slave market, which stood near the center of the city and still stands today. Many of the blacks I passed on the streets, as I rode my bicycle around town, must have been the grandchildren of people who had been herded into the slave pens there, then paraded one by one onto the auction block and sold off to the highest bidders to work on plantations all through the South. I had heard vague stories, like racial memories, of families being separated on that block, of young boys and girls being led away with lips trembling, never to be reunited with parents who were sold to other owners, but these were tales that seemed obscure and without bearing on my own time. I was engrossed in my own era and my own life and the endless swirl of activity that engulfed me: Scouting, music, the jobs I did for pocket money, a quickening and deepening interest in aviation, and a constant round of rehearsals for plays at church and school.

I became a wage earner in those days of rather frenzied boyhood activity. I had my first brush with sex, I did my first work as a boy reporter, and I experienced again and again the thrill of appearing before an audience and speaking lines. All of these things, naturally, taught me some things about life, including, in one instance, the seamy side.

Those were the days before the child-labor laws, and there was nothing to keep an eager boy from earning money if he could find a job. I spent Friday afternoons and Saturdays bagging groceries and stocking shelves at the A&P, earning fifty cents an hour, and I delivered the Charleston *Evening Post* to the homes of 120 customers on Route No. 112, earning between three and four dollars a week.

Then there was the long, hot summer when I was a Western Union messenger boy, bicycling all over Charleston to deliver and pick up telegrams. Among the places I went to, frequently, was Charleston's red-light district, and one of my calls there was instructive in a fascinating way.

There were three "houses of ill repute," as we called them, on Beresford Street, a one-block-long, cobblestoned, dead-end street near the docks and wharves of the waterfront. I learned early that, whenever I had a telegram for one of the ladies in these shuttered houses, my tip was likely to be a handsome one. A delivery there was always worth the bike ride.

I had a telegram for No. 7 Beresford Street on a particularly hot afternoon. The temperature was high in the nineties. I was perspiring freely when I climbed the steps and rang the doorbell. The young woman who answered wore a flimsy kimono, which she clutched around her body with both arms.

"Telegram, ma'am," I said.

She smiled and reached out to take the message and sign for it, and as she did so, moving her arms, her kimono fell open. She wore nothing underneath. My eyes popped and my breathing almost stopped. I stared. So that's what they look like, I thought.

When she had signed, I tried to ask if she wanted to send a reply. I had some trouble getting the words out.

"Maybe," she said, still smiling. She had not yet read the message.

She ran her eyes over the words. She looked up and said:

"Yeah. Take an answer."

Her kimono was still wide open.

I was hardly able to write down what she was dictating. In fact, I was hardly able to hear what she was saying. I had to ask her to stop and repeat. My voice trembled.

She gave me the name and address of a woman in Norfolk, Virginia. Her message read:

"Mabel, come immediately. Fleet arrives tomorrow."

Fortunately, I knew the rate for ten words to Norfolk. I didn't have to look it up.

"That'll be sixty-three cents," I said, my voice still quavering.

She reached into her kimono pocket and fished out sixty-three cents in change.

"Sorry, sonny," she said, "can't tip you this time. Business ain't been so good lately."

I nodded and stumbled down the steps. My bicycle wobbled a bit as I rode away!

I did my first work as a reporter in those childhood years (I may be glorifying it just a bit by calling it reporting). The job came about because of my interest in the Boy Scouts. Interest? It was an obsession! Scouting became a way of life for me. At the age of eleven I had been eager to join, but a boy had to be twelve to be eligible. Most of my older friends belonged. I felt left out. I badly wanted to share their fun and experiences. In the weeks before my twelfth birthday, Troop Six at Sacred Heart Church permitted me to attend its meetings as a prospective member, and I prepared myself for the tenderfoot test before I was old enough to take it. I passed it as soon as I joined. I bought a Scout uniform immediately with money I had saved. Putting on that uniform was one of the thrills of my boyhood.

I plunged into Scouting with such fervor that my grades in school began to suffer. Dad warned me that I would either have to shape up at Julian Mitchell Elementary School or ship out of the Boy Scouts. I shaped up at school by diligent cramming. But I pressed on with Scouting. I slept out in my backyard pup tent often enough to earn the camping merit badge, and I earned badges in such subjects as aviation, weather, music, and dramatics.

I was an eager and dedicated young Boy Scout, and the thought occurred to me that what the Scouts were doing was news, or ought to be. So as scribe for Troop Six, I sent into the Charleston *Evening Post* an account of our troop's activities during one week, and lo and behold! They published it. So each week after that I wrote my piece for the paper and it got published. It was exciting and gratifying to see my own words in print. Other troops began sending their reports to the *Evening Post*, too, and before long we had a whole column on Scouting once each week in our local newspaper. I co-ordinated the effort and made sure the other troops in town reported their activities. My efforts paid off. I got to know the people at the newspaper office and began learning a little something about communicating. I felt I had a toehold in journalism.

Working toward a merit badge in aviation also deepened my interest in flying.

I made toy airplanes out of balsa wood and they flew, powered by rubber bands. I collected a stack of aviation magazines and followed developments, insofar as I could understand them, in every phase of the aviation industry. The great aviators of the time were my heroes: Wiley Post, Richard E. Byrd, Jimmy Doolittle, Amelia Earhart, and, of course, Charles Lindbergh—the Lone Eagle. Dad had bought our first radio, an Atwater Kent, before Lindbergh took off on the first nonstop solo flight across the Atlantic in 1927. He and I monitored the radio repeatedly during the thirty-three hours and twenty minutes of the flight. When the *Spirit of Saint Louis* landed at Orly Field, I cheered loudly and joyously. I told Dad I knew that Lindy would make it. I enjoyed calling him Lindy. It gave me a feeling of camaraderie with a national hero.

In my first year of high school I entered a combination essay and oratorical contest. The contestants were to write five hundred words on the subject, "Old Glory's Greatest Glory." The winners of the essay contest would take part in the oratorical contest, which would be held on the stage of the high-school auditorium.

Five hundred words! Even after hours of researching the history of the flag, it took me three days to get five hundred words on paper. They looked like good words to me but, nevertheless, I was surprised when, a few weeks later, I was told I qualified to enter the oratorical phase of the competition.

I memorized my five hundred words, and I practiced my delivery over and over again in front of my bedroom mirror. Professor Horace Early, my high-school English teacher, gave me some pointers on elocution and suggested some gestures I might use. I worked at it, and I worked hard.

I was nervous when the night of the contest came. I sat there on the stage waiting my turn to speak and perspiring.

But when I was introduced, my fear suddenly vanished. I went through my five hundred words without a fluff.

The next day my picture appeared in the Charleston *News and Courier*. I was the winner! My ego swelled. I discovered that I liked writing, and even more, I liked speaking before an audience.

At about this time the old Atwater Kent radio in our living room began claiming more and more of my attention. I became enthralled with it. A voice that came out of that loudspeaker was making a deep impression on my mind. It was the voice of Lowell Thomas broadcasting the news. His calm and the clarity of his language fascinated me, and the news itself began to hold a deep interest for me. If I became more aware of what was going on in the world than most of my fellow students and more concerned with national and world events, it was because of Lowell Thomas.

Every evening when Lowell signed off with the familiar words, "So long until tomorrow"—words that were his trademark—I went to my bedroom to study. But before I settled down to study, I used to stack a few books on the table and put my Big Ben alarm clock on top of the stack. To me, the clock became a live microphone that would carry my voice around the world. I propped my history book alongside it and read my history lesson aloud, pretending I was Lowell Thomas broadcasting the news. When I signed off and prepared to go to bed, I would always say, "So long until tomorrow."

I dreamed that someday I would broadcast the news, like Lowell Thomas.

In later years, when Lowell and I became good friends, he told me about the circumstances that led to his becoming the country's foremost newscaster. His story confirmed something I felt for a long time: Success depends not only on hard work and talent, but also to a large degree on being in the right place at the right time. I'll tell you Lowell's story later.

While I dreamed of broadcasting the news, Mother had very different ideas about a career for her only child.

"Francis is going to be a doctor," I used to hear her telling her friends at the bridge table. There was pride and hope in her voice.

About the time I was going into the second year of high school, mechanical transmission was coming into the telegraph business, and Morse code—which had been a profession to some men, like my father—was on the way out.

Dad was sent off to a Western Union training school in Rome, Georgia. Mother and I joined him as soon as he had found us a place to live. I was put in the Darlington School for Boys, a private boarding school that also accommodated what we called "day hops." It was a fine school with small classes. Students could get individual help from the teachers if it was needed. I did very well there. The one problem was that it was on the outskirts of Rome, and Mother had to drive me to and from school every day. Even though her eyesight was poor, she could see well enough to drive a car. She never had an accident.

I went to the movies one Saturday in Rome, mainly to catch the newsreel. I really wasn't aware of what the feature was. The "talkies" had just come in then, and there was a movie house in Rome that, they claimed, had been built especially for sound. This intrigued me, and I wanted to see what it was like.

It was that Saturday that I fell madly in love with a vision on the silver screen. The leading lady in the feature movie was a young woman named Lois Moran, and the moment I saw her, I adored her. I sat through three showings of her film.

On the way home that night I thought it would be great to

have a job in the movie house and see Lois Moran as often as I wanted to. The next day was Sunday, but I went around to the home of the theater manager, anyway. I had gotten his name from a notice on the door: "In case of fire notify Charles Lamb." It gave a phone number. I looked up his address in the phone book.

When I rang the doorbell a short, balding man appeared and said, "Yes?"

I said, "Mr. Lamb, my name is Francis Blair, and I'd like a job in your new theater—the DeSoto. I think I would make you a good usher."

He put his hands on his hips, looked at me, and said, "Well, I'll be damned—on Sunday?"

"Well, sir, you see, I . . ."

Mr. Lamb interrupted: "Anyone who has gumption enough to come around on Sunday looking for a job deserves it. Come around and see me tomorrow in my office!"

Wow! I left Mr. Lamb's house with my head in the clouds.

Next day after school I went to see Mr. Lamb, and he gave me a job working from 3:00 P.M. to closing. I would get six dollars a week for a six-day week. The theater was closed on Sundays because of the Georgia blue laws. Mr. Lamb said I'd find a uniform in the locker room that would probably fit me and I could start to work at once. I was overjoyed. The Lois Moran movie would be playing for three more days. It was tough going to school and working until eleven o'clock every night, but I made good use of the study periods in school, and I had an inspiration—I was in love.

Dad's first assignment after he had completed training school was as manager of the Western Union office in Hartsville, South Carolina. We moved again, and of course I had to give up my job at the DeSoto Theater in Rome. That gave me time for Scouting again. I worked hard; on August 16, 1930, I received my reward. I was made Eagle Scout at a Court of Honor in Darlington, South Carolina.

We were there only a few months when Dad was transferred to Charleston to be manager of the King Street branch office. It meant going home again and getting back into the High School of Charleston and Professor Wichman's orchestra.

The moment we arrived in Charleston I telephoned the Pastime Amusement Company, the operator of the movie houses in Charleston, and told them I was an experienced usher and I would like a job. They put me to work the next day at the Majestic Theater, the same one my cousin Ranny and Uncle Nick and I had patronized as small boys. The pay was six dollars a week, but I had to work only half as many hours as I did in Rome. Out of that, I was able to buy most of my own clothes and still have pocket money, which I tried to save.

I felt I was outgrowing the bicycle stage, but I needed transportation for school and for work. I bought a Model T Ford coupe for seventy-five dollars, using my savings and money I was able to borrow from dear Grandma Pinckney on condition that I would take her for a ride around the Battery and Hampton Park once a week. That I was glad to do.

As a high-school student in Depression times, I saw what I thought might be another opportunity to make a bit of money. Dances in the social clubs and parish halls of Charleston were regular things in those days before television, but some of the organizing committees were often low on cash and unable to afford the well-established local orchestras. I thought a dance band that charged cut rates might clean up. Thus was born the aggregation we billed as Curly Blair and His Charlestonians. I organized some of my fellow high-school musicians and formed a band that people might actually be able to dance to. Carl Pollock was our pianist because he actually *was* talented. Russell Long played saxophone. Thurston Steele was our drummer because he had a set of drums. Like most of the rest of us, Thurston was not cut out for a career in music.

We rehearsed in the Sunday school auditorium of St. Johannes Lutheran Church, Russell Long being the son of Rev. Dr. I. E. Long, the pastor. When the auditorium was not available, we rehearsed in the homes of whomever among us had a piano. In time, we were playing at the local dances.

We had to scrounge for our musical scores. In the 1930s, the music publishers gave complimentary copies of their orchestrations to local radio stations around the country, hoping for plugs. Charleston's radio station, WCSC, had no use for the free copies it received, and when I heard about that I began dropping in at the WCSC studios and cadging the orchestrations for Curly Blair and His Charlestonians.

At first, Jack Hearne, WCSC's bookkeeper, salesman, control operator, and announcer, offered to sell them to me, but I was able to explain that my orchestra was not yet solvent.

We had played a few dances in the Charleston area when it occurred to me that we could benefit from publicity. When I next called at the station to pick up orchestrations, I told Hearne I would be glad to have my band play over WCSC in return for the music he was giving us. Jack had not heard us play. This perhaps explains why he agreed to put us on the air.

WCSC, like most small-city radio stations in those days, operated in a casual way. Its studio consisted of one room on the mezzanine floor of the Francis Marion Hotel. The control booth was the size of a clothes closet. But to us it was big time, and when we arrived to perform we were more than a little excited. We set up our music stands and borrowed folding chairs from an adjoining room. When we were finally ready, I nodded to Jack in the control room. In reply, he simply faded out the record he was playing and introduced Curly Blair and His Charlestonians. (What a thrill to hear that go out over the air!) He nodded to me to begin.

That was my cue to point to Thurston Steele, and my pointing was Thurston's cue to tap out four-four tempo on his wood block for our theme song, a piece called "Deep Night." We played that fairly well, I thought; it was one tune we really knew. Next, I signaled Thurston to beat out the tempo for "Walkin' My Baby Back Home." That one, too, we played in a more or less acceptable way.

Some of us were gaining confidence, but Thurston Steele was not. I could see he was deeply moved by the thought that our music was going out over the air. He was perspiring freely and there was a vacant stare in his eyes.

Jack Hearne told Charleston that as our third number we would play Wayne King's theme song, "The Waltz You Saved for Me." Again I pointed to Thurston.

Thurston, a chubby and sometimes bumbling young man, was not the most talented drummer in Charleston. He would beat out the tempo—tap-tap-tap-tap for a fox trot, BOOM-chow-chow for a waltz—and he could keep time when we got started, but he had his failings, and among them was a tendency to cave in under pressure.

When I signaled him for the tempo for the Wayne King waltz, he tapped out not waltz time, but four-four time.

One of us (I forget who) turned to Thurston and shouted, for all Charleston to hear:

"Not that, stupid: BOOM-chow-chow."

Then, after we had finally gotten the right beat from Thurston and I had finished playing the violin solo in "The Waltz

You Saved for Me," Jack Hearne stole out of the control room while the orchestra was in the closing strains, and whispered in my ear:

"Curly, is your violin in tune?"

That ended the broadcasting career of Curly Blair and His Charlestonians.

I was still doing high-school dramatics when the Peruchi Players approached me and asked if I wanted a job on the professional stage. Did I! The Peruchis would pay me thirty-five dollars a week for each show I was cast in. And if I bent the truth just slightly, I could think of myself as a professional actor.

The Peruchi Players were a stock company that had thrived in Charleston and elsewhere in the South until the "talkies" replaced silent movies. At that point, the Peruchis, like countless other professional stock companies in America, went into an eclipse. They performed only occasionally now, and they rounded out their casts with local and essentially amateur talent.

The Peruchis gave me bit parts and supporting roles, and I found myself gaining confidence on the stage. Watching the pros, I learned little tricks of stage "presence," tricks that would be important to me in later years.

In the beginning the Charleston critics were barely tolerant of me. The Charleston *News and Courier* said I "showed promise" as Billy Caldwell in Barry Conor's comedy *Patsy Gets Her Man*, a big hit in those times. Reviewing the same performance, the Charleston *Post* critic said only that I showed "fine stage presence." When I played the role of Herbert Price in Arnold Ribley's *The Ghost Train*, one critic said I "met requirements capably." Charleston had had a long theatrical tradition, and I suppose the critics had mellowed with the years and were reluctant to be too caustic about a local player.

Finally, however, after I had played the role of Kenneth Wayne in Allen Langdon-Martin's *Smilin' Through*, the *Evening Post* wrote:

"A pleasant surprise was the marked improvement in the acting of Francis Blair, Jr. Mr. Blair rose from a rather distinct amateurism in previous parts to a capable performance last night."

Ah! Such sweet-sounding words. I read them over and over again. It seemed to me that I was learning a skill that could only be of value to me if I ever did manage to break into radio broadcasting.

V

MEDICINE AS A PROFESSION never had any great appeal for me; nevertheless, because Mother wanted it, an M.D. degree was my objective when I enrolled at the College of Charleston, which at that time was a municipally endowed school for day students. I paid what seemed to me to be an exorbitant tuition—sixty dollars a semester. I kept my job at the movie house to pay my own way.

I was never a brilliant student. I was always too busy. I did well in English and adequately in French. Trigonometry I could not master at all; it remains a mystery to me. I did get a "98" in physics, but chemistry I could not fathom. I had enjoyed biology as a high-school student, studying plants and bugs; in college, a biology-related course was my downfall.

We were assigned to dissect a rat and identify its parts.

I have a thing about rats. Sometimes even to think about a rat gives me an involuntary shudder. I think this is a prejudice that I developed in an outhouse at Long Lake, Minnesota.

My Uncle Earl, Dad's brother, ran the general store there, a big, rambling country store where you could buy almost anything from a horse collar to an ice-cream soda. Uncle Earl's apartment was above the store, and the family outhouse was in the backyard. Dad and Mother and I visited Uncle Earl and his family during my early childhood.

My mother was always a stickler about regular, daily bowel movements, although the term itself was one she avoided.

"Francis, did you go *out* today?" she would ask each evening as she came to tuck me in. I knew that to "go *out*" meant to move one's bowels. If my answer was in the negative, I had to get out of bed and go to the latrine.

One evening at Uncle Earl's, Mother asked the predictable question; I had to answer "No." I was instructed to get the lantern from the kitchen and make my own way to the small outhouse out there in the moonlight.

While I was sitting there in the dim light with my short pants down around my ankles, a huge rat appeared on a rafter. I screamed. The rat leaped. On its way to the floor it struck me on the left shoulder. I screamed again. The rat disappeared through the open door. I was too frightened to pull up my pants. I ran back to the house shouting and crying and tripping. I had nightmares for a week.

With that in my background, I was asked to dissect a rat at the College of Charleston. I refused to touch the damn thing.

This was when I quit college. I had flunked rat.

It took me several days to get the courage to tell Mother and Dad I was no longer a student, and I didn't until after I had seen my father's boss and gotten a job with Western Union as a delivery clerk. I was still listening to Lowell Thomas every night, still reading the Charleston papers from front to back, and still dreaming of a job as a radio newscaster, but a job in radio, it seemed, could only remain a dream.

Western Union sent me to training school at Bloomfield, New Jersey, and paid me $56.50 a month to learn the telegraph business and to operate and maintain the teletypes.

Those were trying days in Bloomfield; $56.50 a month was a modest income even then. I often went without meals.

But in due course I returned to Charleston as a qualified operator. I was assigned first to the King Street branch office, of which my father was manager.

It was spring in Charleston, and the azaleas, wisteria, magnolias, and camellias were coming into bloom. Northern tourists would soon be arriving to see the sights in what we called "America's most historic city." Western Union opened a branch office in the lobby of the Francis Marion Hotel to accommodate the travelers, and I was assigned to man it. The assignment was a delight because the studios of WCSC were right there in the hotel. They had been moved to the twelfth floor, but they were just an elevator ride away. I began going up to the studios during my lunch hour and at the end of my working day.

As in many radio stations then and now, the announcer at WCSC was on public view. He worked behind a plate-glass window that separated the studio from occasional spectators. At first I stood on the wrong side of that window, watching while the announcer talked and played phonograph records. But in time I found the courage to step into the studio itself.

I knew most of the people there, although only casually. I had met them when delivering their occasional telegrams, and some I had known during the days of Curly Blair and His Charlestonians. So, as a hanger-on at WCSC, I was accepted. And very shortly I must have been appreciated, because I became the station's most diligent unpaid staffer.

I was a kid trying to get a break, and I had a genuine, all-absorbing interest in radio. I took to doing everything that could be done to help around that studio. I emptied the wastebaskets, swept out the place, and ran errands, meanwhile learning what I could about broadcasting. I was not getting paid, but I was learning, and for a boy of nineteen in those Depression years, the opportunity to learn might be worth more than a salary.

WCSC was not much of a radio station in those days. It couldn't afford to be. Commercial radio was still relatively new and still groping for format, and WCSC was still struggling for financial stability in the depth of the Depression. Its programming consisted mainly of phonograph records, although occasionally a band of hillbilly musicians, or spiritual or gospel singers would stop by, and the station would interrupt whatever it was doing and put them on the air. It had no network affiliation, no news wires, no reporters—in fact, no newscasts. It went on the air at eight o'clock in the morning, signed off at three o'clock in the afternoon, and came back at 6:00 P.M. to broadcast until 10:00 P.M.

Hugh Deadwyler, the manager, was an affable man in his late twenties with an engaging smile. He tolerated me. After all, I was being helpful and costing him nothing.

Walter Speight, the program director, and Wylie Calder, the announcer, were especially kind to me. There came a time when Walter and Wylie let me make a station break (station identification). I still recall the words. "This is WCSC, atop the Francis Marion Hotel, in America's most historic city, Charleston, South Carolina." What a thrill that was! However, in seconds, the control-room door burst open and there stood Hugh Deadwyler!

"What in hell is going on here? Who was THAT?" he asked in a loud voice.

Walter said, "It was Curly here. We just thought we'd let him try it."

Deadwyler stood there for a moment and said, "Not TOO bad." He closed the control-room door and went back to his office.

I was shaking in my boots. I asked Walter what Deadwyler had meant.

"I think he didn't mind it too much."

"Oh."

After that they occasionally gave me other things to do on the air, and Deadwyler never said any more about it. I think Walter and Wylie were glad to have me around. They seemed to enjoy watching my struggle to learn. Sometimes when they put on a transcribed program, a WPA concert for instance, that lasted fifteen minutes, they would let me sit at the control board while they went down to the drugstore for a Coke. Darn it, they always returned just in time to sign off the program.

When the station was off the air, they allowed me to operate the control board and play records and transcriptions and do "make believe" programs that only I could appreciate.

Walter had a dance band, Walter Speight's Blues Chasers, the most popular in town at the time, and Wylie played saxophone. Sometimes, to fulfill engagements, they would need to leave the station before sign-off time. They began getting Deadwyler's permission to let me take over.

On one of the sign-offs I did while Walter and Wylie were away, I used my name for the first time: "Francis Blair speaking—good night!" While I was turning off the lights, the phone rang. A man asked: "Francis?" He just laughed. This puzzled me. I thought about it as I was trying to get to sleep that night. Next day I told my father about the anonymous phone caller. Dad just smiled and said, "Why not change it to Frank?" Dad himself had been called Frank as long as I could remember. I liked his suggestion. From then on I became known as *Frank Blair*. It seemed to be a better name for a radio announcer or newscaster. Walter and Wylie encouraged me, and I started studying the structure of network programs and building programs of my own, choosing music and improvising introductions. Sometimes they joined me when I sat listening to the great network announcers of the time—Ben Grauer, Jimmy Wallington, André Baruch, George Hicks, David Ross, Don Wilson, Pierre André, Norman Brokenshire, Graham McNamee, Ed Herlihy, Milton Gross. I studied their delivery, trying to perceive what it was about their voices that put them at the top.

It became painfully obvious to me that one of the things the network announcers had that I didn't was no regional accent. I knew that if I were ever going to get ahead in radio I would have to sound as if I came from anywhere, and nowhere in particular. I began reading the newspapers out loud when I was alone in my room at home and when I was sitting in front of WCSC's dead mike, and I read news in a hushed voice sometimes when I sat at the telegraph desk in the Francis Marion lobby. I listened to every sound I made, and if it seemed to reflect my southern origins I corrected myself and read and reread until the new pronunciation became programmed in my mind. I was trying to teach myself to articulate and use all my speech facilities. It was hard work, believe me, and it was frustrating. Just when I thought I had learned to say "house" or "milk," for example, I would find myself lapsing into old ways and saying "hoose" and "mulk."

I did not immediately overcome my accent, but the constant reading aloud did bring an important payoff. I began reading with fluency. It became a rarity for me to stumble over a word or a phrase. And I was learning to speak "from the stomach, not from the throat"—the classic dictum of voice teachers.

I thought I was really ready for at least a local newscasting job. The problem was that no such job existed in Charleston.

WCSC was Charleston's only station, and WCSC had no regular newscasts.

I went to Hugh Deadwyler's office one afternoon when WCSC was off the air, and I made my pitch.

"Wouldn't a daily news program help us build audience?"

Deadwyler studied me from across his desk.

"Maybe," he said.

"Then why don't you let me put a news program together for you?"

He smiled. I am sure I sounded naïve.

"Where in hell would you get the news?" he asked.

Transradio Press was in operation then—a sort of wire service serving only radio stations, but for WCSC it was out of reach. It was too expensive for a small station with a limited budget.

"I think I could get all the news we need," I said.

"How? Where from?"

"By listening to the network newscasts and making notes. By checking around every day at City Hall, police headquarters, the hospitals, places like that."

"You could do all that?"

I could guess what was in Deadwyler's mind. If he hired me, he would be relying on an untrained nineteen-year-old to collect, write, and broadcast news of the city and the world. If I made mistakes or aired unfounded local reports, the station would make more enemies than friends. On the other hand, he must have thought of me as an earnest and diligent youngster who might just do the job.

"It *is* an idea," he said. "Let me think it over."

I walked out of his office thinking I had at least a chance.

But before he could come to a decision, Western Union interrupted my assignment at the Francis Marion Hotel and sent me to a temporary job at Beaufort, South Carolina, about seventy-five miles away.

Apart from a few decisions that were made for me by my commanding officers during World War II, I suppose the Western Union's decision to send me to Beaufort was the most fateful thing that ever happened to me.

Beaufort is a lovely little town snuggled on the curved shore of Beaufort Bay. Nearby were the Sea Islands of the Carolina low country, steeped in Revolutionary War and Civil War history. Shrimp boats and fishing boats were docked along Bay Street, the main thoroughfare. Beautiful antebellum homes fronted on the bay. Marines in training at nearby Parris Island were constantly on the streets and in the restaurants and bars, using Beaufort as a "liberty" town when they couldn't get to Savannah or Charleston.

Inland the fertile soil and abundance of sunshine made the Beaufort region one of the most productive tomato-growing areas of the country. During the tomato season, Western Union traffic in Beaufort was heavy. Buyers would send quotations to their brokers and stand by awaiting instructions. I was sent there to help with the flow of messages.

Apart from work, there wasn't much to do in Beaufort for a nineteen-year-old stranger in town. I knew practically no one there.

On my first evening in Beaufort, a balmy spring evening, I went out strolling the streets, idling away the time. A sign in a drugstore window caught my eye. It said the senior class at the Beaufort high school would be staging a play, *Patsy Gets Her Man*, one of the plays I had appeared in with the Peruchi Players.

I went up to the local high school hoping to find a rehearsal. There was, and so I slipped into the darkness of the school auditorium.

As I watched, two things about it intrigued me.

First: The girl playing Grace, the ingenue, was lovely.

Second: Everything about the performance was wrong.

I don't understand how I had the courage to do what I did that evening. Well, it *was* spring, and I *was* just turning twenty, and I *did* want to meet that girl.

And, of course, it *would* please my vanity to introduce myself in front of her as an occasional professional actor.

I had a budding craftsman's interest in the theater, and would genuinely enjoy helping to shape up the ragged rehearsal I had been watching.

When the cast took a break, I walked to the stage and brashly presented myself to the young woman who was directing, a Miss Fore, the school's English teacher. I told her I knew the play, had appeared in it with the Peruchi Players, and would be glad to help her in any way I could.

She looked at me with surprise—and I think gratitude. I think she knew her play was heading toward a first-night disaster. The actors and actresses were fouling their lines. Some of them sounded like first-graders reading a fairy tale. Beyond that, the set was all wrong. An actor wouldn't come onto the stage without stumbling over a chair or a sofa.

When Miss Fore accepted my offer, I rearranged the set to conform with the configuration the Peruchi Players had used. Then I began working with the cast.

I had thought I was much too old to blush. I liked to picture myself as far too urbane and sophisticated for anything like that. But when Miss Fore introduced me to the girl playing the part of Grace, I felt my cheeks beginning to burn. It may sound corny. This was love at first sight. When "Grace" looked at me with her big blue eyes and smiled her happy smile, my heart thumped.

"Grace" was Lillian Stoddard. After the rehearsal, I asked if I could walk her home. We strolled along the waterfront and—apologies if I again sound corny—I kissed her by the light of the Carolina moon. We decided that night to keep "steady company," as it was called in those days.

Lil was warm and gentle and gay. She loved to laugh; and she had a firmness of mind, a capacity to look reality straight in the eye and live with it, without flinching. She's still that way today. We are still "going steady," forty-four years later.

Lil was born in Charleston on December 9, 1916. Her parents were John and Marie Stoddard. Her father ran a dry-cleaning business in Charleston. She had a younger sister and had a brother who had died in infancy. When Lil was in her preschool years John Stoddard moved his family to Parris Island Marine Base and became manager of the laundry there under civil service. Lil started school there on the base. She loved the island and the military atmosphere. As a small child she would often go to the retreat ceremony, when the colors were struck for the day, taking with her her terrier, Jack, who barked throughout the ceremony.

Lil was one of the victims of a strange military order issued on Parris Island during her grade-school days.

The commanding general decreed that the children of enlisted men and civilian employees would not be permitted to attend the same school with the children of officers. Instead, they were to be transported to the Beaufort Public School by boat. Well, Beaufort Bay can be rough in the winter and, because of that, Lil's mother refused to let her make the twice-a-day crossings. She was kept out of school until the general's strange segregation order was rescinded.

Lil and her family moved to Beaufort when she entered high school. Her ambition was to be a nurse. The Navy nurses she had seen on Parris Island in their crisp, white uniforms, their blue capes, and their perky caps had inspired her. She had earned a scholarship at Columbia (South Carolina) College with a B-plus scholastic average, and her intention was to enroll there after she finished high school and then go on into nursing.

When our romance was a few weeks old, I wanted to tell her to forget all that because she was going to marry me. But I didn't quite have the nerve to propose and, besides, I didn't have the income to support a wife.

We were still sharing our dreams when the teletype in the Western Union office in Beaufort typed out a message for me from Charleston—signed "Deadwyler, manager, WCSC."

"Come and see me at your convenience," it said.

I was excited and elated.

Deadwyler, I thought, could want to see me for only one reason: to offer me the job I had dreamed of, at WCSC.

I don't think it took me more than a minute to get back to the teletype machine and punch out a message to the district manager of the Western Union. I told him I needed an instant leave of absence from Beaufort "due to the press of business elsewhere."

The reply I got said my message was tantamount to a resignation.

I had to look up "tantamount" in the office dictionary.

In the jargon of today, I would have answered him now with something like: "Yes, sir, you bet your sweet bippy."

But those were gentler times. My reply to the district manager said something like, "Yes, I understand, and when may I be relieved?"

I was not sure I had a job in Charleston. And at the back

of my mind there was an ugly fear that in breaking off with Western Union, in giving up a steady job in the midst of the Depression, I had done something I might spend years regretting. I pictured Dad calling me a damned fool, and I wondered whether I was.

But in a day or two, I accepted my "release" from Western Union.

Saying good-bye to Lil was a sad moment, because we were going to be separated, but an exciting moment, because I felt that I was going to begin a career.

I hurried to Deadwyler's office atop the Francis Marion Hotel in Charleston the next morning.

"Francis—I mean Frank," Deadwyler said, "I've been thinking over your idea, and the more I think about it the better I like it."

I tried my best to look calm.

"We do need news at WCSC," Deadwyler went on, "and I do think you may be able to do the job."

"Yes, *sir*," I said.

"So let's give it a try."

"Fine!"

He hadn't mentioned money.

"This is experimental," he said, "and you know I am not running the most prosperous business in Charleston."

"Yes."

"And times are hard."

"I know."

"What I can do to start you . . . just to start you, while we see how it goes . . . well, I'll pay you five dollars a week."

I remember saying something stupid in the best Horatio Alger tradition. But it came straight from the heart.

"Okay," I said. "It isn't the money I want. It's the opportunity."

We shook hands, and that same day I went to work, realizing the dream I had first had as a high-school student reading history aloud and trying to sound like Lowell Thomas. I became a radio newscaster, for five dollars a week.

If anyone had told me then that, one day, I would be making more money in one second than I made then for a hundred-hour week, I would have thought he was utterly mad.

VI

IN MY EAGERNESS FOR THE JOB, I hauled myself into those studios every weekday morning at seven o'clock, and I worked until signoff time at ten at night. Then I would listen to newscaster Paul Sullivan from WLW in Cincinnati, studying his style and trying to understand just how he built his news programs.

In the mornings and afternoons I covered my beat. I made friends at the places where news was likely to break—City Hall, fire and police departments, hospitals. I wrote my programs and I aired them, trying always to sound as good as Lowell Thomas.

Shortly after I had started my full-time job with WCSC we were able to make a deal with United Press. I would phone their bureau in Charlotte, North Carolina, twice a day, and someone there would read the highlights of the day's news. The phone calls were expensive and the system was not the best, but at least it was a step in the right direction.

I tried to convince Deadwyler that the Transradio Press Service teletype would be a good investment. With it, our newscasts would always be up to the minute. He agreed to refer the matter to G. Richard Shafto, the general manager of the Liberty Life Insurance Company's radio properties.

Shafto's office was in Columbia. I had never met him. The

only thing I knew about him was that he was the big boss. Everything had to be referred to him if a major expenditure of money was involved.

One day, Deadwyler informed me that Shafto had approved and that we would have the Transradio teletype in about a week. I was thrilled. Almost every day I'd inquire if anything had been heard from Transradio. At long last, the big day arrived. The telephone men came and installed the teleprinter. I couldn't do much work that day. I just wanted to watch the installation. What a thrill when they finally plugged it in and it started printing out news copy. Its clickety-clack was music to my ears. I stood there in front of it and watched it typing out the news—story after story. It was fascinating. Occasionally, five bells would ring, indicating an "URGENT"—a story of extraordinary importance. Everybody at the station gathered around to watch and marvel. It was like Christmas morning. The news was in short, crisp sentences written to be spoken and readily understood. The long, involved, complex sentences of newspaper copy never appeared. I was to learn a lot about how to write news for radio, the development of one thought in a clear, concise manner, without embellishments that would tend only to confuse the listener. That evening at six o'clock, using the news from Transradio, I delivered the best newscast of my fledgling career.

Despite the excitement of the job and the long hours, I missed Lil. On an occasional day off, I was able to borrow Jack Hearne's car. He was the station's salesman. I would get over to Beaufort to see Lil.

My newscasts began to attract some interest in Charleston. People talked especially about the local news they heard on our air. Deadwyler began to feel pretty good about his experiment. He raised me to the stupendous salary of fifteen dollars a week.

That, I thought, was enough to support a wife, especially if we watched the pennies.

Lil would once in a while on Saturdays or Sundays drive her dad's car to Charleston, accompanied by her mother. Her mother would visit friends, and Lil and I would spend the afternoon hours in the studios, playing phonograph records while the station was off the air. Almost always we would be alone. It was during one of those romantic sessions that I asked her to marry me. After all, I was making fifteen dollars a week! She said "Yes" right away, and we kissed. She said I'd have to tell her parents. I didn't mind doing that too much. Her father and I had become good friends, and he and her mother knew that Lil and I were in love.

Lil was graduated from Beaufort High School in June of that year, 1935, and we immediately made our plans. I rented a furnished apartment for us on Green Street, opposite the College of Charleston. It wasn't much, but it was adequate. It consisted of a bedroom and a small kitchenette. (The community bathroom was down the hall.) It cost twenty dollars a month, all I could afford.

I was Catholic and she was Methodist, so we planned a kind of double wedding ceremony (ecumenism was working ever so slowly, even in those days). On Sunday, October 20, 1935, we were married at St. Peter's Roman Catholic Church in Beaufort by Father Kamler, and then we went to see Lil's pastor, the Reverend Dr. Watson, who witnessed our vows again. I wore my good blue suit and Lil wore a lovely white chiffon dress. She looked gorgeous.

It was a small wedding with just families and close friends invited. Walter Speight was to have been my best man, but his car broke down on the way and he didn't make the ceremony. We had to call on former mess Sergeant Ellis Testima Walters, an old friend of the Stoddards, to stand in.

Speight did get there for the reception at the Stoddards' house. After we cut the cake, I saw him talking with my father. I eased closer to overhear the conversation.

"What about this radio business?" Dad asked. "Do you really think there is any future in it for a young man?"

Dad sounded skeptical.

"Yes, sir, Mr. Blair," Walter said, "and I think Frank's future in radio is very bright."

He paused and smiled.

"Someday," he went on, "I think he's going to be a great newscaster."

Hearing that, I think, was the best wedding present I could have had.

VII

LIL AND I WENT TO CHARLESTON on the afternoon of our wedding day. I was anxious to get back for a very obvious reason and also because I was about to cover the first big national story of my career. In three more days, President Roosevelt was paying an official and ceremonial visit to Charleston. I still had a lot of coverage planning to do, and I was nervous about it. I was twenty years old and still green, and I was deeply afraid that something would go wrong. On our wedding night in our one-room apartment on Green Street, we talked about the story for a time. But not for long.

That was the shortest night I'd ever spent. It seemed as if I had just dozed off when the alarm sounded on my Big Ben, the same clock I had used as an imaginary microphone while reading my history lessons. It rang for a long time before I reached over and stopped it. I was in a daze, but I sensed vaguely that something strange and unusual had happened to me. Had I dreamed something that I couldn't recall? My eyes half opened, I glanced at the clock. Six-five! That's about right, I thought, but still I had the notion that there was something unusual about this awakening. I was in a place I had never been before. My eyes popped open and I looked around. Where in hell am I? It was then that I smelled coffee perking and bacon frying. Quickly, I sat up on the side of the bed, and in the tiny kitchenette adjoining our one-room flat I saw her. She looked like something out of a story book. Her brown hair was neatly brushed and just touching her shoulders. She wore a sheer negligee over her nightgown.

"Good morning," she said. "Sleep well?"

"Hi," I replied. "How about you?"

"Just fine, thank you."

"That's good."

"Oh my God, look at the time. I've got to get moving."

"The bathroom's down the hall, first door on the left, remember?"

"Thanks. Be right back."

As I brushed my teeth I was humming a little tune and recalling what had happened during the night.

When I got back to the room, bacon and eggs and toast and coffee were set out for me. I sat down at the table still wearing my new pajamas. It seemed that we had been there for years and that we belonged there together. The strange feeling I woke up with had vanished.

She sat down across from me and I reached out and held her hand.

"You all right?" I asked.

"Yeah. How about you?"

"I'm fine, I think."

Still holding hands, she stood up and came to my side. With one arm around my shoulder she leaned over and kissed me on the forehead. I knew then that everything was all right. I took her in my arms and kissed her tenderly.

I glanced at Big Ben. It was a quarter to seven.

"Wow! Gotta get going." I dressed quickly.

"Thanks for the breakfast. See you around noon if all goes well. Will you be okay?"

"Don't worry about me, I'll be fine. Got a lot to do and so have you. Remember, the President is coming Wednesday!"

"Yeah, I'd almost forgotten."

"I'll walk you to the door."

We stood there looking at each other. I took her in my arms and kissed her long and hard and felt her all over. Oh, she felt good through those sheer things she was wearing.

"Oh, I wish I didn't have to go to work today—of all days."

When I got to the studio that morning, I went immediately to the Transradio teletype to make sure it had functioned properly through the night. Then I turned on the broadcasting equipment and checked it out with the transmitter engineer. The transmitter and tower were across the Ashley River in St. Andrew's Parish. I tried to settle into the routine I had established. I had to put together the eight-o'clock newscast, but for once my mind was not on my business. I was thinking of Lil.

But I wrote a newscast. I told the people of Charleston what had happened since they went to bed—everything, that is, except what happened to me. As soon as I signed off with "This is Frank Blair speaking," I called Lil.

"Did I sound okay?"

"Yes, just fine. Your mother called and wants to take us to lunch."

(Fine, I thought, that's one meal I won't have to pay for.)

"That's good. Want to go?"

"Sure—that is, if you stop calling every fifteen minutes so I can get the bed made before she comes."

(I wanted to say, "Why bother with it? We're just going to mess it up again.")

"Okay," I said. "See you right after the noon news."

I went to my desk and tried to concentrate, but it was

difficult. I kept thinking of Lil and what our life together would be like. I was determined to advance myself and increase my earnings. Suddenly the idea struck me. Why not call Transradio Press in Washington and ask if I could cover the President's visit to Charleston for them? I crammed and made my proposal to Herbert Moore, the founder and president of TPS.

"Yes, by all means," he said. "And file your dispatches *press rate* collect to my attention."

The words *press rate* took me back to the days when I used to watch my father transcribing Morse-coded news copy for the newspapers in Charleston.

Was I proud!

I hurried out to the small printing shop where Lil and I had had our wedding announcements printed. I designed something a little larger than a business card that stated that I was an accredited press correspondent for Transradio Press Service and asked that I be accorded all the privileges of the press. I pleaded with the printer to let me have the finished product by the next day. When he asked how many I wanted, I replied ten. He said I could get a hundred for practically the same price. I had a "devil may care" attitude that day. I ordered a hundred.

I got back to the studio just in time to write the noon newscast. As I was broadcasting, I glanced up at the clock and saw Lil and my mother and father watching me through the plate-glass window. I got a tingly feeling all over and almost lost my place in the news copy.

It was the day before the President's arrival. I sat there at my desk in the office area of WCSC boning up on details of his career. If I had to "pad" on the air the next day, I did not want to be at a loss for words.

Deadwyler walked in.

"Just talked to Shafto," he said.

The name "Shafto" always riveted my attention. I sometimes thought the "G" in "G. Richard Shafto" must stand for "God."

I felt a sense of dread while waiting for Deadwyler to go on. Thoughts of our whole coverage plan being canceled popped into my head. How could Shafto do that?

"About Roosevelt's visit," Deadwyler said.

"Yes?"

"He's decided to put a line in to us. We'll feed our coverage to WIS."

"Whee!" I yelled, and my papers went flying into the air.

I would be reporting to a network—a two-station network, but still a network.

"Calm yourself," Deadwyler said. "This could be a big break for all of us."

"Wow! Will it! You bet!"

"So," Deadwyler warned, "do a good job."

"Yes, sir, you can count on it."

I had gotten off to a slow start in writing the six-o'clock news, but I took time out, anyway, to telephone Lil and break the news. I was more excited then about broadcasting to two small radio stations than I would be later about broadcasting to the entire nation.

I suppose I did not do the most brilliant job in journalistic history in reporting the President's visit to Charleston that day. The story was almost too rich in color: Mr. Roosevelt arriving at the Navy Yard aboard the battleship *Houston* . . . the Navy Band playing his favorite song, "Home on the Range," as the big ship docked . . . flags flying . . . crowds lining the streets . . . the President speeding to The Citadel in an open limousine, then beginning his speech with his standard greeting, "My friends" . . . Franklin Delano Roosevelt holding his chin high and rocking his head from side to side in a mannerism that had become known around the world. There was so much to say and so much to write in my dispatches to Transradio that I felt almost overwhelmed. But I must have done something right.

When it was all over, there were two telegrams waiting for me from Transradio: one from Herbert Moore and one from Wallace Werble, the Washington bureau chief. Both extended congratulations on my work.

And, of far greater importance to me, Hugh Deadwyler called me into his office and said there had been a telephone call from Columbia—a personal call from G. Richard Shafto. Mr. Shafto had asked him explicitly to tell me on his behalf that I had done a very nice job.

Furthermore, Deadwyler said, G. Richard Shafto was coming to Charleston in another two days, and would like to see me.

In my mind's eye I had Shafto pictured as an older man, middle-aged, the executive type, stern, hard, strictly businesslike. I had been schooled on phrases like: "I'll call Shafto and ask him," or "I'll consult Shafto," or "Shafto called and said . . ."

Well, when I was summoned into Deadwyler's office that Friday afternoon—was I ever surprised! A handsome man in his early thirties, well dressed, immaculately groomed, stuck out his hand and said:

"Hi Frank. I'm Dick Shafto."

I mumbled something like, "Pleased to meet you."

He immediately put me at ease. He wore a warm smile.

"Sit down, Frank," he said.

I sat. I had been right about one thing: Shafto was strictly business. He came right to the point, and I was thankful for that.

"Nice job on the President's visit," Shafto said.

"Thanks," I said.

"I listened to your newscast at noon while I was driving into Charleston. I liked it. In fact, I recorded it."

"You recorded it?"

"Yes, I have a recorder in my car hooked up to the radio. It operates off the car's battery."

"I didn't know that could be done."

"Well," Shafto said, "it isn't the best quality, but at least I can get what I want, usually. Now let's get to the point."

He did.

"Frank," he said, "you have a marvelous voice. Well suited for news. Sounds authoritative."

"Thank you, sir."

I was bubbling inside.

"Hugh tells me you really dig the news. He says your newscasts have balance and interest and command a lot of attention around town."

"Thank you, sir."

"You know, Frank, Columbia, as the state capital, is more news-oriented than Charleston. More news happens there. News can be more important to us in Columbia than it is here. I want to build up the news at WIS, and I think you could contribute to that."

I was about to explode.

Shafto went on, "Hugh tells me you're recently married. Congratulations."

"Thank you, sir."

"Would you and your wife consider moving to Columbia?"

I was aghast.

Shafto went on, "You're getting fifteen dollars a week here

at CSC. We can offer you twenty-five dollars at IS. (This was another thing I was learning. The pros in the business usually referred to station call letters without the "W"—so it was CSC and IS.)

"We'll fly you and your wife to Columbia and pay whatever moving costs you have. Of course, you'll be concentrating mainly on news coverage and newscasting, but you'll have other duties."

For the first time in the few minutes we had been together I said something coherent. I said, "That's fine. I want to learn all I can about this business." And I meant it.

Shafto smiled.

"Good. So it's all set then?"

It was half a question and half a statement.

"Yes, sir, and thank you. I'll do my best."

I had not consulted Lil, but I knew she would be pleased.

Shafto and I shook hands again. I liked the way he shook hands. His grip was firm, the kind to seal a bargain. I had always thought you could tell a lot about a man by the way he shook hands.

I walked out of Deadwyler's office with my head in the clouds.

In less than one week, I had married a beautiful girl, covered my first big national news story, gotten commendations from the top executives of Transradio and from G. Richard Shafto—and I had been offered and accepted a big new job. And with a substantial raise!

But then a sobering thought struck me: How would I make out covering local news in a strange city? I didn't even know the name of the mayor. And could we find a decent place to live at a rent we could afford? Would we be able to live from payday to payday without the groceries that Dad had brought us every evening since we married?

We were to leave within the week. We felt both excited and frightened. We had lived in our first home less than two weeks. That rather set a pattern for us. Years would pass and a war would intervene before we could feel we were really settled.

We arranged to fly to Columbia on Delta Air Lines. I was thrilled about that. Lil was frightened. It would be her first airplane trip. I was an old veteran, having had three round-the-field rides in Charleston at one dollar a ride.

Lil's parents drove from Beaufort to see us off. My parents, of course, were there at the airport, too.

None of them really believed in airplanes. Any one of them would have driven us to Columbia rather than see us board our airliner, a trimotored, fabric-covered Stinson that could accommodate ten passengers.

My mother made me promise I would send her a telegram the moment we arrived. There were tears in her eyes, and I knew she would be reciting her rosary from the moment of our departure until my telegram arrived.

We kissed good-bye and the plane took off. Lil and I held hands all the way. As we looked out over the beauty of the South Carolina low country on that golden autumn afternoon, it seemed to me that life was good and exciting and I would be able to cope with whatever problems lay ahead of us, although for a long time now I had had an uneasy feeling about the problems of the world at large. I had been studying the world news every day. Mussolini had invaded Ethiopia, Hitler was making warlike noises in Berlin. I had an uneasy feeling that war was on the way. Every American generation had had its war, and there really was no reason to believe that mine would be an exception. As we flew on over the rolling midlands near Columbia, the thought occurred to me that if

I ever did have to go to war and leave Lil, I would rather do so as a flier than as a guy slogging through the trenches.

Vic Lund, the WIS program director, met us at the Columbia airport and escorted us to the Jefferson Hotel. The WIS studios were situated there on a lower level.

Lund walked up to the reception desk.

"You have reservations for Mr. and Mrs. Frank Blair," he said.

The language thrilled me.

I signed in for us, writing "Frank Blair and wife." That thrilled me, too.

Lund told the clerk that our expenses were to be billed to WIS.

Another small thrill. It was my first experience of expense-account living.

Lund said good-bye, and a porter took us to our room. He was an elderly black man, distinguished-looking, type-cast for the role of an old family servant in a movie about the Old South. I tipped him a quarter. Shafto had advanced me a week's pay to cover expenses, so I was loaded. A quarter was nothing—a snap of the fingers.

The porter thanked me and left, and suddenly Lil and I were alone. A strange feeling came over us. I could sense it in her and I was sure she could in me. We felt like strangers. It was the first time either of us had been alone in a hotel room with someone of the opposite sex. It seemed so different from our little honeymoon apartment in Charleston. Here, strangeness surrounded us. It was an awkward feeling. Suddenly we both started to speak at once, and then we laughed, and I took her in my arms. That broke the spell.

I kissed her again, and then went downstairs to meet G. Richard Shafto.

I was twenty years old when I went to work for Mr. Shafto in Columbia and he was thirty, but to me he seemed much older. He was a perfectionist. His manner was businesslike. I admired his conservative clothes and his almost perfect grooming. I held him in awe, and so did the others who worked for him. To us, he was "*Mr. Shafto.*" No one ever called him Dick. I never addressed him without saying "sir."

In his earlier days Mr. Shafto had been a radio technician, a new and rare breed in the twenties and early thirties. In 1927, he built his own ham radio station and proceeded to study "electronics"—the word hadn't come into use in those days. He studied radio engineering at Columbia University and Georgia Tech and New Orleans Radio Institute, where he earned a first-class radio operator's license. He went to sea for a year and a half as a ship's radio operator. Then he became a salesman for Graybar Electric Company, a subsidiary of Western Electric. His territory covered eight southern states. He sold broadcasting equipment and public-address systems and speech equipment in general. As a salesman, he used to call on Frank Hipp, president of Liberty Life Insurance Company, which owned WCSC, WIS, and WNOX, in Knoxville, Tennessee. Hipp was impressed with young Shafto's knowhow, his personality, drive, idealism, and business sense. Hipp hired Shafto to oversee the operations of Liberty Life's radio properties, and that started him on a brilliant career as a broadcasting executive.

I was to learn more from him than from any other broadcaster I would ever know. His background was technical, but he had an innovator's vision and the courage to experiment in other areas—programming, news, music—and the willingness to let his mind roam along unexplored corridors.

As the new and untried member of his staff, I walked into

the WIS outer offices and asked Margaret Bouzard, the office manager, in a half whisper:

"Where's Mr. Shafto's office?"

She nodded toward a closed door.

"Is he in?" I asked cautiously.

Margaret nodded in the affirmative.

"Why don't you go in and let him know you're here," she suggested.

"You think it would be all right?"

"Sure. I think he expects you. But knock first."

"You sure?"

"Sure."

I approached the door timidly and tapped gently three times. Margaret was watching me. We smiled at each other. A voice from inside said briskly, "Come in."

I was in, and I started to say, "Mr. Shafto, I'm here." But I didn't get that far.

Mr. Shafto was on his feet.

"Frank, welcome. Glad to have you with us. Everything all right? Accommodations okay?"

He put out his hand at the same time he was talking, and we shook hands. It was that same firm grasp I had liked when I shook hands with him in Charleston the week before.

I was saying something like, "Glad to be here," and "Yes, sir—yes, sir," when he said, "Sit down." I felt he was really glad to see me.

His office was unpretentious, like the man himself, but comfortable and designed for efficiency.

"How would you like to do the noon news?"

"Sure, fine. I'd like to get started."

He depressed a key on an intercom and said, "Vic, Frank will do the noon news. Give him a hand—will you?"

"Yes, sir," Lund's voice came back.

I glanced at the clock on the office wall.

"Well, I'd better get started," I said.

"Good luck, and again, welcome."

We shook hands again.

I went out smiling, and Margaret asked, "How was it?"

"Fine," I said, half over my shoulder as I passed her desk, "I'm going to work."

"Good, and good luck."

The Program Department office adjoined the business office, and I went directly to my desk. I found everything a desk should have: sharpened pencils, a pen and holder, a desk blotter, a dictionary, two trays marked "In" and "Out," and a sharp-edged ruler for separating the news wire copy.

I inspected the three drawers on the left of the desk, and found them supplied with stationery, paper, rubber bands, paper clips—the works. On the right side, there was a door that opened to reveal a new Underwood typewriter mounted on a platform. There were springs that raised it to desk level as it was pulled.

There was a telephone and an intercom, too, on the desk.

I was eager for Lil to see my new setup.

Vic Lund appeared with reams of news copy from the Transradio teletype. He deposited the pile on my desk and said:

"Okay, go to it."

I did just that. I started by scanning the latest material. Each item was numbered at the top and carried the date and time at the end. I separated the material into piles: international, national, regional, and features. I was sorry to see there were no items pertaining to South Carolina. I thought—I'll have to do something about that.

I said to Vic, "What do we do about local news?"

"Nothing yet. That's why you're here."

I picked up the local morning newspaper, *The State*, and skimmed through it. I had remembered seeing earlier a couple of stories that I thought could be developed by means of a few phone calls. One pertained to an automobile accident—they call them "wrecks" down South—an automobile wreck in which several people were injured. That was easy: Call the hospital and get the latest information on the conditions of the victims. That's what I did. I enjoyed telling the hospital, "This is Frank Blair with the WIS News Department." I put together a five-minute newscast, and I got through it without a fluff. Mr. Shafto was at my desk when I returned from the announce booth.

"Fine," he said. "I particularly liked the local item you carried. We want to do more of that." He returned to his office.

I had done my first newscast in a strange town. I closed my desk and went to our hotel room to see Lil.

Lil had good news. She had found a furnished apartment. Like our first home in Charleston, it consisted of one room, with a kitchen at the end of a hall, curtained off. But it was near the bathroom and it would do for now. It was eight blocks from the hotel. She said she had walked it and it wasn't too bad. We could move in the next day. And the rent was twenty-five dollars a month. Living costs evidently would be higher in the state capital.

I used the twenty-five dollars Transradio Press had sent me for the coverage of Roosevelt's visit to Charleston to pay the first month's rent.

I had notified Transradio of my transfer to WIS, and Transradio executives were pleased. Columbia was a more important news town. They asked me to stay on and to report anything of importance from the southeastern states as a whole as well as from Columbia itself. I considered myself a regional correspondent for Transradio.

Before we moved into our new home, Lil and I had three more good meals in the hotel, and I signed the tab for them. I was still on an expense account.

We moved into our apartment the next day, and I began to feel pretty proud of myself. I was the head of a household, I was doing a new and important job, and I was making a name for myself with Transradio. I was edgy and apprehensive in a strange studio, but I thought my future looked bright.

I had my comeuppance in my first week. I cannot imagine how I could have made a more embarrassing goof.

One of the most popular radio programs of the day was "Major Bowes' Amateur Hour." Major Bowes was a showman who put amateur entertainers on the air to compete for honors. Some would go on to professional careers. But for those who failed, Major Bowes sounded a gong. The phrase "given the gong" became part of the language. It was synonymous with failure.

The sound of the gong signaled the opening of each of the major's programs.

I was doing the newscast that directly preceded the major's program. I was engrossed in what I was reading, and I failed to watch the clock. The control operator saw I was not going to sign off in time. He made a snap decision. While I was still in the middle of a sentence, he cut me off the air and switched to the network just as the gong sounded, the symbol of failure.

Burroughs "Buck" Prince was the city editor of the *Record*, Columbia's afternoon newspaper. He was a short, barrel-chested man, a southern gentleman of the old school with a strong southern accent and the manners of the Old South. To him Furman University, his alma mater in Greenville, South Carolina, was "Fumman" University. He called Lil "Miz Lillian," and his own wife was always "Miz Ruth," even, I suspect, in the privacy of their bedroom. Buck and I became close friends. He loved to talk about radio. He told me over and over again that I was involved in the coming thing in journalism—radio newscasting. He helped me whenever he could without being disloyal to the *Record*.

Buck was also a tease. During my time in Columbia he teased me mercilessly about having gotten the gong from Major Bowes.

Years later (because journalism is a small world), Buck and I met again, he in the role of night news editor of the *Today* program, and Buck became responsible for one of television's classic all-time boo-boos.

Those were the golden days of radio. Everybody listened. Here was escape from the drab world of the Depression into an exciting world of imagination, of fun and frolic and tingling fear and suspense. There was something for everyone. For women listeners there were the soap operas. "The Romance of Helen Trent" featured radio's most incurably optimistic heroine, dedicated to proving that romance was still possible for a woman past thirty-five. Helen was past thirty-five when the program began in 1933, and was still hopeful in 1960, when the program went off the air. There were "Vic and Sade," "Young Widder Brown," "Our Gal Sunday," "Backstage Wife," "Lorenzo Jones," "Big Sister," "Stella Dallas"—forever dedicated to her daughter's happiness—and there were many more.

Hillbilly music, live and recorded, was popular, and so too were hymns and gospel songs. Radio preachers thrived.

The big bands were tops. There was Guy Lombardo—"the sweetest music this side of heaven"—and the Dorsey Brothers, Benny Goodman, Artie Shaw, Glenn Miller, Ray Noble, Charlie Spivak, Glen Gray and his Casa Loma Orchestra, Vaughn Monroe, Russ Morgan, and Hal Kemp with Skinny Ennis. The truly great were Louis Armstrong, Duke Ellington, and Count Basie. The Lucky Strike "Your Hit Parade" was one of the most popular music programs on the air. You could win a carton of Lucky Strike cigarettes by sending in a postcard listing the top ten tunes in the order in which they would be played on the show. Phonograph records were acetate and easily breakable, and a surface noise was broadcast with every one played on the air. Nevertheless, listeners accepted them because, despite the noise, it was the sound they wanted to hear.

There was the NBC Symphony Orchestra, which broadcast live, conducted by Arturo Toscanini. Radio was so popular that people were staying home to listen. The movie theaters began to feel the squeeze. They resorted to Bank Nights and Free Dish Nights in a sometimes faltering effort to compete. NBC and CBS (ABC and Mutual had not yet come into being) were dominant in American life. Stations welcomed network affiliation, even competed for it.

Now radio stations prefer to go it alone. There is no full-time radio network programming. Radio networks exist mainly for news, sports events, and Sunday religious services. But in the thirties! It was a great time to be breaking into radio.

But those were lean times, too. It wasn't easy getting by on our twenty-five dollars a week. We learned that potatoes were cheaper and pancakes could make a hearty meal.

More and more people were listening to our newscasts, and more and more people were talking about them in the hotels and restaurants and barber shops of Columbia. Mr. Shafto's emphasis on news was clearly paying off, and now he was insisting on more and wider coverage. He made a business deal with *The State*, Columbia's morning newspaper. I would have access to more world and local news. That was a coup for Mr. Shafto. In those times newspapers were resenting radio's invasion of the news field. Radio was robbing them, they said, of advertising dollars. Some would not even print the schedules of their local radio stations, in spite of strong demands from readers.

Under arrangements Mr. Shafto worked out, I would do most of my news work in *The State*'s editorial offices, and I would broadcast the news right from there by remote control. I would have the full wire services of the Associated Press and United Press at my disposal as well as access to the files of the paper and their local and regional sources. I was given a small office where I could both write the newscasts and broadcast them. I would be closely associated with the newspaper people and would be indirectly involved in the workings of an active newsroom.

I was inundated with wire copy—reams and reams of it. Transradio's stories were written expressly to be read aloud. They were written in short, simple sentences. But AP and UP copy was long and involved, with complex sentences. That was the difference between writing for the print medium and writing for broadcast.

A reader can reread a sentence if it is too complex for him to understand at first glance. In radio, a listener understands the first time or not at all. Any distraction, no matter how slight, can cause the listener to miss part of what was said. Looking at the mass of wire copy on my first day in *The State* newsroom, I determined that my broadcasts had to be clear, concise, and that the words had to be enunciated so that there could be no misunderstanding. I was no longer involved in a "rip and read" operation. I would no longer be ripping the copy off the Transradio teletype and reading it unchanged over the air. It was a much more exacting task now. The reams of newspaper wire copy had to be read and culled and whole sections eliminated and the newscasts had to be "processed" for the air. The newscasts from *The State* offices were scheduled at 7:55 A.M., 12:00 noon, 6:55 P.M., and 11:00 P.M. I'd get home around eleven-thirty at night and be up at six the next morning. I could get home for lunch and a nap most afternoons unless there was a breaking local news story. My main concern was about Lil being left alone so much, but she enjoyed listening to the radio and she was an avid reader. I would get home for dinner in the evenings and sometimes Lil would bring along a book or a magazine and walk back to the newspaper offices with me. She would read while I prepared and broadcast the eleven-o'clock report. It was good to be able to turn to her and ask:

"Honey, what do you think of this?"

"That's good, hon," she would reply, or, "I think you can make it clearer."

She became my severest critic.

Time and events were moving swiftly for us now, and we were very happy in spite of the grind.

But soon I began to notice that Lil wasn't feeling up to par. She seemed tired and she seemed to need a lot of rest.

When I arrived home one evening I found her still in bed.

"Hon, can you fix yourself something to eat? I just haven't felt like getting out of bed today. I'm so tired lately."

I wondered what could be wrong. She had also complained of nausea. That should have been my clue, but it wasn't.

My parents came the next weekend, and without my knowledge they took her to a doctor.

Well, when I got home that night after the six fifty-five news, Mother and Dad and Lil were sitting there grinning.

"What's up? Why is everybody grinning like that?" I asked.

"Son," my dad said, "we've got news for you."

"Yeah—about what?"

Almost in one voice the three of them blurted out:

"You're going to be a father!"

"What!"

"I'm pregnant," Lil said. "We're going to have a baby!"

Once the shock wore off I was overjoyed.

But I could not quite see how we could manage with a baby in a one-room apartment, and I could not see how we could get by on twenty-five dollars a week.

Lil has often said, "Don't tell Frank anything you don't want broadcast. He can't keep a secret."

True. I mentioned at WIS that Lil was expecting, and the word got to Mr. Shafto. He called me into his office, congratulated me, and gave me a five-dollar-a-week raise.

It was that spring that Walter Knobeloch appeared at station WIS.

I suppose there is a Walter Knobeloch in every man's life— a good friend and, at the same time, if you will pardon the cliché, the bane of one's existence.

Walter had grown up in Charleston. His father ran what was called a "Plain and Fancy" grocery store at the corner of Calhoun and Coming streets. I had never known Walter very well. He was four years older than I and had graduated from the High School of Charleston when I was still in grade school. He was a young man of less than medium height, with a thin frame and markedly effeminate mannerisms. He was an earnest student. He was graduated from Vanderbilt

University with honors. When I was transferred from Charleston to Columbia, Mr. Shafto had hired him to take my place at station WCSC. Apparently he had done well there. We had heard in Columbia that Mr. Shafto regarded him as a good writer, a man who could write commercial copy as well as news.

Thus, as the news operation expanded in Columbia, Mr. Shafto transferred him to WIS. Mr. Shafto thought he and I would make a good team.

We did in fact work well together, although at times I thought he was too pushy, overly aggressive, with an approach that sometimes rubbed people the wrong way. His voice was not the greatest in broadcasting, but it was adequate, and Walter himself was diligent. We got along well. He began doing small favors for Lil and me. He loaned me his 1934 Ford coupe occasionally so I could take Lil for a ride or run errands. But Lil's intuition was sounding small alarms. She told me one day, "Walter is a nice enough fellow, but there's something in his makeup I don't like or understand."

Walter had been with us in Columbia only a few months when I got an important telephone call, and made the mistake of telling him about it.

I was hard at work in my office in *The State*'s Editorial Department. The telephone rang and I reached for it muttering under my breath. I hated the interruption. The caller identified himself as B. H. Peace of Greenville, South Carolina.

The name commanded my attention. The Peace family owned radio station WFBC in Greenville. The Federal Communications Commission had just granted it a power increase from 250 watts to 5,000 watts. That lifted WFBC out of the strictly local class and made it an important regional station in the South. The Peace family also owned the Greenville *News* and the Greenville *Piedmont*, the morning and afternoon papers, respectively, in the city that called itself "the textile center of the South." B. H. Peace was the youngest of three brothers in the family. Roger and Charles devoted themselves to the newspapers. B.H. was left as the overseer of the radio property. He was known only by his initials. I never did learn his given names.

On the telephone, B.H. came quickly to the point. He said he had heard me on the air, he was expanding the WFBC Program Department in view of the strengthening of the station's signal, and he asked if I would like to take part in that expansion. He was not offering me a news job, but a job announcing and creating local programs.

I told him I was happy where I was and liked what I was doing in broadcasting. I said my wife was expecting a baby and it would be a bad time for me to contemplate a move. I thanked him, but said I didn't think I would be interested.

Then he asked how much money I made. I resented the question. I thought it was none of his business. I felt that if Peace or anyone else wanted a new employee, he should offer whatever he thought the employee would be worth to him. On the other hand, I had no reason to be ashamed of my salary. I told him, finally, that I was making thirty dollars a week.

He offered me forty dollars.

That was a 33.3 per cent increase, and we had a baby on the way.

Peace asked me to think it over and get in touch with Beverly T. "Bevo" Whitmire, general manager of WFBC, if I found myself interested.

I thought about it, of course. The extra ten dollars a week was tempting. But I could not bring myself to move Lil again, and with the baby coming I was reluctant to leave the security of a job I knew. I was on the fence, unable to make a decision.

And then I told Walter Knobeloch about it.

He said nothing about WFBC for several days. Then he offered to drive me home, and on the way he broached a subject:

"Why don't we look into that WFBC business?"

"What do you mean, *we?*"

"Well, Peace said they were expanding, didn't he? Maybe they would take us as a team."

He paused a moment, and then added:

"Let's drive up there one day and see about it. It's more money, and with your baby coming you could use it."

"Let me think about it."

I told Lil about it. I could see she was skeptical of Walter's proposition. She didn't trust him.

A few days later Walter brought it up again and I agreed to go, mainly out of curiosity, to see what they had in mind for me.

I made an appointment with "Bevo" Whitmire and we drove to Greenville in Walter's car.

"Bevo" was a large man. He wasn't fat, he was just large. He was charming and affable, and he had an explosive laugh. I liked him. Our meeting took on an air of informality, and in just a few minutes we were on a first-name basis.

As we talked, Walter worked himself into the conversation, and before long he was dominating it. He pointed out how well we worked together as a team, and before I realized what was happening he was talking himself into a job as WFBC's program director. I would be his assistant and the chief announcer—titles that meant very little. My thoughts were more on the additional money I would make, and which I certainly needed, and I was sure I would enjoy working for Bevo. I told him Lil was expecting the baby. He asked when it was due. I told him we thought about the middle of September. He suggested October 1 as a starting date, and before I realized what I was doing I had agreed to take the job.

Almost immediately I had qualms about what I had done. I dreaded having to tell Mr. Shafto.

When I told Lil about it she said what she would say so many times again through the years of our marriage:

"If that's what you want."

Telling Mr. Shafto would be more difficult. When I had to face up to it I felt I had made a mistake. He had been good to me. He had given me many opportunities. I liked him and his way of doing things. I thought seriously of backing out of the deal.

But I mustered up my courage and went in to see him. I wanted to tell him before Walter got to him. At first he was annoyed. Then he said:

"I half expected this would happen. I think we should have had a chance to match the offer."

I was sure then I had made a mistake. But I had already committed myself. We shook hands and he wished me luck. If he had ranted and raved and chewed me out it would have been better for my morale, but that was not the nature of the man.

The middle of September came and there was still no baby —and I was due on the job in Greenville in just two weeks. I was getting nervous about the whole thing.

Lil's mother came from Beaufort to help us. And finally, with October 1 at hand, I asked her advice, and Lil's. Should I call Whitmire and dump the job, or at least try to delay it?

They told me, in effect, to stay cool. I should go on to

Greenville, Lil would stay behind with her mother. Her labor was bound to begin soon. They would keep in touch by telephone.

So at Lil's insistence I traveled to Greenville and joined the staff of WFBC on October 1.

1918—Charleston, South Carolina. Dad, Mother, and me. Dad was a telegrapher in the Navy, stationed at the Charleston Navy Yard. I was three years old.

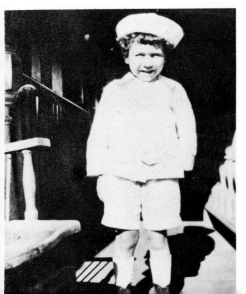

1919—Charleston, South Carolina. That's me on Mama Pinckney's piazza. I was four years old. How about my sharp outfit?

1920—Mother and me. Moth[er] always was the dressy type. I w[as] five years old.

1923—I posed for this in my good suit. Mother liked to see me dressed up. I was eight years old.

930—Right after I had won an atorical contest. Note the bow e and the two-tone shoes.

1935—Charleston, South Carolina. A freshman at the College of Charleston in premed. That's where I flunked rats and quit. The beanie was part of freshman indoctrination.

October 1935—Lil when our engagement was announced. This is the picture that was printed in the Charleston *Evening Post*.

Lil and me shortly after we were married and were living in Columbia, South Carolina. She was pregnant—but we didn't know.

1939—at WOL, Washington. MBS on microphone is for Mutual Broadcasting System. I was very proud to be considered a network announcer at twenty-four years of age.

May 9, 1941—The day I took delivery of my own airplane. Lil, John inspecting the wheel, Mike looking things over. It is the sixty-five-horsepower Aeronca that John Gantt and I flew to the West Coast and back a few weeks later.

1941—WOL, Washington, D.C. A Fulton Lewis, Jr., broadcast to the Mutual Network. Notice the time cards. Fulton couldn't keep track of the time from a clock. As his announcer, I had to get him off the air on time.

1943—Lil in a gimmick photo. I was in Navy flight training at Naval Air Station, Corpus Christi, Texas.

Fall of 1943—Naval Air Station, Hutchinson, Kansas. I was a Navy flight instructor. Good duty. I loved it.

1946—WOL, Washington, D.C. Interviewing Sid Caesar and friend about their experiences in *Tars and Stars*, the Coast Guard show that toured the war. I don't know the attractive lady's name— I wish I did.

1948—Scranton, Pennsylvania. I was general manager of Radio Station WSCR—"The one-grand station." *Photo by Jim Leo.*

1948—Scranton, Pennsylvania. Left to right, Tommy Dorsey, me, Ann Culkin, and Frank Mansuay, who was interviewing T.D. We carried the Tommy Dorsey syndicated radio program on WSCR. *Photo by Jim Leo.*

1951—Washington, D.C. "The American Forum of the Air" (NBC). Senators Purtell and John F. Kennedy.

1951—"Youth Wants to Know" (NBC). West German Chancellor Konrad Adenauer answers questions of high-school and college students through an interpreter who sits at left. *Photo by Reni Newsphoto Service.*

VIII

AND THE TIME DRAGGED. I called home every day. My telephone bill exceeded my ten-dollar-a-week increase. Every day Lil and her mother urged me to keep calm.

In the middle of the second week, Lil's father telephoned. He too had gone to Columbia. He said the labor had begun. He had taken Lil to the hospital that morning.

My heart pounded.

I told Whitmire. He told me to take time off. Walter loaned me his car, and I drove the 150 miles to Columbia in three hours. I went directly to the hospital. Lil was in bed, looking lovely—and resting comfortably. The pains had subsided. The doctor said it had been a false labor. He told me I might as well take her home, and I did.

But what to do now? I had a job in a city 150 miles away. I called Bevo Whitmire and explained, and he told me to stick with it.

Another day passed before the labor pains began again.

In those days a father was not allowed in the delivery room. I spent the first day in that hospital in the waiting room and in the hall pacing and waiting and pacing and asking questions and worrying and praying. Lil's dad brought me coffee and sandwiches, and I spent the night on a couch the nurses let me use in the hallway. Also, I spent the second night there

—and the third night. I didn't leave that hospital until the third agonizing day of Lil's labor. On the third day, Lil's father told me I had better go home and clean up.

Okay. I did. I went home and took a bath and shaved off a three-day growth of beard and put on some fresh clothes, and I hurried back.

When I got there, Lil's father and mother greeted me with broad smiles.

"Congratulations! It's a boy! And a ten-pounder!"

"My God! How's Lil?"

"Fine!"

"Thank God!"

I nearly fainted.

Suddenly, I felt guilt. I had caused Lil all that pain. She had been in labor seventy-two hours. But my anguish was short-lived. A nurse approached and said I could go in now and see my wife.

I opened her door and there she was, propped up in bed, a ribbon in her hair, smiling and looking lovely. She took my hand and kissed me and said:

"Thank you for our baby."

We named him Francis Samuel Blair III. He was the first in a long line of new arrivals at our house.

When I got back to Greenville and WFBC I had been gone four days, but Bevo Whitmire, bless him, did not dock my pay.

I found a neat little furnished bungalow for rent on Ruth-erford Road at the edge of Greenville, and soon after, Lil and the baby arrived. We also acquired a roomer.

Walter moved in. He took over our spare bedroom. It was not a bad arrangement. We welcomed his rent money. Also, it was comforting to me to know he was at home with Lil and the baby on the nights when I had to work at the station. Furthermore, I appreciated having occasional access to his car. We had not been able to afford one of our own.

Walter and I worked well together. We were given a free hand, and we created a number of local programs that were welcomed in the Greenville area. In a way it was a satisfying job. But I missed doing the news. There were only two newscasts a day over WFBC. Each was done at the Peace newspaper offices by a fellow named Dan Crosland. I sat in for him occasionally, but not often enough for my tastes. However, I managed to keep my hand in as a part-time journalist. I was still the regional correspondent for Transradio. And Transradio seemed to like my work. There were occasional commendations for my coverage as well as occasional Transradio checks, which always seemed to arrive just as Lil and I were running out of money.

Only a few months had passed when I received a peculiarly provocative letter from Transradio. The signer was Wallace Werble, now the southeastern regional manager. I still have that letter in my files:

"Dear Frank: Am driving through the South and expect to be in Greenville on Saturday. It is very important that I see you about a matter that might be of great personal interest to you. Kindest personal regards."

I had no idea what he had in mind.

He arrived at WFBC a few days later, on a cold, windy Saturday in February. We shook hands, and he told me he would like to talk with me in private. I did not have an office of my own; I used a desk in Walter's office. Walter's office was free, however; Walter himself was in the studios. We went in and sat around my desk, and Wallace Werble broke the news that was to transform my life—although by no means very soon.

He told me that station WOL in Washington, a major affiliate of the Mutual network and an important subscriber to the Transradio Press Service, was looking for a newscaster. They wanted somone young and aggressive, with experience and with a good voice.

We had hardly started the conversation when Walter walked in. He nodded and took his seat behind his desk and bent over his papers.

But, without thinking, I pursued the discussion with Werble. He suggested I get in touch with William B. Dolph, the WOL general manager. He gave me WOL's address and suggested I write to him at once. I thanked him and walked him to the door. It was hard to contain my excitement as I returned to my desk.

What Werble had dangled in front of me was an opportunity that seemed almost beyond hope. The job, if I could possibly get it, would mean not only a return to newscasting, it would also mean doing the news in the most important news city in America and perhaps in the world. Washington was where the big news was made. Furthermore, I would not only be doing newscasts for Washington radio audiences. WOL was an important Mutual affiliate, and the chance to broadcast over the network, to listeners all across the country, would surely come my way.

I glanced at the clock. I had time to get off a quick letter of application to William B. Dolph. I was just about to thread the paper into my typewriter when a voice from the next desk interrupted my thoughts.

"That sounded interesting," Walter Knobeloch said.

"What sounded interesting?"

"The opening at WOL."

"Yeah."

"I have an idea."

I think I knew what was coming.

Walter smiled and went on glibly:

"Why don't we write a joint letter to Dolph? Offer our services as a team?"

I gulped.

"A team may be just what they're looking for," Walter said.

"Yeah."

I had not had time to think.

Walter put paper in his machine and began typing.

"What can we lose?" he asked. "It's worth a try."

I was still half dazed.

Walter wrote a quick letter and handed it to me.

"Here. How's this?"

I read it, and it sounded good. Walter had outlined our backgrounds and emphasized the successes we had had together as a team. He said we complemented each other. And, he said, we would like to call at WOL for a joint interview.

I made another of my big mistakes.

"Okay," I said. "Send it."

Walter mailed the letter, and I immediately developed a strong guilt feeling. I felt I had betrayed Wallace Werble, and I felt I had in some way betrayed myself.

The predictable reply from William B. Dolph arrived a week later. There was only one vacancy on the WOL staff, but if one of us could come to Washington, an audition and an interview could be arranged.

Walter and Lil and I talked it over at home that evening, and we came to an unshakable conclusion. I could not afford a trip to Washington. But Walter could. So he would go without me and while there he would try again to sell us as a team.

So Walter went off to Washington, and in his absence I did his work as well as my own. He was gone three days.

When he returned, he walked into the living room and sat down with Lil and me and there was a quiet smile on his face.

There had indeed been only one opening at WOL and he, Walter, had taken it.

He gave Bevo Whitmire his notice, and when he left, I was made program director, a job I did not particularly want. I was even farther away from the news.

IX

I GOT ANOTHER BIG BREAK only three months after Walter left for Washington, and once again I muffed it.

The football season was approaching, and the Atlantic Refining Company was organizing a regional network of radio stations to carry play-by-play accounts of the important college football games. Dode Phillips, a former Erskine College football star, had been hired as an observer and commentator. He was a big name in the South. He had recently been voted the Greatest All-time Palmetto State Athlete. But he was not a skilled broadcaster. Bevo Whitmire alerted me: Atlantic was looking for a professional to complement Dode and do the play-by-play. Rather, the N. W. Ayer Company, the big ad agency, was looking in Atlantic's behalf. N. W. Ayer had consulted Bevo, and Bevo suggested a sort of mass audition for the job. Anyone at WFBC who had done announcing would try out, and so would Jimmy Thompson, sports reporter for the Greenville *News*, who had done WFBC's sports work—what there was of it—in the past.

I knew practically nothing about football. I hardly knew the rules of the game. I was aware of the records of a few of the top stars and the top teams in the Southeast, but beyond that I was ignorant.

Atlantic Refining would pay twenty-five dollars a game—

and that was big money. It was powerfully tempting. But I was a football dunce and I knew it. I told Bevo I would not even try out for the job.

In due course two N. W. Ayer executives, Les Quailey and Wallace Orr, appeared in the WFBC studios and auditions began. Each candidate was asked to dream up a mythical football game and describe it in front of a microphone. I sat in the control room, monitoring. Bevo and the N. W. Ayer people listened in Bevo's office. They went into a private huddle when the last audition was completed. I watched from the control room. The door was ajar. Their conversation was in muted voices. In a moment or two, Bevo left the others and approached me.

"They want you to take the audition," he said.

I was astonished.

"But I told you! I know next to nothing about football."

"Take the audition anyway. What can you lose?"

"Everything."

"Well, take it anyway."

It was something close to a command.

It meant an extra twenty-five dollars a week, on top of a forty-dollar salary.

I went into the studio and dreamed up what must have been the damndest game in the history of football. I was never entirely sure of what I was talking about.

When it was all over, Bevo and the agency people went into a huddle again, and then came to me.

"Congratulations," Bevo said. "You've got the job!"

When I shook hands with Quailey and Orr, I was in a state of mild panic. The first game on the Altantic network was less than three weeks away. I had barely three weeks in which to learn a game I had hardly even played. But I would be earning an extra twenty-five dollars a week.

Lil and I had never owned a car. After Walter Knobeloch left for Washington, we had had to move in order to ease our transportation problems. We had moved from the outskirts of Greenville to a small furnished apartment in the city. I was able to walk to work. I could even get home for lunch.

But we wanted a car. And now, through the football season, at least, I would be making sixty-five dollars a week. That looked like big money.

Well, I saw it one day on the way home for lunch. It was a beauty. Yes, it was on a used-car lot. Someone else had had it first. But to me it looked fresh and precious. I knew enough about cars to see that it was a 1935 sedan, a Chevrolet.

I went in and talked to the salesman. Yes, he said, the Chevy was a cream puff. He told me in the manner of used-car salesmen everywhere that I obviously had a good eye for a bargain, because the price was only three hundred dollars.

"Three hundred dollars!"

"And a real bargain, sir! A real bargain!"

It would have been no more within my reach had the salesman said three thousand dollars.

"The good thing about it," the salesman said, "is that you only need a hundred dollars cash. The rest can be financed. No problem."

Well, a hundred dollars was still more money than I had.

I told Lil about it over lunch. She said it sounded like a nice car, for anyone who had a hundred dollars.

On the way back to the studio I stopped at the used-car lot again. The beauty was still there. But a hundred dollars!

As I walked away, I began thinking more about money. I would be getting twenty-five dollars a game for the football broadcasts, assuming they did not fire me after the first quarter of the first game. In four games I would have a hundred dollars. But by then someone else would have bought my Chevy.

So I asked Bevo Whitmire for a hundred-dollar advance on the football games, and he gave me the money on the spot. I drove the Chevy home the next day. But on the way the thought occurred to me that in only three more weeks I would be broadcasting play-by-play on a game I hardly knew; my hands gripped the wheel and I could feel my palms perspiring.

Well, N. W. Ayer didn't fire me after the first quarter of the first game. But when the game ended—The Citadel vs. Newberry College at Newberry—I was shaking. I had been out of my element from the first kickoff. Without Dode Phillips to turn to with queries, I could never have made it. I fared just slightly better on the second game a week later—Georgia vs. South Carolina. But only slightly. I thought for the first time that, given a season or two of intensive study, I might actually be able to do the job. Meanwhile, I had paid off fifty dollars of my advance from Bevo Whitmire.

My third game would be The Citadel vs. Furman. And word came that Les Quailey of N. W. Ayer would be joining us in the broadcast booth. We were told he wanted to "observe." I knew what that meant. He wanted to observe Frank Blair. Les really knew the game. He had been a spotter and statistician for Ted Husing, a top-notch CBS sportscaster. I felt that if Les observed me in action for only a few minutes, I would be out on my ear. The money I had been counting on for my car would be gone. But there was nothing I could do to keep Les away.

The night of the game arrived. Quailey and I were in the announce booth at Johnson Hagood Stadium in Charleston. The stadium was crowded, the fans were eager and excited. A roar went up as the teams trotted onto the field. Dode Phillips was broadcasting statistics and naming the starting players. I was idle.

Les leaned over to me and said: "Aren't you the least bit excited? Hell, Frank! There's going to be a football game down there!"

"Yes, I know, Les, but I don't see anything to get excited about. A bunch of guys kicking a football and running around down there and warming up. Maybe when they start playing I'll get excited. I hope."

Les nodded.

I knew immediately I had said the wrong thing. You don't tell an ardent football fan that the game doesn't move you.

The whistle blew. Someone kicked off and the game began, and all through it I was conscious of Les Quailey's presence. I did as bad a job as I had done at my first game—perhaps a poorer job.

Les and I were at a cocktail party in Bevo Whitmire's home the next evening. Les took me aside.

"You don't like being a football announcer, do you?"

"No. Sorry. You remember at the audition I told you I'd never done it before and wasn't at all sure I could make it."

"Yes. But we liked your audition best. We thought you might get to like it."

"Thanks, but I'm afraid it's not my cup of tea. I wish it were."

I thought I knew what was coming. I was about to lose the job. I had earned seventy-five dollars against my advance, but I still had twenty-five dollars to go. However, I would make it some way.

"You know, Les," I said, "I think the guy you really want is Jimmy Thompson, the sportswriter."

Les nodded.

"You wouldn't be offended if we made that change?"

"Not in the least. I'd only be disappointed in myself."

"Okay. We'll do it."

I thought those were his last words on the subject. Instead, he said:

"But we liked the way you handled the commercials."

"Thanks."

"And we'd like you to continue on the broadcast team, as the commercial announcer."

"Glad to," I said.

Les smiled and added:

"And at the same salary. Twenty-five dollars a week."

I would have my advance repaid in another week.

X

WALTER KNOBELOCH WAS DOING WELL in Washington. We had heard as much via the grapevine, and Walter himself had said as much in his occasional letters. He was doing news and special events, the work I loved best. I envied him.

Walter was not a man to let small things stand in his way. The name Knobeloch had a German ring, and by now Adolf Hitler's antics in Germany had given rise to an anti-German feeling in the United States. More and more Americans were thinking, as I did, that a war against the Nazis was inevitable. It was in that climate that Walter changed his name. He broadcast the news as Walter Compton. The name Compton had a nice, English-sounding ring.

I first heard him use his new name when he telephoned from Washington one afternoon that December. I took his call at what had once been his own desk in the WFBC offices.

"Frank," he said, "I *told* you I would keep my eyes open for you."

"Yeah?"

"There's a job opening up here. An announcer's job, and I've recommended you for it."

I felt a quick jolt of excitement. Walter suggested I make arrangements to come to Washington as soon as possible for an audition and an interview. I told him I would think it over and get back to him soon.

It was hard to contain my excitement. I made myself calm down and think it through. I would be an announcer, not a newscaster, but it would be a foot in the door; I would be on the staff of a major radio station in the capital city, and the station was affiliated with the Mutual network, which was steadily growing in popularity and prestige. It was likely that once there I would be given opportunities on the network and in newscasting. I would be in the big leagues.

But I was only twenty-two years old. Could I compete against men with years of experience behind them? Also, I would be moving with a fourteen-month-old baby, and I would be taking Lil to a big, strange city far away from her parents. The cost of moving would be high. And would I draw an adequate salary? Money was tight for us already, in a town with living costs that obviously were lower than those in Washington. But still . . . a job on WOL, in Washington!

When Lil and I talked it over, her reactions surprised me. She was twenty-one years old, she had the responsibility of a small child, we were very nearly penniless, and apart from Walter Knobeloch—now Walter Compton—neither of us knew anyone in Washington.

And, beyond all that, we suspected that Lil was pregnant again. If she was, I would want the best medical care possible for her, and the expense would be great.

"I'd love to go," Lil said. "I'd love to live in Washington. If you want the job, and I think you do, let's do it!"

I felt a sudden new surge of love and ambition.

"And hon," she said, "you know they do have babies in Washington."

But I could not afford to make a false step. I did not want

to be carried away in a blue-sky dream. It would be a new city, a new job, and we had another baby on the way.

I sought Bevo Whitmire's advice. By now Bevo was my friend as well as my boss. I trusted him.

He stood up when I walked into his office, his huge frame dwarfing his desk.

"Hi, Frank! Welcome! What's on your mind?"

I told him.

"Hell, Frank, take it, take the damned job if you can get it! Don't think we wouldn't miss you. Damn it! You'd leave a big hole in this staff. But sure, you try for that job. You've got to."

I thanked him and asked if I could have the weekend off to go to Washington and take the audition.

"Sure," he said. "Go ahead."

He glanced down at my shoes. They were the only pair I had and they were scruffy—shined, but with the cracks of age in the leather.

"If you're going up to Washington, you'd better get yourself a new pair of shoes."

New shoes? I could hardly afford new laces.

"Bevo," I said, "right now I haven't enough money for new shoes."

Bevo looked at me for a moment, then reached down and took off one of his own shoes.

"Here," he said, "try this for size."

I smiled and tried on Bevo's shoe; it was a size too large, but it was comfortable.

"Nice," I said.

He nodded.

"Good," he said, "because you can borrow those shoes for your trip. I've got another pair and these might bring you luck."

So I called Walter in Washington and arranged for an audition that coming Sunday morning. And I traveled to Spartanburg, South Carolina, thirty-five miles away, where my father was now the Western Union manager, and borrowed the train fare from Dad and Mother.

That Saturday night, I sat up all night on the day coach to Washington. The day coach was all I could afford.

William Dolph had an office befitting his stature in broadcasting. It was sumptuous and elegant, with fine mahogany furniture, magnificent drapes, and wall-to-wall carpeting that felt ankle deep when Walter and I walked across it. I was nervous when I was shown in. I felt small and clumsy and alone, even though Walter was with me. I was a small-town announcer in the presence of one of the wheels in the radio industry. A young woman sat with him.

Dolph was in his early forties, balding. He got up from behind his massive desk and shook hands. He had a warm, friendly smile. As we exchanged greetings I began to feel at ease. He introduced me to the woman with him—Madeline Ensign, the program director, who would be my boss if I got the job.

He glanced at his watch.

"Okay," he said, "let's get on with it."

He explained that he had a date on the golf course.

"Walter," he said, "get some copy for your friend here to read and ask Steve to come in."

Steve McCormick was WOL's chief announcer. He was a handsome man a few years older than I. He beamed when he smiled, and his eyes sparkled. I liked him immediately. We shook hands and he wished me luck. I left for the announce booth, with Walter at my side. Steve stayed behind with

Dolph and Madeline Ensign. They would listen to my audition on a monitor.

In the studio, Walter handed me some commercial copy and news copy and introduced me to Bellum Miller, WOL's big, bald-headed control operator.

"Just give Bellum a signal when you're ready and he'll patch you through to Dolph's office," Walter said.

I was anxious to get it over with. I had never really taken an audition before—not at Charleston, nor at Columbia, nor at Greenville. I read through the copy, rehearsing one or two phrases under my breath. When I thought I was about ready to go, Walter stuck his head in the studio door.

"When you're through reading," he said, "give them a description of the studio. They just want you to ad-lib. There's a lot of that to do around here."

"Okay," I said.

I signaled Bellum Miller. A light came on over the window looking into the control room, the signal that my microphone was live.

I read the copy without a fluff, although I mispronounced one word. I put the accent on the wrong syllable in "ephedrine" in a commercial promoting a nose drop. But otherwise, no flubs, and I felt I was reasonably fluent in my ad-lib description.

Walter led me back to Dolph's office to hear the verdict.

Dolph, Madeline Ensign, and Steve McCormick were straight-faced when I walked in.

"You mispronounced 'ephedrine,'" Dolph said, but there was a gentle smile on his lips.

"I know. I'm afraid I was nervous."

"Anyway," Dolph went on, his smile broadening, "we liked your work. We liked it very much."

He asked if I could start work in two weeks.

"Yes, *sir*," I said. "Yes, sir."

"We can pay you fifty dollars a week."

"That will be fine," I said.

I hoped it really would be. Living costs in Washington concerned me, and Lil being pregnant, I would have doctor and hospital bills to pay.

"Over and above that," Dolph said, "we try to get a commercial fee for our announcers. It's not much, but it all adds up."

A commercial fee of even a dollar or two for a program or two a day would raise my income significantly.

We shook hands and I left Dolph's office.

If I had been wearing a hat, I think I would have thrown it in the air once I had closed that door. I was exuberant. I was in another world. I had a bubbly sensation in my stomach. I was coming to the most important news town in the world and joining the staff of a radio station there. I would not be broadcasting the news—not for a while, but I was still only twenty-three. I had plenty of time. I was determined to make it.

Walter shook hands and congratulated me. He said he would try to find Lil and me a place to live.

At Union Station, I filed a telegram to Dad. I sent it collect. As a Western Union employee, he could make it a "deadhead" telegram and it would cost us nothing. It read:

"ARRIVE 1:15 A.M. ALL SET FOR JANUARY FIRST. CALL LIL. LOVE."

In my exuberance, I signed it: "THE MUTUAL BROADCASTING SYSTEM."

Aboard the train, I thought I was in for another sleepless night. I would have to sit up for eleven hours. I took off my shoes. *My* shoes? They were Bevo's. Maybe he had been right. He had said they might bring me luck.

I put my feet up and I fell asleep before the train left the station.

I returned to Greenville with mixed emotions. When I told Bevo I had taken the job, he smiled and congratulated me.

XI

AT SOME POINT IN HIS BABYHOOD, we began calling our son "Mike," a nickname that has stuck with him through life.

It was early on a cold December morning when Lil, Mike, and I got into our Chevy and left Greenville for Washington. Walter had found and rented a small furnished apartment for us and we had packed our meager belongings into the trunk and on the rear seat of our old Chevrolet. The little old Chevy performed beautifully on that long journey.

We approached Washington in late afternoon. About six miles from the city, along Lee Boulevard (now Arlington Boulevard), we noticed some attractive small houses under construction, the first stories of fieldstone and the second of lap-strake siding. They looked warm and inviting, and we wondered how much they would cost. But whatever the cost, they would be beyond our reach.

We rounded the long curve on the boulevard that took us past Fort Myer and wound up on a bluff overlooking the city of Washington. I shall never forget the sensation I experienced. There it was—the nation's capital—beckoning to me. There was the Lincoln Memorial, the reflecting pool, the Washington Monument, the Mall, and the Capitol itself off in the distance. The sun was setting in back of us, and its rays gave those historic buildings and shrines a golden glow. The gnawing little feelings of doubt and insecurity that I had felt, disappeared. I felt a glowing ambition to succeed in Washington. Great things were happening there. I wanted to become part of it all.

Walter Compton had told me the apartment he had rented for us was at 127 Carroll Street, S.E., two blocks from the Capitol grounds, so I drove toward the Capitol building. Near there, I found Carroll Street.

There was a parking space right in front of No. 127.

"Well, I guess we made it," I said.

"I guess we made it," Mike echoed.

The neighborhood was unimpressive. In those days Southeast Washington was not an elite section of the metropolitan area. Nevertheless, we had a place to live.

Lil and Mike stood by the car in the cold of that fading December day. I went up the steps of the row house and rang the bell.

I heard children's voices yelling:

"Somebody's at the door, Grandma!"

"I'll get it," an older woman's voice yelled back.

The door opened. There stood a disheveled, grimy-looking woman in her late sixties.

"Yes?" she inquired.

"My name is Blair and Mr. Compton—" That's as far as I got.

"Oh yes, Mr. Blair. Expected you yesterday."

"Yes, ma'am, the trip took longer than we planned."

By this time the two noisy kids were at the door staring at me and poking at each other.

"Well, do come in. Everything is ready for you," the woman said. I motioned to Lil to join me. We stepped inside.

The house was in complete disarray, and there was a musty odor about it.

"My God," I thought, "what has Walter gotten us into?"

"Your place is on the second floor. Just follow me," the woman said. "Oh, I'm Mrs. Gimmel—first name, Agnes—and these are my grandchildren, Buddy and Janie. They live with me since my daughter left her husband."

The odor faded away as we approached the second floor. At the head of the stairs was a kitchenette large enough to accommodate a small table and two chairs. There was a living room and a bedroom and an antiquated bathroom. It was neat and clean—a far cry from what I'd observed on the first floor. With Lil's touch, we could make out there for a while.

"You must be frozen," Mrs. Gimmel said. "While you're bringing your things in I'll send up a pot of tea to warm you up."

"Thank you," I replied. Anything to get Mrs. Gimmel and her two grandchildren out of there so we could relax and look the place over.

Lil had some jars of baby food for Mike, but nothing for her or me. I walked up to Pennsylvania Avenue, found a White Tower, and got us a bag of hamburgers which, in those days, cost fifteen cents apiece. I bought coffee for us and milk for Mike.

When I got back I plugged in the little radio set we had. I was eager to find out what Washington radio sounded like. To me it sounded good. It was sophisticated and urban.

That was our first night in Washington, and thus began some of the happiest, busiest, most rewarding years of our life together.

I was twenty-three years old and Lil was twenty-one, and we were in a strange and big city with a small baby, hundreds of miles from home, with one friend in town, Walter Compton—and with a problem that kept me awake through much of that first night in Washington in the December cold of 1938.

We were practically broke.

Walter had paid our first month's rent—twenty-five dollars. However, he was doing well at WOL, and he had said he could wait awhile for me to return the cash he had laid out for me. Nevertheless, Mike had to have baby food, and Lil and I would have to eat, too—and I had exactly twelve dollars. I would not be paid for two weeks.

That first morning I went to the A&P store a block away and bought a few staples. We had a breakfast of sorts in our drab little apartment, and then I finished unloading the car. It was bitterly cold as I brought in the last of our possessions —some dishes, bed linen, blankets, Mike's toys, and some personal things. Among them were a few books and my violin, which I had hardly touched since Curly Blair and His Charlestonians had disappeared from the dance halls and the radio three years before.

After unloading, I put on my best suit and left five dollars with Lil "in case you need anything." Then, when Lil wasn't looking, I slipped my violin out of the apartment and back into the car.

On the way to WOL to check in, I found a pawn shop on Seventh Street. I hocked the violin for twenty-five dollars. Then I tossed in my high-school ring for another three dollars.

We could keep eating for another two weeks.

The immediate problem that remained for me now was to get a good start in the big leagues of broadcasting. I wanted to be something more than an announcer on WOL. I wanted to do newscasting, and I wanted to be heard coast to coast on the Mutual network.

The Mutual Radio System had been organized in 1934, the year before I got into broadcasting. As the name indicated, it was set up as a system by which radio stations might mutually meet the cost of producing radio programs. In the beginning only three stations were involved—WOR in New York, WGN in Chicago, and WLW in Cincinnati. Each operated on fifty thousand watts, the strongest radio signal allowed under FCC regulations. By 1938, when I began settling down in Washington, other stations had been added, including, of course, WOL, a vital cog. Mutual was growing into a coast-to-coast linkup of four hundred radio stations, and WOL was a kingpin because it was through the WOL facilities that Mutual covered the news of Washington at a time when the Washington dateline was dominant virtually every day. Those were the times when we were struggling to recover from the Great Depression and when the world was building up to another war.

Mutual had many of the top names in newscasting. H. V. Kaltenborn was on NBC with his peculiar, labored delivery. Dorothy Thompson was on CBS (Barbara Walters had not yet been born). Lowell Thomas was on both NBC and CBS. Yes, Lowell's popularity was such that he could command contracts from both networks at the same time. But Mutual competed against both NBC and CBS with men like Raymond Graham Swing, the very popular Edwin C. Hill, who did what he called "the human side of the news," and the always optimistic Gabriel Heatter—"Ah, there's good news tonight," his usual opening line. Among Mutual's strongest entries was a conservative-minded commentator, Fulton Lewis, Jr., who made himself famous by denouncing President Roosevelt. Fulton was so controversial that some of the affiliates, including one of the network's founders, WOR, refused to broadcast his views.

Fulton's commentary was offered first as a sustaining program—that is, one without sponsorship; then as a co-operative
program. Stations were free to sell sponsorship to their local
advertisers. When they did, a fee became payable to Mutual,
and a part of the payment went to WOL.

In the beginning and for several months Fulton operated
alone, gathering news himself and writing his own scripts, but
as his power and prestige increased he assembled a staff to
work with him. His volume of mail from listeners was on the
increase, and requests for him to speak around the country
started coming in. His attacks on the New Deal were paying
off. He investigated, probed, and cajoled to get news for his
broadcasts. The conduct of government was his target—
Roosevelt his bull's-eye—and Fulton successfully conveyed to
a large number of listeners the notion that he was keeping
his eye on Washington and his ear to the ground in their behalf and that he considered it his patriotic duty to serve as a
watchdog for the people. He said Roosevelt was leading the
nation toward socialism.

By the time I arrived in Washington, a considerable number of affiliates were selling the program to sponsors, and Fulton was getting wealthy.

The actual technique of broadcasting, however, was not his
forte. In time I would be coaching him in phrasing, inflection, and where to take a breath while reading. We became
close friends—although politically I don't think we ever agreed
about anything.

Fulton had become a national figure, a man who
influenced the thinking of many Americans, partly by reason
of the fact that he was a good fisherman.

He had been a reporter for the International News Service,
a wire service that later merged with United Press to become

United Press International. He had gained a reputation around Washington as an investigative reporter.

The fishing editor of the Washington *Times Herald* was a regular broadcaster on station WOL. Every Friday night, he broadcast fishing information, such things as where the fish might be biting in Chesapeake Bay.

Then came a Friday when the fishing editor was ill and unable to broadcast. Fulton heard about that and immediately offered his services to WOL as a substitute. He would fill in, he said, until the fishing editor recovered. WOL accepted, and Fulton became acquainted with WOL executives, including General Manager Bill Dolph. Fulton and Bill Dolph began talking politics in the studios and corridors of WOL and I suppose at an occasional lunch, and Dolph was impressed by the provocative nature of Fulton's views. Dolph was an enterprising radio executive. Recognizing an interesting journalist when he saw one, he became Fulton's manager and he put Fulton on the air once a night to do a Washington commentary. Not only was he on WOL, he also went on Mutual as well.

Mutual's news operations were under the command of one of the early greats of broadcast journalism, Abe Schechter. Like most radio news executives of that and later eras, Schechter had begun his career in print journalism. He had been night editor of the Associated Press based in New York when radio news began slowly coming into its own. Spotting opportunity in a new and growing field, he had left the AP to join NBC. His first assignment at NBC had been to set up a news operation. In a sense he had been a one-man News Department there; he had collected the news of the world by telephone, calling news sources in the United States and abroad and then putting the information into the words that announcers would put on the air. In time Mutual had hired him away from NBC and, if he had been the father of NBC News he became the adopted father of Mutual News. (There would come a time when NBC would hire him back so his name and talent could add luster to a struggling new early-morning TV program.)

Schechter became a legendary figure to me in my first days at WOL. I developed a nodding acquaintance with his news-casting stars, who were in and out of WOL regularly. I felt flattered to be on the same team. I stood in awe of these men. I made it a point to study their styles, and I dreamed of the day when I also might bring the news to the entire network, signing off with my own name. But my own duties in those first few days were of a much lower order. I did routine staff-announcer chores. I made station breaks; delivered commercials; prepared, transcribed, and recorded music programs and, occasionally, handled a local newscast. I became totally absorbed in my work. Lil listened to me when possible at our apartment on Carroll Street and offered her criticism and encouragement when I got home in the evenings.

"I couldn't tell you were reading," she would say at times, her highest form of flattery. It meant that I appeared to be talking to the listener rather than reading from a script.

Each day we counted our dwindling supply of cash, but two weeks passed and we survived. We were almost entirely out of money—I barely had carfare left—when my first pay-day rolled around. I received a check for a hundred dollars minus the Social Security deduction. That check was a blessed relief. We celebrated by going to the movies.

Little Mike loved the movies, and the picture playing at the neighborhood movie house three blocks from our apart-ment was *Snow White and the Seven Dwarfs*, which we knew Mike would especially enjoy. Snow White was one of his favorite story-book characters. He knew all the seven dwarfs by name and could recognize their pictures.

We enjoyed ourselves in that darkened movie house. Mike sat on the arm rest on my seat or stood up in his own seat, pointing occasionally at the screen and identifying the dwarfs —"See Sneezy! See Dopey! See Bashful!"

Then the newsreel came on. President Roosevelt appeared on the screen. Mike stood up in his seat, pointed at the President, and yelled, "See Dopey! See Dopey!"

There were shouts and screams of laughter all through the audience. My God, was that embarrassing! We left in the middle of the newsreel. We didn't wait for the selected short subjects.

It was only a week later that I got my first commercial assignment. I was hired to introduce, insert commercials and sign off a news program—well, it was billed as a news program —which I don't think would be allowed on the air today. It was called "Five-star Final." It was not on the Mutual network. It was on a regional network that operated only along the Atlantic seaboard. It was called the Intercity Broadcasting System. Intercity linked together several stations in key cities, including New York, Philadelphia, and Washington. It carried a number of programs, but "Five-star Final" was its principal attraction.

On "Five-star Final," professional actors dramatized the news events of the day. In a sense, the program consisted of re-enactments of news events. An unsuspecting listener might think he was hearing the actual event as it took place. One of the actors did an almost perfect impersonation of President Roosevelt. Another sounded very much like Eleanor. Others played the roles of whatever public figures were involved in the day's events. It was an ingenious idea and the program acquired a large audience, but the line between truth and fiction, between drama and reality, was fuzzy and blurred. Today most news directors would veto that program as irresponsible. That was a point that scarcely crossed my mind in those days. I was much too impressed having a commercial assignment, and I was even more impressed by the rewards. I was paid twenty-five dollars a week as "Five-star Final's" announcer. That twenty-five dollars a week made all the difference. However, it hardly meant that we were out of the woods, financially. Lil was well along in her second pregnancy, and we would soon face some medical bills. And over and above that, with another baby we would be hard-pressed to make it at 127 Carroll Street. The apartment would be too small.

Our thoughts kept going back to the small new houses we had seen driving along Lee Boulevard when we had first arrived in Washington. We began going out there on Sunday afternoons to see how the builders were progressing and, most of all, to see whether the "For Sale" signs were still there—or whether the last of those houses had been sold. A house of our own seemed far beyond our reach, of course, but still we could dream, and we could entertain at least a faint hope, however unreal it might seem, that one day we could muster the money for a down payment. I was surrounded by men earning what apparently were colossal incomes. My talents perhaps were more modest and my experience was certainly limited, but I felt there was at least the possibility that my earnings might continue to rise, if only slowly and by nominal increases.

As the weeks passed that in fact was the case. I began getting small fees for doing local commercials, and I even got my first and long-awaited assignment to do an announcing job on the Mutual network. Frances Perkins, President Roosevelt's

Secretary of Labor—the first woman Cabinet officer in American history—asked for Mutual time to broadcast a short message about Labor Department policy. I was assigned to introduce her to the network. It was a great thrill.

But of course I was still a local announcer and I was immersed in the day-by-day operations of Washington local news.

The star of Washington radio in those prewar days was a man with a style all his own—a talk-show artist who sounded like your next-door neighbor gossiping over the back fence, feisty and irreverent, but one with a full measure of warmth and friendliness. His name was Arthur Godfrey.

Arthur was the "morning man" on station WJSV (now WTOP). His program consisted of news, weather information, music, and his own delightful chatter. He was the bad boy of Washington radio. He poked fun at his sponsors—sometimes even insulted them. One of his advertisers was a furrier named Zlotnick, whose trademark was a huge stuffed bear mounted at the entrance to his shop. Over the years the weather had aged and soiled that monster. Arthur took delight in inviting his lady listeners to call on "Zlotnick the furrier, at the sign of the dirty old white bear." Arthur's chatter was irresistible, and I found myself listening to him as much as to WOL's own morning man, Art Brown, who was himself a strong entry in the competitive morning field; he ranked second only to Godfrey.

Godfrey filled much of his time with stories of flying. He talked constantly of Beacon Field, a bumpy cow-pasture air field three miles south of Alexandria, Virginia, where his small plane was maintained. It was called Beacon Field because an FAA Airways light beacon stood alongside one of its hangars.

Something happened to me as I listened to Arthur's morning programs. First I would hear the news from Europe—always ominous news—pointing toward war. Then I would hear Arthur's tales of Beacon Field and his flying out there. His stories quickened my own interest in flying, and the growing fears of war made me realize once again that if war came, I would rather fight in the air than on the ground. I longed for enough money to go out to Beacon Field to take flying lessons.

But I had more immediate worries. Spring was at hand, and only a few months remained before our second child would be born. We urgently needed more living space.

There came a Sunday afternoon when I made up my mind to find out if there was any possibility whatever of our buying one of those new small houses on Lee Boulevard. We had very little in the bank, but I felt I had to try.

We drove out there again. The name and address of the real-estate broker selling the houses was on the "For Sale" sign. I copied it and we drove to the broker's office.

A few minutes later a salesman took us back to Lee Boulevard and began showing us through one of the unsold houses. It looked like a palace to us. It had a living room with a fireplace, a dining room, and an acceptable kitchen on the first floor, and three bedrooms and a bath on the second. Our hearts leaped at the thought of living there, and we played along with our dreams. The house would cost $6,500.

Back in the broker's office, the salesman told us he was sure we could get a $5,000 mortgage from the Arlington Trust Company. We would need only $1,500 in cash, plus settlement costs. Only $1,500! I thought he might just as well have said $15,000 or $150,000. I leveled with the man. I told him we had just come to Washington on a new job, my income was modest, and my assets were nil. Moreover, as he could well see by now, Lil was pregnant and we would have hospital and doctor bills to face.

That salesman nodded his understanding, and then taught me to believe in miracles.

He asked me if I had twenty-five dollars. I told him I could write a check for that amount and asked what good that would do. He replied that I could put down a twenty-five-dollar deposit and sign a statement of intent to buy, provided financing could be arranged. That, he said, would take the house off the market. We could then apply for a mortgage, and if the application were approved, "we'll proceed from there."

I glanced at Lil. She had tears in her eyes. My heart melted. I resolved on the spot to get that house for her and our babies by any means I could conceivably devise, short of holding up a bank. I wrote out my check for twenty-five dollars.

A few days later the realtor called and said our mortgage application had been approved.

And, he said, the builder would take a second mortgage for the $1,500 we would still owe.

I could hardly believe what I was hearing.

Two weeks later, with Mike sitting on Lil's lap because we couldn't afford a baby sitter, we signed the papers and closed the deal. The broker himself paid our settlement costs. He said I could repay him when I got around to it.

The smile on Lil's face when we walked out of the office must have been reward enough for that kindly broker.

Once outside, both of us were so excited we could hardly find our car, and once inside the car we kissed and hugged each other and cried with joy.

"What's wrong?" Mike asked. "Aren't we happy?"

"Son," I said, "we haven't been happier since you were born."

"Why are we crying then?"

"These are tears of gladness, son. You'll see."

We drove directly to the house. I find it difficult to describe the feeling I had when I turned the key in the lock. There it was, all new and clean with just a faint smell of fresh paint. We wandered through every room. The kitchen was already equipped with stove and refrigerator and ample cupboards. Lil loved it. Mike and I examined the full basement and the furnace and the washtubs. It would make a nice playroom for Mike on cold, damp days, I thought. Mike was as excited as we were.

He said, "You mean this is our house? We're going to live here?"

"You said it, son, we're really going to live here."

In all the excitement we hadn't given thought to the fact that we had no furniture. I found myself practicing what Roosevelt was doing to get the country back on its feet— "deficit financing." I bought furniture from Montgomery Ward, on the installment plan.

That was in April. On July 18, 1938, our son John was born at Sibley Memorial Hospital. When the doctor told me I had another son, he said:

"Young man, your wife really loves you. All through the delivery she was calling for you and saying over and over again, 'Hon, I love you.' You must be hon."

"Yes, doctor, I'm hon," I replied.

XII

MORE AND MORE ASSIGNMENTS were being offered me at WOL, and also at Mutual. I welcomed them.

My day started with the 6:00 A.M. newscast on the Art Brown "Rise and Shine" program. And, of course, that meant early rising for me each day, something I was going to have to get used to. The really tough part of it was that I usually did the news at eleven o'clock at night as well. And sometimes I was the Mutual announcer for the remote broadcast of dance bands.

Mutual was famous for its late-night broadcasts of the big bands from hotels and ballrooms all around the country. The broadcasts began at 11:30 P.M. and continued in half-hour segments until 1:00 A.M. The other networks were competing, but Mutual dominated the field. The roster of bands Mutual broadcast reads like a Who's Who of the big-band era. In fact, Kay Keyser's Kollege of Musical Knowledge, with vocalists Ginny Simms, Harry Babbitt, and Ishkabibble, got its start as a dance-band remote on Mutual.

The big-band leaders were folk heroes—men like Benny Goodman; Harry James; Glenn Miller; Artie Shaw; Tommy Dorsey, who introduced a skinny young singer named Frank Sinatra; Jimmy Dorsey, who featured Helen O'Connell and Bob Eberly; Ozzie Nelson, who married his vocalist, Harriet

Hilliard; Sammy Kaye; Louis Armstrong; Woody Herman; Glen Gray; Guy Lombardo; and Freddy Martin, the band Mike Douglas sang with for several years.

Of course, many of the bands came to Washington to play the hotels or the theaters, and when they did, WOL was responsible for originating the broadcasts to the network. In spite of the hours, dance-band remotes were fun to do. When it was time to take the air and I'd cue the orchestra leader and a familiar theme song went out over the airwaves, a chill would run up my spine. At the appointed time I'd step up to the microphone, the leader would soften the music slightly, and I'd cup my ear with my hand in order to hear my own voice over the music and say something like this:

"Good evening, ladies and gentlemen. From the beautiful Shar Zad Room of the Carleton Hotel in your nation's capital the Mutual network is proud to present the music of . . ."

Lil used to come with me on those assignments. She enjoyed the big bands, too, and she loved to dance. Moreover, the management was always good for a couple of free drinks. Yes, it was tough getting up at five o'clock the next morning, but I always made it, and, apart from the fun of it all, the job always meant an extra fee.

WOL also had the contract to broadcast the Washington Redskins football games on Sunday afternoons. Tony Wakeman, the WOL sportscaster, was the play-by-play reporter, although he was no Ted Husing or Bill Stern. When the season began that autumn of 1938, I was given the job of broadcasting the "color" on the games, handling the commercials, and serving as Tony's spotter and assistant. I don't think I was given the job because of my short-lived career as a football announcer in Greenville. I think the assignment came my way simply because there was no one else available to do it. Steve McCormick had "American Forum of the Air" every Sunday evening, and therefore couldn't do the traveling to the cities that was necessary; also, I think, Walter Compton felt it was beneath his dignity to assist in broadcasting football games. Furthermore, he knew even less about the game than I did.

The job had its rewards. I received a talent fee of twenty-five dollars for each game, and when I had to travel, my expenses were paid. I began taking an interest in football, although I hardly became a fan.

These were the days of Redskin stars. "Slingin'" Sammy Baugh, famous No. 33, could throw a pass half the length of the football field. There were two great end receivers, Wayne Millner and Charlie Malone. Andy Farkas was the Redskins' running back. I remember Wakeman describing Andy's legs "working" like pistons when he'd set out to charge down the field. Another famous name in the Washington lineup was Turk Edwards, a guard, who was built like a Sherman tank.

No team ever got more loyal support from its fans than the Washington Redskins, unless maybe it was the Brooklyn Dodgers baseball team.

The "Skins," as they were called, were owned by George Preston Marshall, who had made his money as owner of the Palace Laundry, the biggest in Washington. He was married to Corrine Griffith, the heroine in the epic motion picture *The Birth of a Nation.*

The halftime entertainments he staged were theatrical spectacles—pageants. It was my duty to describe these festivities for the radio audience.

We had no modern, heated broadcast booth to work in. We worked out in the open, and on some of those really cold, damp Sunday afternoons we very nearly froze to death. At Griffith Stadium, for example, we broadcast from a balcony that overhung the railing at the second tier of the grandstand on the fifty-yard line. Just climbing into it was to risk your life. Once there we never dared budge, no matter how urgent the call of nature. We wrapped ourselves in blankets to try to keep warm, and because we were out in the open, exposed to the crowd noise, we had to shout most of the time to be heard. Yes, the conditions were primitive.

By that winter I was well enough established at WOL and with Mutual to be assigned for the first time to cover the White House.

How do you describe the emotions of a young man of twenty-three, woefully conscious of his inexperience and his inadequacy, when he is asked to go to 1600 Pennsylvania Avenue, listen to the words of the President of the United States, perhaps ask a question about anything not quite clear, and then return to a radio studio and quickly summarize the news conference for an audience of millions? My feelings were so intense that the memory of what the President said at my first White House press conference has long since been blotted out of my mind. Whatever it was, it seemed momentous to me.

Roosevelt's news conferences were cut-and-dried affairs. They weren't held in an auditorium with a couple of hundred reporters firing questions at the President, each trying to make a name for himself before the television cameras. The press corps was much smaller then. The news conferences were held in the President's office.

Steve Early, the President's press secretary, had established a fine working relationship with newsmen early in the Roosevelt administration. The President believed in maintaining that relationship. As the threat of a European war increased, presidential press conferences were held twice each week—on Tuesday afternoons for the following day's morning newspapers, and on Friday mornings for that day's afternoon newspapers. Reporters would assemble in a room set aside for the press in the building adjoining the White House.

At the appointed time Steve Early or one of his aides would announce, "Gentlemen, the President will see you now." We would file into the President's office to receive the Roosevelt greeting. Always he would be smoking a cigarette.

The President would begin with a short statement—"Today I have informed the Congress," or "I have advised the Secretary of Defense," etc., and then ask, "Are there any questions?" I was always amazed at Roosevelt's ability to handle any question fired at him. We made notes and I often wished I knew shorthand. I had developed a method of quick writing using abbreviations, but still it was difficult to get every word.

At a point when he felt we had the information we had come for, Merriman Smith of the United Press, the senior wire-service correspondent at the White House, would say, "Thank you, Mr. President," and we would scurry out of the President's office, some to private telephone lines.

My problem on Friday mornings was to get a report of the news conference on the network by eleven o'clock. I often ran the three blocks to the WOL studios.

Soon I was being assigned frequently to introduce Roosevelt to Mutual audiences when he gave his famous Fireside Chats, the radio talks by which he tried to rally the nation.

Walter introduced many of the Fireside Chats, pulling rank to take the assignments in his role as head of WOL news operations. He used to refer to himself as "Mutual's presidential announcer," which was something Steve McCormick and I both resented.

Introducing the President was of course a prestige assignment. John Charles Daly usually did the job for CBS and Carleton Smith for NBC. Both were much older and better experienced than I. The work itself was relatively simple. One man might easily have done it for all three networks. But each network, of course, wanted its own man on the scene. Print reporters were there too, of course.

The Fireside Chats originated in the Oval Room of the White House. The announcers' booths consisted of drapes, with isinglass windows to allow a view of FDR. The drapes kept each announcer's voice away from the other announcers' microphones. When we arrived we were given copies of the President's speech.

At perhaps ten minutes before air time, a Secret Service man would enter the Oval Room and move among us announcing, "the President is on his way down." A moment or two later we would hear the elevator door open in the hallway, and shortly the President would be wheeled in, flashing the familiar Roosevelt grin, the familiar cigarette holder held at a jaunty angle between his teeth.

"Good evening, gentlemen," he would say, without removing his cigarette.

"Good evening, sir."

"Are we ready?" he would ask.

Each of us would nod. Then he would greet us, each of us, by name. He would be wheeled to his place behind the desk and, while looking over his script, he would light up a fresh Camel cigarette. There was a battery of microphones in front of him.

"One minute to air, Mr. President!" someone would say.

He would snuff out his cigarette in his big ashtray and prepare himself for his cue.

At that moment, the announcers would take their places behind the drapes and await the signal from the technicians to begin. We were allowed precisely thirty seconds—no more, no less—to identify ourselves, our networks, and our locale, and conclude with the magic words, "Ladies and gentlemen, the President of the United States."

Like most of the newsmen present, I used to follow the President's script as he delivered it. Roosevelt was a master of the broadcasting art. His voice was strong, his delivery superb. He rarely fluffed. At times he deviated from the language written for him to shade the meaning just slightly, or increase the clarity, or insert some small point.

Luckily for me, it was that spring—the spring of 1939, when I was not yet twenty-four and was just building a name for myself in Washington—that radio finally won official government recognition as an integral part of the American news establishment. Until then, we had been barred from the press gallery in Congress. Radio newsmen were hopelessly handicapped in the struggle to cover the activities of the country's legislators. The newspapers and wire services, with all their influence, were jealous and wary of radio's growing strength and popularity, and there was no disposition on their part to help us to an even break. Radio newsmen were regarded simply as announcers. The legislation that had set up the press gallery a century earlier had limited membership to journalists, and radio people were not put in that category.

That spring a number of influential radio journalists—Fulton Lewis, Jr., among them—approached the Senate Rules Committee and the House of Representatives and got resolutions introduced to set up a new *radio* news gallery. The House resolution was adopted on April 20, and the House radio gallery came into being. A Radio Correspondents Association was created to help administer the gallery. Fulton was elected its first president. Steve McCormick, Walter Compton, and I became charter members, representing Mutual.

Bob Menaugh became the first superintendent of the gallery. He held the job for nearly forty years.

Our new status helped me enormously in the coverage of two big news stories that came my way just after the radio gallery was established.

The first was the *Squalus* disaster. The *Squalus* was a new, diesel-powered attack sub that had just been launched by the Navy. She was making her nineteenth test dive off the Isle of Shoals on May 23 when a valve failed. The vessel sank to the bottom like a stone, and fifty-nine men aboard were trapped.

Steve McCormick and I were in the WOL newsroom watching the teletypes when the first bulletin came over the wires.

We dropped everything and rushed over to the Navy Department, which was then housed in a series of low, yellow, stucco buildings left over from World War I, located on Constitution Avenue between the Washington Monument and the Lincoln Memorial. We relayed our first meager reports from there by telephone to Walter Compton in the WOL newsroom. Walter put the information on the network. That afternoon, with a dramatic rescue operation under way and the nation eager for every scrap of news, we persuaded the telephone company to break precedent and install a *broadcast* line in the Navy's public-information office. Thus Steve and I could broadcast live from Navy headquarters. The Navy Department was in direct and constant communication with the Portsmouth Navy Yard. Hence we were able to get firsthand information without delay. Steve and I, spelling each other, stayed on the job around the clock. When we had nothing new to report, we rehashed the story of what had gone on before.

That night *Squalus'* sister ship *Sculpin* (SS191) located the stricken submarine and established communications. Immediately, instead of occasional bits of new information, we had a running story.

A newly developed McCann rescue chamber, a revised version of the Momsen diving bell, was put into use, and thirty-three survivors were rescued. But twenty-six men were still trapped in the flooded after portion of the ship.

If anyone thinks a reporter doesn't find himself personally involved when he's reporting the news, he doesn't understand human nature. Steve and I were definitely affected. When the survivors were brought up and we were able to announce their names, we felt a sense of relief. But when we were finally informed that the other twenty-six were presumed dead, we were affected as if a personal tragedy had befallen us. It was my first experience with that ominous sentence "Other names are being withheld pending notification of the next of kin."

Another major news story requiring ad-lib descriptive reporting came our way a few weeks later.

King George VI and Queen Elizabeth came to the United States. Ostensibly, their purpose was to visit the New York World's Fair and call on President and Mrs. Roosevelt in Washington. Most of us in the Washington press corps were aware of deeper motives. The news from Europe was more and more ominous. World war seemed inevitable. It was easy to perceive that George VI and his Queen wanted to show themselves in America and build good will with a powerful ally whose help in war might be vital.

The royal couple first visited Canada. After three weeks of pomp and ceremony there, they crossed into the United States on June 7, at Niagara Falls. They were due in Washington by train on the morning of June 8. It was a beautiful spring morning.

To cover the arrival for Mutual, I was given a special State

Department ID card and, in addition, special authorization to "enter and remain on the radio stand at Union Station Plaza." I had to get there early. In spite of the credentials provided for radio journalists for such events, there was always a hassle for the best possible vantage point. I staked out my claim well in advance of the royal arrival time and stood by while the crowd around me built up. Soon it stretched far down Pennsylvania Avenue. Security agents and uniformed policemen were everywhere. Secretary of State Cordell Hull arrived to extend the government's official welcome. The President himself remained at the White House to greet the King and Queen there. Walter Compton was with the White House radio news corps. Steve McCormick was inside Union Station.

A pilot train had been dispatched ahead of the special train as a safety measure. Around ten o'clock the pilot train was sighted. The train transporting the King and Queen and their entourage would be only ten minutes behind it. Steve took to the air and described the scene in the concourse as the pilot train pulled in. Then he threw it to me and I described the scene outdoors—the huge crowds, the newsreel cameramen and still-picture photographers in position, the hordes of uniformed policemen and security agents. And then I threw it to Walter at the White House, and by this time the *special* train was arriving, and Steve took over again. He held it for as long as he could see the royal party, and then it was my turn again. My first sight of the Queen was thrilling. In dress and manner she was very much as I'd seen her in newsreels, but she was so much more beautiful in person. I hope I did justice to her in my ad-lib description. To Mutual, however, my work apparently was satisfactory. Abe Schechter telephoned from New York to extend congratulations. The assignment helped to enhance my reputation as a newsman.

Late in 1939 we discovered that Lil was pregnant again. She already had her hands full with our two sons, Mike and John, both lively, healthy youngsters who required a lot of attention. I thought the strain of another pregnancy and looking after those two hombres would be too much for Lil. She needed good help.

One afternoon I went on Tony Wakeman's Sportspage—the race-results program on WOL—and announced that we were looking for a maid. In a few minutes I got a call from a woman named Ethel Mattingly. She said she might be interested in the job. I made an appointment for her to come out to the house the next afternoon. I would be home then. She could meet Lil and me and discuss details. Were we in for a surprise!

The next afternoon a big car, better than anything we could afford, pulled into our driveway and an attractive black woman, light-skinned and buxom and in her late forties, got out. She was wearing a fur coat. As she slammed the car door we heard her say to the man behind the wheel:

"Be back in a little while. Wait for me."

"Oh-oh," I said to Lil, "look what's coming. This can't be the woman coming about the job!"

The doorbell rang. I answered it apprehensively.

"You Mr. Frank Blair?" she asked.

I nodded.

"My name's Ethel and I come to see about the job."

My eyes must have been big as saucers.

"Come in," I said.

The minute Ethel crossed our threshold she was in command. She took off her coat and casually threw it on a chair and looked the place over. The two boys and Lil and I were staring at her in amazement.

She said, glancing at the boys, "So these are the boys I'll be looking after? Come here, boys, and say hello to Ethel. I gonna take good care of you."

The boys ran to her as if she were a favorite aunt. She picked up John and held him in her arms and put her other arm around Mike's shoulders and drew him close to her.

Lil and I still hadn't said anything. We couldn't.

Ethel said, "Okay, when you want me to start? Tomorrow?"

I stammered, "But—but we haven't talked about pay or anything like that."

"We do that later. You need help. Ethel's here to help. I'll be here tomorrow around eleven o'clock and I'll cook you the best dinner you ever ett."

She kissed each of the boys on the cheek, picked up her fur coat, and headed for the door saying, "See you tomorrow."

Lil and I were flabbergasted. We collapsed in a chair. It was like the second-act curtain in a good comedy.

"Think it'll work out?" I asked Lil.

"I don't know. But it's sure worth giving it a try."

"If it does," I said, "we'll have the classiest maid in all of Arlington County."

The next morning at eleven o'clock Ethel got off the bus in front of our house, came in, took off her fur coat, hung it in the closet, and proceeded to get the place and everybody in it organized.

Ethel became as good a friend as we ever had. She loved us and we loved her. We could never have paid her what she was worth. There was no way. She stayed with us until the day we broke up housekeeping.

XIII

On September 3, 1939, Britain and France declared war on Germany. I was sure it wouldn't be too many months before our country would be involved. I made up my mind then that I was going to learn to fly. I thought that if war came my conscience would somehow force me to help, and if need be, I could be a flight instructor. I had my two sons to answer to if they should ever ask, "Daddy, what did you do in the war?"

I came home on a crisp, bright afternoon in November and said to Lil:

"Let's take a little ride out to Beacon Field; it's just south of Alexandria. The boys might enjoy seeing the airplanes."

Lil said, "Maybe Daddy wants to see the airplanes."

I said, "Maybe."

From the time we met, Lil had known of my interest in aviation.

So we bundled up the boys and got into our car. By this time we had traded our good, old, reliable Chevrolet for a snazzy, black Ford convertible with an automatic top and the gear shift mounted on the steering wheel. I loved to drive it.

We drove out to Beacon Field. There were two hangars situated in one corner of the field near the beacon. Several light planes were parked in front of the hangars, mostly Aeroncas and Piper Cubs—all sixty-five-horsepower or under. There were a couple of planes shooting "touch and go" landings—students practicing or taking instructions.

We walked around and looked at the airplanes. The boys were excited.

Lil said, "They look awfully small."

"Well," I said, "they're what are called light planes, but they're perfectly safe and a lot of fun. I'll be right back."

And I strolled off in the direction of a sign that said "Office."

I met Bob Ashburn and his wife, Betty, who ran the office, and a young flight instructor named Jimmy Millan. When Jimmy got up from his desk to shake hands with me I noticed that he was bent over. He couldn't stand erect. I learned later that he had been in an airplane crash several years before and his back had been broken. I liked him immediately; he had a great smile and good handclasp.

Bob Ashburn was exactly as Arthur Godfrey had described him when he talked about him on his morning radio program. Bob looked like a flier, and talked and acted like a man who knew a lot about flying.

I told them I wanted to learn to fly. They told me the cost and what would be involved. I would have to have a flight physical before I could get a student's permit. I told them as soon as I got the physical I'd come back.

When I returned to the car, Lil asked, "What did they say?"

"About what?" I asked.

"About your taking flying lessons. That's what you came here to find out, isn't it?"

"How did you know?" I asked.

"Oh, hon, you're so obvious about everything. You've been thinking about it for some time, haven't you?"

"Yes." As I started the car and headed for home I told her

what my thoughts had been and asked how she felt about it.

She gave her usual answer, "If that's what you want."

Mike chimed in with "Hon, will you take us for a ride in your plane?"

"Son, I haven't got a plane and I haven't even learned to fly yet, but one of these days—yes, I'll take you for a ride."

The next afternoon I went to a doctor who was certified to give flight physicals and got a student's permit to fly.

I took my first lesson on November 3, 1939. And from then on I was out at Beacon Field as often as possible, taking lessons and loving it all. Most times Lil and the boys would go with me and sit in the car, watching and waiting. Lil once said she should have logged the time she spent in the car while I was learning to fly.

The day I was scheduled to solo, January 8, 1940, it was snowing and cold, but Lil and the boys and I went to Beacon Field anyway. I was surprised to find that they were flying. Frankly, I had hoped for a better day. The grass field was covered with snow, and the rotating beacon was operating.

I went to the office. Jimmy Millan said, "Ready to go?"

"In *this?*" I questioned.

"The snow shouldn't bother us. We're just going to fly around the field. Ceiling's high enough and we've put skis on the planes."

"I've never flown with skis," I said.

I was trying to beg off.

"No different from wheels," Jimmy said, "but more fun."

I bolstered my courage and said, "I'm ready if you are."

I was apprehensive, but we went.

Jimmy had me make five landings and take-offs in the snow on the skis. I was surprised at how easy it was. After the fifth landing he said:

"All right, think you can do it by yourself?"

"I guess so," I quavered and tried to smile. Jimmy opened the door and got out.

"It's all yours," he said. "Don't go above five hundred feet, keep the beacon in sight, and don't forget your carburetor heat when you throttle back on your final approach."

I was trembling a little, maybe it was from the cold, as I sat there and waited for Jimmy to walk away and get clear of the prop wash.

I turned the plane around and taxied for the takeoff position. I swung around into the wind. I could see Jimmy standing out there in the snow, and I could see that Lil had gotten out of the car and was standing alongside it. We had a cheap, little 8mm movie camera, and I knew she was going to try to get pictures. We didn't get any, however, because the film froze in the camera.

I said a little prayer and pushed in the throttle and I was on my way. The little plane lifted gracefully into the air. I flew straight ahead, climbing to five hundred feet. Then I got the strangest feeling of loneliness. I missed Jimmy sitting alongside me and telling me what to do.

At five hundred feet I made a left turn and spotted the rotating beacon, went a short distance and made another left, lining up the plane with the field and the landing area I was planning to use. All was going well and I realized I was smiling and the nervousness had disappeared. Another gentle left turn and then another and I was on my final approach. I throttled back, put on the carburetor heat, and began to descend. "This is it," I thought. The plane touched down just as it was supposed to do and slid along the snow on its skis, just as it had done when Jimmy had been with me earlier.

I glanced at Jimmy and he was waving me on. I pushed in

the throttle again and took off. The next landing was just like the first. Again I got a wave from Jimmy. I did the same thing over again, but this time when I landed, Jimmy waved me in and started walking toward the office. I taxied the plane to the parking line and shut off the engine. I got out and ran to the car. I was so happy. I had done it. Lil had a big smile on her pretty face, and she gave me a big kiss. Mike yelled to me out of the car.

"Can we go for a ride now?" Lil and I laughed.

"Not yet, son," I said, "but soon. Instead let's go into the office and get something warm to drink."

Bob and Betty congratulated me, and Jimmy signed my log book indicating that I was "safe for solo."

"We picked a fine day for it," I said.

Bob Ashburn replied, "The worse the conditions the better pilot you'll make."

As we drove home my head was still in the snowy clouds. Frankly, I was proud of myself. I was more determined than ever to get my license and become a good pilot.

When we got home and Ethel heard the news, she was as proud as the rest of us.

Lil produced a package from the closet and handed it to me.

"This is for being a good boy," she said.

I opened it and there was a beautiful, brown leather jacket like those I had seen worn by Jimmy and Bob and some of the famous fliers—Lindbergh, Amelia Earhart, Wiley Post.

I had tears in my eyes.

I still had a long way to go to get a private license. During the next months, I spent all my spare moments, which were few, studying, attending ground school, and flying. Then, on July 31, 1940, I got my private license: No. 18066-40.

I was now authorized to carry passengers on a noncommercial basis. The day I got the license Lil was my first passenger. She didn't like it very much. She said that it was noisy and we didn't seem to be moving. She never flew with me again.

XIV

IT WAS THAT SAME SUMMER that Congress authorized the first peacetime compulsory military service in American history.

It was determined that the fairest system of calling men to military service was by lot. So, on October 29, 1940, the first "draft lottery" was held on the stage of the Departmental Auditorium in the Labor Department Building in Washington.

Steve and I were assigned to cover it for Mutual, and therein hangs a memorable tale.

The President was there with General Hershey, director of Selective Service, and the members of the Cabinet. Also on hand were senators and congressmen whose committees were concerned with armed forces matters. On stage was a huge glass bowl full of small capsules each containing a slip of paper with a number on it. The draft became known as the "fishbowl lottery." The numbers drawn would determine which American men would be drafted into the armed forces and, roughly, when. The lives of many, many Americans would be changed forever by that lottery.

The drawing was ceremonial. First the President made a short talk. It appeared to be impromptu. He spoke about the need for a draft and of the fairness of the lottery system.

Then Secretary of War Henry L. Stimson was blindfolded with a strip of yellowing, old linen that had been cut from the cover of a chair used in the signing of the Declaration of Independence. Stimson fished out of the bowl the first capsule. He used a ladle carved from a rafter in Independence Hall in Philadelphia. The capsule was handed to the President. The President opened it, lifted out the slip of paper, and read the first number drawn. It was No. 158. Then more numbers were drawn and posted on a huge board, the size of a highway billboard, on the stage.

Henry Morgenthau, Jr., Secretary of the Treasury, was the second man to draw, followed by Attorney General Robert H. Jackson and Secretary of the Navy Frank Knox. And so it went hour after hour.

Steve and I were at the side of the stage reporting the numbers as they were drawn and posted. Occasionally we cut away for other network programming, but the nation's interest was centered there on that stage.

On the nineteenth drawing No. 105 came up. For some reason that number sounded familiar to me.

At that moment Steve was recapping the first numbers drawn. He did not hear the number just called. Suddenly it dawned on me. No. 105 was Steve's number. I said to him:

"Steve, what is your number?"

He leaned away from the microphone and half whispered: "A hundred and five." I pointed to the board.

Steve looked, and on mike in full voice blurted out:

"Omigod, that's me."

He was stunned. Steve is no prude, but he later admitted that it was a horrible thing to say on the air. In those days you just didn't say things like that. In fact, "damn" and "hell" were never used, and even the words "pregnancy" and "rape" were avoided in newscasts.

The word got around the auditorium that Steve's number had come up; apparently, of the people assembled there, he was the only one to suffer such a blow. Photographers rushed over and snapped Steve's picture as he pointed to the board with a look of amazement on his face.

I stepped up to the microphone and interviewed Steve— one announcer interviewing another announcer. It was probably the first interview of a "draftee" on radio.

One of the press services circulated a picture of Steve, and next morning it got a big play in newspapers all over the country. In one paper, it was captioned:

ON AIR—CAUGHT IN DRAFT

Steve was called up several months later. I myself was immune from the draft, at least temporarily. As a married man with three children, I had a 1C classification. But like hundreds of thousands of other Americans, I had no immunity from my conscience. The day would come when Steve and I would meet again, quite unexpectedly, on an atoll in the Pacific with World War II raging all around us.

On January 20, 1941, President Roosevelt was inaugurated for his third term. I don't know what the weather records show for January 20, 1941, but as far as I was concerned it was the coldest day I had ever experienced, partly because of the temperature and partly because of the assignment I was given.

Walter Compton was to be at the White House to cover the President's departure for the Capitol. Walter would describe the parade as it passed the reviewing stand along Pennsylvania Avenue. Steve would be at the Capitol to cover the swearing-in ceremony. Gabriel Heatter, who came down from New York, would be atop the Federal Trade Commission Building for a "bird's eye" view. Other reporters were at positions along the parade route designated by the Secret Service.

Their reports would be fed back to the studio by remote control over telephone lines.

My assignment in the coverage, I thought, was by far the best. It was certainly the most unusual. I was assigned to broadcast from a troop-carrying vehicle that would move along directly in front of the President's open-air touring car. He had refused to ride to the White House in a limousine despite the cold. It had rained during his inaugural four years earlier and he had refused then to ride in an enclosed car. He said the people had turned out to see their President and he'd be damned if he'd deny them the privilege.

I was required to wear the Army uniform in order to be inconspicuous aboard the troop carrier. I had to go to Fort Myer to be outfitted. Fortunately, I was provided with a heavy overcoat and heavy infantry shoes. The Army was cooperative. For two days before the ceremony we rode up and down Pennsylvania Avenue from the Capitol to the White House checking out the equipment to find the spots where our radio signal would be strongest. We had prevailed upon the Signal Corps to set up a portable radio transmitter on the vehicle for my use. We figured we had really scored a coup. We hoped the other networks wouldn't try to do the same thing.

The sun shone brightly that day but the air was crisp and cold. Thank God it wasn't raining. We sipped hot coffee while waiting for the parade to begin, and that did wonders for the inside of man but little to combat the biting cold on the outside. I wondered, too, what would happen when that coffee got to working on my kidneys and bladder while we were in the middle of the moving motorcade.

The body of the troop carrier was made of heavy steel, and that steel was really cold to the touch. Our uniforms stuck to the seats. If we touched the steel our gloves would stick to it just as fingers stick to the bottom of an ice tray when it's removed from a freezer.

All the discomfort vanished, however, once the ceremony at the Capitol was over and the parade got under way. I monitored the goings-on by portable radio using headphones. That's how I got my cues to go on the air. From my position in the rear seat of the carrier I could see the President easily and observe his reaction to everything that went on. The entourage moved slowly. The Secret Service men flanking the President's car walked at a brisk pace, but they didn't have to run. It's a long walk from the Capitol to the White House at any pace. No wonder those guys are in good shape.

When I got my first cue to go on the air we were just leaving the Capitol Plaza. Steve, broadcasting from the Capitol, said:

"The Inaugural parade is just beginning to move out of the Capitol Plaza, and for more on that here is Frank Blair in our mobile unit accompanying the President's car."

Hearing that, I hoped our short-wave rig would work as it had when we checked it out. It did. When I started talking I could hear my own voice coming back through my headphones, slightly delayed. My voice was reaching me after having traveled thousands of miles over telephone lines through the network and then back over the air. It was disconcerting at first but I got used to it.

I started by describing the position of our vehicle in the parade. I explained that the listeners were hearing my voice via short-wave radio from a moving vehicle. I thanked the Signal Corps for its co-operation and then started describing everything I could see.

The crowd along Pennsylvania Avenue was enormous, ten or twelve deep on the sidewalk behind the police barriers, in spite of the low temperature. Some of the people had taken their places early in the morning. I knew they must have been freezing. Many of them who didn't manage to get a place on the front lines had purchased cardboard periscopes from street vendors, and these little devices kept popping up in the crowd as we moved along. When the President's car came along the crowd would cheer, and from my vantage point I could see the familiar Roosevelt grin as he waved back to the crowd. Mrs. Roosevelt, who was seated beside him, waved and nodded and smiled as the cheers rang out.

Our vehicle was so close to the President's car that I could see the lap robe that he and Mrs. Roosevelt had over their legs.

I kept talking for as long as I had something to say. Then for a "bird's eye" view I turned it over to Gabriel Heatter atop the Federal Trade Commission Building. He did his bit and passed it to another announcer along the route. And so it went.

When it was all over, the troop carrier stopped at the end of the parade route. I want to tell you I was very careful in getting down to the ground. It was several feet from the deck of it to the pavement. The GIs jumped, as they had been trained to do. Not I. I sat down on the edge and slid down. If I had leaped in the GI manner, I think my feet would have broken off. They were so cold the bones would have to be brittle. My happiest moment came when I got indoors and made it to the men's room.

When I went back to the studio and got out of that itchy Army uniform as quickly as I could, I went to Madeline Ensign's office to listen to the remainder of the coverage. It was then that I learned that Gabriel Heatter had finally deserted his post. When they had cued him for another "bird's eye" view, he had not responded. Heatter had gotten so cold on top of that building that he had gone to Union Station and caught the next train back to New York.

Early in the spring of 1941, I became involved in a cloak-and-dagger operation right out of a story book.

Bill Dolph called me into his office.

"What are you doing tonight after the Lewis broadcast?" he asked.

"Nothing important. Why?"

"I'd like to take you to dinner," Bill said.

"That's nice. What's up?"

"Oh, nothing much. You'll find out later. You'll have some work to do, if you don't mind."

"I don't mind."

"Good. I'll pick you up in the basement parking area right after the Lewis broadcast. Okay?"

"Okay."

I walked out, puzzled.

What in the world was that all about? I'd been to Bill's apartment several times for cocktail parties, but an invitation to dinner on short notice, and without Lil, was baffling, and I was mystified by the statement that I'd have some work to do.

I called Lil and told her about it. I said I'd get home as soon as I could.

When I finished announcing the Fulton Lewis broadcast I went down to the parking area in the basement of our building. Bill was waiting at the wheel of his car. The engine was running. Madeline Ensign, obviously in her role as our program director, was in the front seat with him, and in the back seat was Harold Reed, one of our technicians. There was equipment for a remote-control broadcast on the floor of the car. I sat beside Harold.

"Do you know what this is all about?" I whispered.

"Not the slightest notion," Harold replied. "Remote broadcast is all I know."

Bill spoke up. "Now I can tell you fellows what's going on. Sorry I couldn't tell you before. It had to be top secret. It's the only way we could do it. We're going to a friend's house in Maryland for dinner, where we'll meet Jan Valtin. . . ."

"Jan Valtin!"

He was a defector from the Gestapo and author of *Out of the Night*, a best-selling book that was a sensation all through the United States. Valtin had chronicled his life as both a Gestapo agent and a Soviet secret police agent. Now he was a man without a country. His publishers had said both the Soviets and the Nazis were trying to find him—to kill him.

"We feed an interview with Valtin to the network at nine o'clock," Bill said. The interview would last thirty minutes.

"It wasn't on the schedule," I said.

"Deliberately. We didn't dare tip our hand. He had to have complete secrecy."

Bill kept glancing in the rear-view mirror.

Madeline handed me a sheet of paper bearing some typewritten notes.

"Look this over when we get there," Madeline said. "It's a fact sheet that should be of some help to you."

When we got to our destination, which was a typically suburban Maryland home, Bill drove down a shallow ramp that led to a double garage under the house. The garage door opened and we drove directly in. We parked alongside a big black limousine. We went upstairs and I was introduced to our host and hostess, whose names meant nothing to me in my state of mind. I don't remember them now.

Then I was introduced to Jan Valtin. We shook hands warmly. He was very nervous. Valtin was younger than I thought he'd be. He was tall and well built. He had dark hair and eyes, and he smiled a lot. He spoke with a German accent, but his English was good and readily understandable.

How he had gotten there I did not know—perhaps in that black limousine that was already in the garage when we arrived.

The hostess announced dinner. I glanced at my watch. We had a little over an hour before nine o'clock. I was nervous. A live interview with Jan Valtin would be a national sensation. I took out the notes Madeline had given me and studied them between courses. That was rude and I apologized, but I had no option. I had to be prepared. I wished I had been alerted so I could have read the book.

We finished dinner at about ten of nine. Bill, Madeline, Valtin, Harold, and I went into the den. The microphones were on a table. Valtin and I would be facing each other. Harold's equipment was set up on a smaller table in a corner of the room. Harold turned on his amplifier, put on his headphones, and asked for a mike check. I did the usual "long count" —1—2—3—4—5—5—4—3—2—1. Then I said to Valtin:

"Just say anything, Mr. Valtin, for a mike check."

"Thank you. I am very glad to be here. I hope it goes well."

Harold said, "Fine. Thanks. Sounds good."

It was two minutes to nine. Harold said, "Stand by." Bill and Madeline left, saying they would listen on the radio in another room.

At precisely nine o'clock Harold pointed to me and nodded his head and I began with a prepared introduction:

"The program originally scheduled for this time will not be heard because of the following special broadcast."

Then I introduced Jan Valtin, and told the audience briefly who he was. I wondered if any Nazi or Soviet agents were monitoring or even recording the broadcast.

I began questioning Valtin and listening intently to his answers. I found myself becoming absorbed in Valtin's story. He spoke freely and easily. He was clear and lucid.

After I had signed off, Bill and Madeline and our host and hostess came into the den.

"Great interview," someone said.

I was very pleased.

Two men whom I had not seen before appeared in the room. One had Valtin's coat and hat and the other simply said:

"Let's be going."

I assumed they were federal agents. They took the stairs to the garage, and the black limousine sped off into the night.

Bill said, "We'll wait a few minutes." That was a command. We could not be suspected of following the limousine.

We had drinks while waiting.

Then, driving back to WOL, Bill suggested that I get my car there and drive directly home. He cautioned me not to go up to the studios. He said there would probably be reporters there. He thought it better that none of us say anything.

I did as I was told. Driving home, I found myself glancing in the rear-view mirror frequently. I was glad to get home. I never saw Jan Valtin again.

The next morning, as expected, the interview made headline news.

The middle of May Lil and I received in the mail an engraved invitation to the White House:

THE PRESIDENT AND MRS. ROOSEVELT

AT HOME

on Tuesday evening
May the twenty-first
at nine o'clock

There was also a second card, which said:

Please send response to
THE SOCIAL SECRETARY
THE WHITE HOUSE
at your earliest convenience

An invitation to the White House! Naturally, we were excited.

A few days later while walking along F Street, where the exclusive dress shops were located, I saw a beautiful bright-red formal gown in a show window. I could see Lil in that gown. She would be stunning. I immediately went in and bought it on approval. I could hardly wait to get it home. As it turned out, that gown was made for Lil. She loved it. I thought she would be the most beautiful woman at the White House.

The affair was for the gentlemen and ladies of the press. It was in the East Room.

Mrs. Roosevelt had a friendly greeting for each guest. When Lil and I approached her, she recognized me. I had introduced her when she had given a talk over WOL on one of her favorite charities.

As I shook her hand she said, "Oh, here's that nice Mr. Blair. You were so kind to me when I broadcast from your studios recently."

I was floored by the remark and flattered that she had remembered me.

The President held court at one end of the East Room with groups of people surrounding his big chair.

It was a satisfying experience for both Lil and me.

I was proud to have been recognized as a member of "the fourth estate."

I was proud, too, of how beautiful my wife looked. After

that, whenever we made plans to go out, our boys would ask her:

"Mommy, are you going to wear your pretty 'fire engine' dress?"

It was December 8, 1940. The Redskins were playing the Chicago Bears at Griffith Stadium in Washington. I was doing the PA (public address system).

The Redskins had defeated the Bears earlier that year in the regular season, and this was a playoff game. Everybody was sure the Skins would take the Bears. But as the game progressed it began looking worse and worse for the Redskins. They just weren't functioning according to their usual style.

Whenever there was a time-out I had announcements to read to fill the time. Some were public-service announcements, but Marshall even had some commercial announcements thrown in. That day the way the game was going there were a lot of time-outs for the Redskins, and we were getting close to the bottom of our pile.

It was the last minutes of the fourth quarter—the score was 73 to 0, in favor of the Bears—the ball was deep in Washington territory, and Washington called another time-out. Without reading it beforehand, Leonard Meakin, my assistant, handed me one of the few announcements that hadn't been used yet.

So on the PA system before a crowd of about forty thousand people I said:

"Time-out for the Redskins."

And proceeded to read the announcement. I was well into it before I realized what I was saying.

"Anyone interested in next year's season tickets for the Redskins . . ."

That's about as far as I got when there was such a roar of

boos from the crowd the PA system couldn't be heard. Was I embarrassed? Don't ask.

Immediately the private direct phone from Marshall's box rang. All I heard on my end with the roar of the crowd was:

"That was a goddamned fine thing to say at a time like this." And Marshall slammed down the phone.

I looked at Meakin and asked, "What in hell did you do that for?"

"I didn't do it deliberately," he pleaded. Then we both started laughing.

"It's been a ridiculous game, anyway," I said. "We might as well have put the icing on the cake."

When the game was over—Bears 73, Redskins 0—and before I could get out of the booth, Marshall was there glaring at me, and he really chewed me out. I've never heard such language. Finally I said:

"Mr. Marshall, it was a mistake. It wasn't done on purpose." And I added, "Furthermore, I thought the Redskins' fans were more loyal than that."

The next morning Shirley Povich, in his sports column in the Washington *Post*, wrote, "If ever the State Department is looking for a diplomat we recommend Frank Blair, the PA announcer at the Redskins' games."

It was embarrassing to live with but it, too, soon passed away, and next year Marshall called me to be the PA announcer again. But he cautioned:

"Be more careful this year."

XV

WHEN STEVE MCCORMICK was called up for military service that spring I inherited most of his duties, including "The American Forum of the Air" and the handling of the Fulton Lewis, Jr., news commentaries to the network. I was busier than ever, and I was getting constant network exposure.

Nevertheless, I was flying out of Beacon Field every chance I got, and I wanted my own plane. I was earning more now, and my mother had died and left me the proceeds of a small insurance policy. With that and some financing by the Morris Plan Bank, on May 9, 1941, I took delivery on a brand-new Aeronca Chief, powered by a sixty-five-horsepower Continental engine and equipped with extra fuel tanks for longer cruising range.

John Gantt, one of our engineers at WOL, had become almost my constant flying companion. We made plans to fly that little plane to the West Coast and back when vacation time rolled around. A cross-country flight would be an adventure we both wanted. And I had very much in mind that the experience would be a good thing to have in my background if, as now seemed certain, the country should finally go to war.

We arranged to leave on Friday, May 30, my twenty-sixth birthday. My Aeronca had a cruising range of about 450 miles. We would have to leapfrog across the country. We planned stops at Columbus, Ohio; Indianapolis, St. Louis, Kansas City, Wichita, Amarillo, Albuquerque, and finally Los Angeles. We reckoned the trip West would take a week.

There were two problems. Both seemed minor at the time.

The first was that I was booked to do a weekly commentary on Mutual on Sunday night, June 1, and that was only two days after our planned takeoff. The program scheduled was called "FYI." It was a program that I broadcast every Sunday, and it was important to me. It carried a good fee, and it gave me regular network exposure. It consisted of factual stories of spies and saboteurs in this country and overseas. The material was provided by Transradio Press Service, which did careful research. "FYI" was well received by both the critics and the people. My name was linked to it. It was my program, and I could hardly afford to miss doing the next weekly edition. I reckoned that John and I could make Kansas City in time for the broadcast scheduled for June 1, and arrangements were made for me to originate from the studios of the Mutual affiliate there. Transradio would send the script on ahead of me. I would have time to study it and telephone for the answers to any questions I might have or any additional detail I might want.

Our second problem—and at the time it seemed equally minor—was that I was due in Los Angeles on the following Sunday, June 8, to broadcast another edition of "FYI" and also to appear as a guest on another Mutual program with Deanna Durbin, a popular movie singing star of that era. This was a program called "Nobody's Children." Miss Durbin and I were to be interviewed together with a group of orphans. "Nobody's Children" had had a promotional buildup. It would command a good following, and it would be good for me to be a part of it.

There was always a chance that something might go wrong, but I felt confident that I could fly to Kansas City by the Sunday after our departure and to Los Angeles by the following Sunday.

We had only a light aircraft with no more instrumentation than a magnetic compass, altimeter, and tachometer. We wouldn't have known how to use an artificial horizon, rate of climb, or gyro compass even if we'd had them. As for two-way radio, the cost put it out of the question and, with war threatening, two-way radio equipment was scarce, anyway. We did have a Lear portable, which had a band for aircraft navigation.

The day of our departure dawned overcast, hazy, and muggy, with a distinct threat of rain.

After a couple of hours of phone calls to the weather bureau, John and I decided that it might burn off after a while. We finally decided to go out to Beacon Field, roll out the airplane, and hope.

We drove out with Lil and John's wife, Lola. We had two suitcases, two cameras, a Thermos of hot coffee, and some sandwiches, all of which we stowed in the baggage compartment. We put the radio on the floor between John's feet, the idea being that, inasmuch as it had a built-in loop antenna, he could pick it up by its handle and rotate it in the horizontal plane and obtain a null on a known radio station. Then by reference to the aircraft's magnetic compass, we could figure out the bearing to the radio station.

The ceiling seemed to be lifting and it was not raining, so we decided to get started. Our take-off run was bumpy and longer than normal because of our extra weight. Our climb was slow and a little sluggish, but we got on up to about 800 feet. John gave me a course that would take us to Cumberland, Maryland. I had started a slow turn toward it when I suddenly had a horrible thought. I mustered the courage to say to John, "My God, I think I've got the car keys in my pocket!"

John said, "Huh?"

"The keys—I forgot to give Lil the keys to the car!"

I could tell by the look on John's face that he wasn't anxious to have me set that heavily loaded airplane back down on that rough field. After all, I only had 63½ hours of flying time logged.

But there was nothing to do but start a turn to the left and head back. As we approached the field we saw Lil and John's wife standing around the car and watching us come in. Suddenly, John got an inspiration.

"Hey," he said, "hold on. Give me those keys!"

"What are you going to do?"

"Drop 'em, that's what!"

"You can't do that—they'll never find them!"

"Oh, yes they will. Give 'em here!"

I handed them over. They were on a ring with a small chain. John took out his handkerchief, passed a corner through the key ring, and knotted it tightly.

"Now," he said, "go downwind about a mile, make a left, come back upwind, hold the nose of the plane high to slow her down to about sixty, and try to pass over the car about fifty feet up, but for God's sake don't stall it. Keep your eye on that airspeed indicator and altimeter. We'll see how good a bombardier I am."

Well, it went all right. The handkerchief hit on the grass and spread out. I glanced over and saw Lil pick it up and wave and blow us a kiss.

I poured on the gas and we started to climb to cruising altitude—headed toward Cumberland, Maryland, 175 miles westward.

We made a forced landing only a few minutes later. The mountains just north of "Point of Rocks," Maryland, where the Potomac River passes through, were covered by low-hanging clouds. The danger was great, but we had only started our trip, and it was much too soon to end it.

I found a cow pasture and made a safe landing near the small town of Dobbs, Maryland. Once on the ground, we taxied toward a farmhouse, and as we did, a gray-haired white man in work clothes, and a black man wearing a straw hat and overalls, came hurrying down a knoll toward us.

"Dere dey is! Dere dey is! I seen 'em when dey come down," the black man shouted.

The farmer yelled, "Howdy!"

Their friendly welcome was reassuring. I had been calm throughout the landing, but when John took out the Thermos and poured a cup of coffee and I reached for it, my hand was shaking a little. The farmer took us to his home. I called the nearest weather station and got the bad news. The ceiling would not lift until early afternoon.

At noon, the farmer's wife offered us what she called "lunch," which turned out to be thick slabs of country ham, mashed potatoes, greens, and hot biscuits, with apple pie and hot coffee.

At about 2:00 P.M. the overcast began lifting and we took off, squeezing between the treetops on the ridges and the cloud base, and picked up the Potomac River.

For about two hours, which seemed like eternity, we kept the winding, twisting Potomac in sight. Finally, through the broken clouds, we spotted the sprawling railroad yards of Cumberland, Maryland. I began letting down, looking for the airport. What looked like a landing field showed up a couple of miles west. It was small with only one landing strip, which was short—probably not more than 1,500 feet, with the shoulder of a mound blocking the approach end and railroad tracks and high-tension wires at the other end. The tracks and wires seemed perilously close to any point where I could hope to touch down. But there was a Pitcairn Mailwing biplane and a couple of Piper Cubs sitting on the ground, so we decided to go in.

I flew over the field at low altitude to get a better look and decide how to proceed. I would come in as low and as slow as practicable, and once over that mound I'd sideslip, losing altitude without picking up forward speed. Then I would straighten out close to the ground and land as quickly as possible before we ran out of grass and found ourselves on the railroad tracks.

I think the plan was sound, but I guess, with my inexperience, when I tried to execute it, I chickened out and broke the sideslip too soon. When I straightened out, most of the grass strip was behind us, and the railroad tracks and high-tension wires were coming up fast.

"To hell with this!" I shouted, and gave her full throttle. I held the nose down as long as I dared to gain as much speed as possible, then pulled back on the yoke. The little airplane shuddered. We were very close to a stall. But we cleared the wires. Thank heaven we had used up a lot of fuel on our devious route following the Potomac River, and the plane was a lot lighter than when we took off from Beacon Field.

We landed at the incompleted Cumberland Municipal Airport. In spite of all the construction encumbrances, our landing there was routine, and we tied the plane down for the night.

That was enough flying for one day.

We hitchhiked into town and took rooms at the YMCA, the least expensive place we could find.

When we woke up the next morning the sky was still overcast, and that was bad news. We could not take off, and I was due in Kansas City for my "FYI" broadcast in only two more days.

I phoned Madeline Ensign at WOL in Washington and explained the predicament.

"Sorry, pal," she said, "we can't pick you up out of Cumberland. Think you can make it to Pittsburgh?"

I told her that Pittsburgh, under the present conditions, by air, seemed about as accessible as the capital of Outer Mongolia, but I would do what I could and keep her informed.

So John and I set out for the airport to get what weather information was available. We walked through the gray morning, following one of the railroad tracks we had seen from the air. The weather information was not good at all. There was just no safe way out.

I had not yet missed an important radio broadcast, and the "FYI" program was important. I was determined to make it to Pittsburgh. I checked the train schedules from Cumberland. If the train ran on time I could possibly make it, but with minutes to spare. I took the train, and I made it to Pittsburgh just in time. The script had been teletyped to the station from Washington and was handed to me as I walked in the door by a disappointed announcer who had hoped he'd get to substitute for me on the network. There was no time to edit or rehearse. I went on the air "cold." I "read ahead"— that is, I used a trick I had long since perfected. I kept my mind on the sentence I was reading and my eyes on a sentence or two ahead of my voice. If Mutual had known that I had broadcast a commentary without adequate preparation, I never would have heard the end of it.

In today's broadcast world, I could have put that fifteen-minute commentary on a three-dollar cassette in Cumberland and shipped it to Pittsburgh without ever seeing the place.

I took the next train back to Cumberland, arriving very early the next morning to find the weather lifting. John informed me that the forecast west of Cumberland didn't look too bad. I was tired, but there was no time to lose if we were to make Los Angeles in time for the "FYI" broadcast the next Sunday.

We took off as soon as possible—leapfrogging across the country with overnight stops at Columbus, Indianapolis, and Kansas City. Then, after fuel stops at Wichita and Pampa, Texas, we took off for Amarillo. The sun was getting close to the horizon. With visibility failing, we found our way to Amarillo by flying low over the flat Texas terrain and following the railroad track.

It was dusk when we got to Amarillo. We did not want to buck the traffic at the Municipal Airport without two-way radio. We chose a secondary grass-strip airport. It had rained a great deal in that part of Texas, and when we landed on that field we didn't roll very far. Our landing gear bogged down in mud over the hubcaps. Full throttle and four men lifting and rocking the wings got us unstuck.

Next morning we wanted to get an early start. The weather forecast was CAVU (ceiling and visibility unlimited) to Albuquerque. The sun came up in a beautiful orange-colored sky.

But the sky did not remain beautiful for very long after we took off. We began running into clouds, and we began climbing above them instead of flying through them. The clouds kept building and building and we kept going higher and higher, and very soon we had lost all contact with the ground.

We were running into strong headwinds. But we could not see the ground. We had no way to measure our progress. I kept an eye on the gas gauge.

John picked up a strong signal from the radio range station

at Tucumcari, New Mexico, on our portable receiver. Using it as a direction finder, he gave me a heading to the station. As the signal got stronger and we could identify the legs of the range, we knew we were getting close. We weren't lost above the overcast. The problem was getting down through it. We had no real knowledge of how thick it was. I had heard of fliers deliberately spinning down through an overcast, but we had no way of knowing when we might break out. And if we went down at too steep an angle, our baggage would be thrown all over us. That idea didn't appeal to me at all. But we were lost above the clouds and we were running out of gas.

John came up with an idea.

"I'll hang a screwdriver on a piece of extra antenna wire and suspend it from the trim tab [it was overhead—between us] and let it dangle."

"What the hell good is that going to do?" I asked.

"Well, if the screwdriver swings forward and hangs when we start our descent, at least we'll know we're not upside down."

"You're nuts," I told him.

"Look, pal, you just fly the airplane. I'll watch the screwdriver. Stay on the heading and try to maintain constant airspeed and watch the altimeter and try to keep it unwinding at a constant rate."

My big fear was that we would both get vertigo and wouldn't know what we were doing or why. But I said, "Okay, here goes!" I throttled back and started down.

That screwdriver swung forward and then started swaying like a pendulum. I was scared. We entered the clouds and, believe me, under those conditions, even with your best friend seated alongside, a guy can feel mighty lonely.

It seemed interminable. I'm not sure, but I think I was praying when suddenly the overcast opened up and there was the ground about 1,500 feet below us. Within sight was the orange-roofed shack and light beacon of the Tucumcari FAA auxiliary field. For the thousandth time since we had left Beacon Field, I said, "Thank God!"

We refueled and, with the weather clearing, we flew on to Albuquerque and then headed for Winslow, Arizona.

But the minutes ticked away in the air over New Mexico, and I knew we'd never make Winslow. The sun was setting, and I most assuredly was not going to fly at night in a single-engine plane with no instruments. John studied the chart and located the nearest auxiliary field, at El More, New Mexico. He gave me the heading to it and we landed there just as darkness fell. The El More radio operator with his wife and young son lived in a small, comfortable cottage that also housed the electronic equipment. They put us up for the night. It was Friday night. I was due in Los Angeles to go on the air in less than 48 hours.

The next day, Saturday, we took off early for Winslow, Arizona. We bucked headwinds, making our progress over the ground very slow.

The airport at Winslow, Arizona, was situated on a mesa. It had asphalt runways, which radiated the heat from the desert sun. As I began my approach I knew the winds coming up over the mesa and the heat convection from the asphalt might give us trouble. I told John about it.

"Just do the best you can. We don't have enough gas to fool around," he said. John couldn't have been more right. We were almost entirely out of fuel.

We made a direct pass at the runway, but that little plane just would not settle down. The convection currents and the wind kept it in the air. We went around for another try, and going downwind, I told John, "I'm going to have to use power to buck that wind and try to force this baby down. Hope she stays there."

The wind was strong over that mesa, and it blew in gusts. Coming in again, I was doing my best to "fly her into the ground." But just as we were about to touch down, a gust of wind hit us at a slight angle and we went up again. The wind just lifted that plane right off the runway and onto its left wing. We careened into a cluster of bushes. I cut the ignition immediately. We were shaken, but neither of us was hurt. I looked out over the wing and wondered whether the damage would mean the end of our trip.

A pickup truck came to a screeching halt alongside us, and the driver yelled out, "Anybody hurt?"

John and I were climbing out of the cockpit.

"No, all okay."

A number of men piled out of the truck and surrounded the plane.

"You took a great chance coming in here in a little plane this time of day," the driver shouted. "We don't fly these things except early in the morning or late in the afternoon. That's the only time conditions are right."

The men righted the plane and hitched the truck to the tail wheel. They dragged it out of the bushes and back onto the runway. "You get in, start the engine, and keep a little wind flowing over the wings," the driver said. "My men will hang onto the wings and I'll tow you to the hangar."

On the way to the hangar the plane ran out of gas.

Inside the hangar we inspected the wing. No structural damage. We had only scraped the wingtip and torn the fabric. It was repaired in the time it took the dope to dry on the fabric. The cost was only twenty-five dollars.

The next morning—Sunday—we were airborne for Los Angeles at 6:00 A.M. with two network broadcasts awaiting me there. In eight hours we were in Los Angeles and headed by taxi for the Don Lee-MBS studios.

Luckily, "Nobody's Children" was radio and not television. I arrived in the only clean clothes I had left—a sports shirt and jacket and a pair of worn, linen slacks. My slacks were so washed out that anyone looking closely could see through them to my red-striped undershorts.

Deanna Durbin smiled in a ladylike fashion when she saw me but made no comment about my appearance.

Later, I did my "FYI" broadcast, and the next morning we began leapfrogging home to Beacon Field. We made it home without incident.

It was about 3:30 P.M. on Saturday, June 14, 1941, when we landed at Beacon Field. Six thousand miles of flying experience were behind us, and I had accumulated a total of 140 pilot hours.

When I went to the WOL newsroom and began catching up on the news from Europe, it seemed to me more likely than ever that our country would soon be at war.

XVI

On December 7, 1941, I sat behind a microphone in Griffith Stadium; the Washington Redskins were playing the Philadelphia Eagles, and I was calling the plays over the public-address system. It had started out as an exciting game. Roars of approval rose up from the stands as the Redskins registered gains. Hundreds of uniformed Army, Navy, and Marine Corps men were among the fans, including an array of top brass. For the generals and admirals as for the rest of us there that chilly afternoon, the game was a respite from the high tensions that were gripping Washington. War was threatening. Japan had seized part of French Indo-China. A delegation of Japanese diplomats was in the capital. The Japanese wanted the United States to accept the Japanese conquests. Secretary of State Cordell Hull had refused. Negotiations were to proceed, but to many of us in Washington the danger of armed conflict seemed acute.

The Redskins and the Eagles had played only a short time. I was handed a message. A general, whose name I no longer recall, was asked to report to his office at once. I made the announcement, and a few minutes later another, similar message was handed to me. Now it was an admiral who was wanted. As the game progressed there were more such summonses for military officers of all ranks. What in the world was going on?

Someone passed me a note:

"The Japanese have bombed Pearl Harbor."

My God! This was it! War was here.

But was I to broadcast that ominous announcement? Would my words bring on a panic among those thousands of people jammed together in Griffith Stadium? I could envisage people trampling each other in a rush for the exits.

And what if someone had been misinformed and the report was unfounded?

George Preston Marshall always kept a portable radio with him in his owner's box. I made a quick decision. I turned the microphone over to an assistant and made my way through the stands to Marshall's side. He was listening to his radio.

Marshall looked up as I tapped his shoulder. He had been so busy monitoring the news that he had not noticed the change of voice on the PA system.

I showed him my note. He nodded.

"It's true, Frank," he said.

"But what should I do? Do I broadcast the announcement or not?"

Marshall knew why I asked. He thought for only a moment. Then he said we had no choice. I would have to announce the news. He cautioned me to be as calm about it as I could. Any excitement in my voice could be contagious.

I made my way back to the PA booth. More and more fans were leaving the stadium by now. Many, obviously, had portable radios. The news was spreading.

Even so, I dreaded what I had to do as I sat down at the microphone. I could envisage a mob surging out of control, people crushed together, some getting hurt.

There was a time-out in the game. I steeled myself, and I spoke with all the calm I could muster.

"Ladies and gentlemen," I said, "may I have your attention, please, for an important announcement."

I paused. A hush settled over the crowd.

"We have just gotten word, and we have checked the information: The Japanese have bombed Pearl Harbor."

There were shouts from the crowd. Immediately more people started leaving, but there was no panic. I thanked God. A few men in military uniform did rush for the exits and there was a continuing roar of conversation, but the excitement was contained. The crowd was orderly.

I don't think the few fans who remained paid much attention to the rest of the game. The Redskins won, 20 to 14, but there was only a hollow cheer from the dwindling crowd when the game ended. The news was too sobering. All of us, I think, knew that a formal declaration of war could not be long in coming. Some of those uniformed officers and men who had hurried to the exits would soon be dying in the Pacific and probably also in Europe, and life would never be the same again for any of us.

On October 6, 1942, at the age of twenty-seven, I was sworn in for active duty as an ensign in the United States Naval Reserve, and right away I began learning what millions of men had learned before me—specifically, that military service was never designed for the family man.

I was assigned first to Dietrick Field, at Frederick, Maryland, seventy-five miles from home. A few days after I had begun additional flight training there, I found a few moments to telephone Lil back in Arlington. I only wanted to confirm that all was in order there.

Lil answered.

"Hi!" I said.

She recognized my voice.

"Hon," she said, "would you call back in a few minutes? The firemen are here now."

She hung up.

My God!

Fire trucks! Fire! I began fantasizing. I saw my boys trapped in a smoke-filled room with the flames licking at a locked door. I saw firemen battering down that door and, in so doing, setting up a draft that would engulf my little family in flames! My God!

I called again. Now the line was busy. I was terrified.

If the house burned to the ground, where would Lil and the boys spend the night?

And what in hell, I asked myself, was I doing in Frederick, Maryland, with the fire trucks at my home in Arlington, Virginia?

The phone rang. I snatched the receiver off the hook.

"Hello!"

"Hello, hon," Lil said, calmly.

"What in hell is going on?"

"Oh, nothing much. We had a little fire in the chimney, that's all."

"That's *all*?"

I was angry, and Lil's calm made me more angry.

"It could have burned the house down!" I said.

"No, hon, the firemen said there was no real danger. Just some soot caught fire and some sparks were coming out of the chimney. It was out in just a few minutes."

She paused, then went on:

"All the neighbors came in and we had a nice visit. The firemen were very nice."

Suddenly I was jealous of the firemen.

"My God!" I shouted.

"Oh, another thing."

"What else, for goodness' sake?"

"The boys all have whooping cough."

I swore again.

"And another thing . . ."

"Now what?"

"Your airplane is up a tree."

"What?" I thought we had a bad connection. "What's that about my airplane? What?"

It was not really my airplane any longer. I had sold that little Aeronca, NC33788, the plane I loved so much. I had closed the deal only a day or two before I was sworn in. But we still thought of it as my plane.

Lil said a severe thunderstorm with high winds had hit Calverton, Virginia, just beyond the Washington defense perimeter, where the plane was based.

Bob Ashburn, who now managed the airfield there, had telephoned Lil and told her the plane had been torn loose from its moorings and had blown up into a tree. It had been practically destroyed.

"Hon," Lil said, "I'm afraid I have some *really* bad news for you."

"Really bad? How could it be any worse?"

Well, it could be, and it was. Very much worse.

"It's about Ernest," Lil said.

Ernest was a dear old friend of mine. He was an elderly black man who had serviced my plane and others at Beacon Field. He was a gentle and kindly man, and my feeling for him was warm as I am sure his was for me. He had appeared to take a personal pride in my little Aeronca. He used to point it out to visitors as the plane that John Gantt and I had flown across the continent and back. When Bob Ashburn had transferred operations to Calverton, Ernest had gone along with him to work there.

"What about Ernest?" I asked Lil.

"Well, you'll have to brace yourself now, hon," she said.

"Okay. But tell me. What is it?"

Lil said Ernest had been on the field at Calverton when the storm hit. He had tried to save my plane. He was hanging onto it when the wind shot it up into the air. He rose with it —and then fell. And the fall had killed him.

When Lil broke the news, I broke down and cried.

Christmas 1942. It was a joyous Christmas—joyous because I was home on leave. It was a poignant Christmas, too, because Lil and I were forced to a sad decision. We decided to sell the little house we so much loved. I had just been reassigned to the Naval Air Station at Corpus Christi, Texas, for further flight training, where, if all went well, I would get my Navy wings. There was no way of knowing what would happen to me then. It seemed impractical for the family to try to follow me around and, in any event, with the future so uncertain, I wanted Lil and the boys settled someplace near their own kin. They would move to St. George, South Carolina, near Lil's parents.

Our decision made, I left Arlington on the day after Christmas to proceed to Corpus Christi. I kissed Lil and the boys and hugged them all, and the tears welled in their eyes and mine. Our parting was like a scene from a war movie, the soldier saying his good-byes to his tearful family and going off to war.

There was only one light moment as I left the Lee Boulevard house for the last time.

"Hey, hon!" little Mike yelled, "you look nice in your uniform."

I spent that New Year's Eve alone in my room in the Hotel Driscoll in Corpus Christi, and I think those were the saddest moments of my life. I lay there in bed listening to Guy Lombardo broadcasting from the Roosevelt Hotel in New York, and when the band played "Auld Lang Syne," when the whistles and bells in Corpus Christi announced the arrival of the New Year, I cried again and prayed that I would come through all right and be reunited with my family.

"If it moves, salute it. If it doesn't move, pick it up. If you can't pick it up, paint it!"

That was an old axiom in the United States Navy, and I learned what it meant. The cadets at Corpus Christi saluted every officer who came within twenty paces.

A group of cadets approached me as I was entering the Administration Building at Corpus Christi for the first time. Each one of them saluted me smartly. I was impressed. In fact, I was thrilled. I felt a surge of emotion. I was more determined than ever to be a good naval officer.

The Navy allowed no free time during training. If I wasn't scheduled for a flight, I was expected in ground school, in radio code class, in an aircraft-and-flag-recognition course, in some corollary course, or in athletics. We played badminton on the concrete floor of an airplane hangar. One afternoon I made the mistake of playing while wearing leather shoes. I reached for the bird—and reached too far. My leather soles slipped from under me, and I landed on my chin. It knocked me cold. I woke up in the emergency room at the dispensary. The medics had taken six stitches to seal up my wound; for a time after that, I flew with a helmet strapped uncomfortably over a bandage under my chin. That was my first war wound. And, let me hasten to say, it was my last. I guess it is understandable that I was not awarded the Purple Heart.

I finished primary instruction at Corpus Christi and went into Flight Instructors' School.

March 25, 1943, was my big day. I got my Navy wings. It was a moment of intense emotion. My class lined up in front of the commanding officer. He made a speech congratulating us, and then he pinned wings on each of us and handed us certificates declaring we were now naval aviators.

I got through the ceremony with a tight rein on my emotions. But then the band played "The Star-spangled Banner," and that did it. I cried. I stood there at rigid attention with tears streaming down my cheeks.

I was given another ten-day leave, and I made my way to Lil and the boys at St. George.

Yes, it was like falling in love all over again. Lil and I started what was very much like a glorious honeymoon.

When you change ships or stations in the Navy, you have to make the rounds—that is, you've got to call on each of several departments and check in. I was assigned to the U. S. Naval Reserve Air Base at Hutchinson, Kansas—a naval base right in the middle of the Kansas wheat fields—and on my rounds at Hutchinson I checked in at Flight Squadron 2 as ordered. The commander, Lieutenant Ralph Couser, was absent. So I introduced myself to the second in command. He looked vaguely familiar. When I saluted and approached his desk to present my credentials I saw his name on a plaque on his desk. He was Lieutenant (J.G.) Burt Morris. The name, too, somehow seemed familiar. Then it came to me. Burt Morris reminded me of Wayne Morris, the movie actor.

"Pardon me, sir," I asked after the formalities, "but are you Wayne Morris' brother?"

He laughed and said, "No."

"Well," I said, "these days you never know. What with

Robert Taylor flying for the Navy and Tyrone Power in the Marines and Jimmy Stewart in the Air Force, you never can tell who you'll meet."

He smiled and shook my hand and said, "Welcome aboard."

I saluted and left, and a few moments later, Johnny O'Connor, one of my comrades in arms, explained to me that Lieutenant Burt Morris was in fact Wayne Morris, the star of innumerable "B" movies, now playing a wartime role in real life. Wayne later joined the fleet in the Pacific and became a real-life hero flying fighters off a carrier.

As a flight instructor at Hutchinson, I felt I had a reasonable chance of staying put, at least for a time. So I rented a small house on the outskirts of town and sent for Lil and the boys. We settled in and lived there much like a family in peacetime. The two older boys went to the local school, and Lil lived the life of a local housewife, although perhaps with one important difference: She and the other service wives there were married to fliers, and to the lay mind, flying entailed more than normal risk. Two of our squadron members were killed there in a midair collision. However, if Lil or the other Navy wives at Hutchinson ever had any qualms about our flying, they never showed it.

A rumor (scuttlebutt) started at Hutch that primary training stations around the country were to cut back operations. The rate of attrition among naval aviators was not as high as had been expected. The Navy had a surplus of cadets. Wayne Morris was transferred to a fighter training base and I was ordered, like other instructors, to tighten up at once and let only the best cadets get through. That posed an ugly dilemma for me. The thought of washing out a young cadet with stars in his eyes was abhorrent. A cadet who could not make it might well wind up as a second-class seaman with reduced income and months of hard and grueling training gone for naught.

One of my students was a young man named Stevens. I don't think I ever knew his first name. Stevens was not making it. He was a good flier for "straight and level" landings and takeoffs. But he had a deep fear of putting an airplane into unusual attitudes, such as had to be assumed in aerobatics. Flying upside down, for example, terrified him. Unless he could overcome his fear, I would have to wash him out, and that was something I could not face doing.

I began spending free time with him. I tried to condition his thinking before every flight. Some little time passed, and Stevens began slowly to shape up. His fears were waning, but not entirely gone. One afternoon I flew him to an outlying practice field. We landed and I got out of the plane.

"Now," I said, "you take it. Take the plane up to three thousand feet and do everything I've taught you. I'll be right here watching everything you do."

He paled, and a glazed look came into his eyes, but I assured him he could do it if he could get control of himself. His confidence began to return. I stepped back from the airplane, and he gunned the engine and took off. As he climbed, I said a quiet little prayer for him.

He executed a loop, then an Immelmann, then snap rolls and slow rolls—and then he inverted the plane and did a falling leaf. He executed every maneuver he had been taught.

When he landed and taxied over to where I was standing, he had a big grin on his face.

I stepped over and looked into the cockpit.

"Did you throw up?" I asked.

"No, sir. It was fun."

The next day, Stevens passed his flight check, and late that afternoon, when Lil and I got home from shopping, we found a package waiting for us on our porch. It was a quart of scotch—something not easy to come by in a dry state—and attached to it was a card that said,

"Thanks. Cadet Stevens."

Months later, when I was flying in the Pacific, I met Stevens again. We ran into each other in the mess hall on Manus in the Admiralty Islands. He had become a fighter pilot and had received several decorations.

By early 1944, we had suspended almost all instruction at Hutch, and transfer orders began coming through for the flight instructors assigned there. A number of pilots were assigned to other primary bases. The rest of us began sweating it out.

Finally, orders came for me. I was assigned to an instrument flight school at the Naval Air Station in Atlanta, Georgia. That could mean only one thing—training in multi-engined aircraft. This was fine with me. However, a transfer meant a family problem. Mike was in first grade by now and John was in kindergarten. And my Atlanta assignment was almost sure to be short-lived. We decided that Lil and the boys would stay in Hutchinson until the end of the school term and then move back to St. George to live with her parents.

I had a month of intensive training at Atlanta. One of my classmates was Tyrone Power. He and I spent a lot of time together at the bar of the officers' club. He was a likable man and a first-class pilot.

After Atlanta, I spent a month at the American Airlines instrument training school in Fort Worth, flying DC-3s, and while I was there Lil and the boys moved back to St. George. I was glad they were there. I had every intention of surviving that war, but if God had other ideas I wanted my family in a familiar environment and close to Lil's parents.

"Proceed to Naval Air Station, Alameda, California, *for further assignment.*"

So read the orders cut for me at Fort Worth. The phrasing had an ominous ring. Alameda, of course, was on San Francisco Bay, and it seemed the reference to "further assignment" could only mean one thing: I was on my way to duty in the Pacific.

We had a saying in the Navy: "There are two ways to do things: the right way and the Navy way." I went out to Alameda and found that my "further assignment" was strictly in accord with the Navy way. I was assigned to a squadron of seaplanes. Seaplanes! I had never even ridden in one, much less flown one. My assignment would be flying big four-engined seaplanes into the Pacific area. Why I was assigned to that VR-2 squadron only the U. S. Navy in its wisdom will ever know.

But it was a big break for me. I would be on "permanent" duty in Alameda, as permanent as anything in the Navy in wartime could be, and that meant I would be able to have my family with me. There would be only three problems: (1) finding a home we could afford in that inflated, wartime economy; (2) raising the money for train fares across the continent from South Carolina; and (3) getting train reservations, which in wartime might take weeks.

I found it in the Oakland *Tribune*—a completely furnished house at a "reasonable" rental, the tenants to live with and provide meals for the owner, who was described as an elderly gentleman. There was certainly a chance, I thought, that a reasonable rental would be one that a lieutenant (j.g.) in the

United States Navy could afford, even in wartime Oakland with its inflated prices. I telephoned at once.

The man who answered identified himself as Charles Curran. He sounded not only elderly, but also crotchety. He said his wife was in a sanitarium and he was unable to cope alone but he was determined to stay on in his own home. He wanted a family to move in and take care of things for him, and his charge would be twenty-five dollars a month.

Curran turned out to be a grumpy old man in his late seventies who constantly smoked cheap cigars. His house reeked of stale cigar smoke. It badly needed cleaning and airing. But otherwise it was fairly presentable. It had a well-equipped kitchen and three bedrooms. If we took the deal, there would be one for him, one for Lil and me, and one for the boys.

The problem, clearly, was Curran. He was a fiercely independent old man with fixed and rigid opinions, most of them negative. He hated Franklin Delano Roosevelt and the New Deal, he hated the rent-control board, and he hated the inconvenience of war. Furthermore, he didn't particularly like Navy people, but he said he would not make an issue of that in my case. I did not dare mention to him that we were Democrats and Roman Catholics.

Curran and his wife had never had children, and I got the feeling he thought the world would be a better place to live in if babies could be twenty years old at birth. However, he said he thought he could live with our boys if they were well behaved.

I steeled myself and told the old man I would think over his offer and telephone him soon with a yes or a no.

I did a lot of hard thinking on the way back to the air station. I knew Lil had a phenomenal ability to get along with people and make things work, and perhaps this would be a situation she could manage. Most of the burden would be on her. I would be away in the Pacific most of the time. But I badly wanted her and the boys with me. And it would be a start. Once here, Lil might find something better.

I telephoned her and gave her the unadulterated facts.

Yes, she was willing to try. She said she would try anything that would mean we could be together.

I called Curran at once and told him we would take his deal.

And then I borrowed money on my life-insurance policies to cover the family's train fare from South Carolina.

Train reservations were not easy to come by in wartime. Long waits were the rule. I flew to Kwajalein atoll in the Pacific and returned to Alameda—a round trip which, with stopovers, took eighteen days—before Lil could even begin her trip West. She made reservations that called for a one-night stopover in New Orleans.

It was on the morning of the third day of her journey that I got a telegram from her datelined New Orleans. It said only:

"MISSED TRAIN IN NEW ORLEANS. WILL BE A DAY LATE. LOVE."

My God! What in hell could have happened? When I read that telegram in my room at BOQ, I could have climbed right up the wall. I wondered if she had enough money for an overnight stop. What had happened to cause her to miss the train? Could she get reservations out of New Orleans? A million horrible thoughts went through my head. I spent the rest of that day in a phone booth in the BOQ. I tried every source I could think of to reach her: Traveler's Aid, the shore patrol, the station master at the railroad station. On each call I left implicit instructions for her to call that phone-booth number as soon as she was located. Nothing!

I took a breather from depositing quarters in that pay telephone long enough to have lunch with Father O'Callahan. I told him what had happened and that I was worried that she wouldn't have enough money. He said we could take care of that. He had some money in the Navy Relief Fund and he could advance me a hundred dollars. I could wire it to her in care of Western Union at the station and she could pick it up after she returned my calls.

Then I took up my vigil by the telephone booth again. Every time someone used that phone I went through agony.

At long last, that telephone rang and it was Lil.

"What happened?"

Lil seemed a bit annoyed that I had sent so many people in New Orleans into a tizzy paging her and searching the station for her. She said she had been accosted by practically everyone there in an official capacity when she and the boys had come back from the zoo.

"The zoo?"

My own temper was rising now.

"I took the boys to the Audubon Zoo to kill time."

"To kill time?"

"Yes. Listen and stop interrupting."

"Okay."

"This morning we arrived at the station in plenty of time and I had my luggage checked by a redcap and he put it on the train for me. Then we had breakfast and I didn't hear the announcement about our train."

"Yes?"

"Finally, I thought we better get on board, and on the way to the train I stopped at the newsstand."

"Yes?"

"The redcap, who had taken my luggage, came up to me and said, 'Lady, aren't you taking that train to California? Well, there it goes down the track!'"

"I said, 'My luggage is on it!' And he said he'd try to get it put off at the suburban station and I could take a taxi out and pick it up and try to get another reservation. Well, he did and we did."

"Oh my God!"

"Listen now while I tell you. The station master came to my assistance and said I could check with him at five o'clock when the government reservations were canceled and maybe there would be something good for us. So we didn't have anything to do for several hours so I took the boys to the zoo. I didn't want to worry you until I found out what we could get."

"Worry me? Oh my God!"

"Well, it's all set."

"What's all set?"

"I just saw the station master and I've got a compartment straight through to Los Angeles, and I'll pay the conductor the extra fare on the train."

"A compartment?"

"Yes. When the cancellations came in he saved a compartment for us. The train leaves in an hour. We're fine. Don't worry."

"Worry? Who, me? Did you get the money?"

"What money?"

"I sent a hundred dollars to you care of Western Union."

"Oh I didn't know. I'll go get it and get on the train right now."

"Please, do for my sake. I love you."

"I love you, too." She hung up.

I was exhausted. I went to the chapel and offered some prayers of thanks. Father O'Callahan and I had dinner together. We had a drink on the outcome of the day and I got a telegram from Lil saying:

"THANKS FOR MONEY, MADE TRAIN, SEE YOU TWO DAYS, LOVE."

It was just one day later—and just one day before Lil and the family were to arrive—that I got word I was being transferred to the Admiralty Islands.

An old friend and flying buddy from Hutchinson, Lieutenant Bud Dyas, burst into my room at the Alameda BOQ while I was at long last enjoying a sound sleep, free of worry about the family.

"Wake up, Frank!" Bud said, tugging at my shoulder. "I got news for you."

"Yeah? What news?"

"A new squadron has been formed. It's going into the Pacific with R4Ds (DC3s). It'll be VR-13 and it'll be based in the Admiralty Islands and do island-hopping."

"So?"

"Well," Bud said, "you've been selected to be one of the plane commanders in the squadron."

I thought I was having a nightmare.

Lil and the boys would be ensconced with old Charlie Curran while I was permanently based in the Pacific!

Bud had even worse news.

"We're shoving off tomorrow morning," he said. "Bright and early."

Lil and the kids were due in Los Angeles in the afternoon. I wouldn't even be there to meet them.

"You've gotta be kiddin'," I said, hoping.

"No," Bud said. "It's for real."

I scrambled out of bed in a rage. Who would meet Lil and the boys? How would they manage in a strange city, living in the same house with an irascible old man, a total stranger?

I got dressed hurriedly and dashed off to the office of the

commanding officer of VR-2, Captain William Millage Nation.

I told his aide that I had urgent business with the captain and had to see him right away. I was seething with anger at William Millage Nation and the entire United States Navy. The aide saw by the look on my face that I was in no mood to be trifled with. He admitted me to Captain Nation's office. I stood in front of Nation's desk at attention. He didn't look up. He continued to sign papers. I thought, "Oh my God, my orders are probably among those papers he's signing."

When he was through he tossed the papers in his "Out" box and looked up and said, "Yes?"

"Sir," I said, "I'm Lieutenant Blair. I've been told that I've been selected for this new VR-13 squadron and that they're shoving off tomorrow morning."

"Yes. That's correct."

"Begging the captain's pardon, sir, may I ask how I was selected for the assignment?"

"Yes. We selected qualified R4D pilots who had training at the American Airlines School in R4Ds."

"But sir," I said, "I have been assigned to this squadron under your command and I like it here, and furthermore I have been assigned to a crew and have already made two trips."

I didn't stop. I went right on.

"And furthermore, sir, my wife and three small sons are on their way right now and due to arrive in Los Angeles tomorrow afternoon. Sir, this is a disaster. And if I may continue, sir, I don't like the idea of being drafted. In fact, it's worse than being drafted; at least there's a lottery involved there. I volunteered for duty in the Navy in time of war and it seems to me that there are many qualified R4D pilots in this squadron, single men, who would jump at this chance for adventure. Frankly, sir, I'm worried about my family. They have no one to meet them and break the news and turn them around and send them back home. You can see I'm in a helluva jam—Sir!"

"Where's your family coming from, Lieutenant?"

"From South Carolina, sir. They've been traveling by train now for five days."

"I see." He studied me coolly.

I said, "I thought I would have permanent duty here. That's why I sent for my family."

Captain Nation's eyes met mine.

He said, "Lieutenant, when you got your commission in the Navy, you left your family and family obligations behind you. The Navy comes first now."

I returned his stare. Our eyes locked on each other like radar.

"Sir," I said, "it may be that way in your home, but it isn't that way in mine."

His expression did not change. I went on:

"My family comes first and the only reason I'm in the Navy is because my family comes first and I feel an obligation to them to serve and help get this war over with so we can return to a normal life. I would welcome this assignment if circumstances were different."

Captain Nation's face was set in a rigid mold. Nothing I had said seemed to have penetrated.

"Lieutenant," he said sternly, "your orders have been drawn. Now you may leave my office and report to the Naval Air Station at Oakland at 0800 tomorrow for final indoctrination and departure with VR-13. Transportation to Oakland will be furnished."

He stared at me with his eyebrows raised.

"That is all, Lieutenant."

I saluted and walked out.

On my way back to the BOQ I was a defeated man. I didn't know where to turn, what to do. I was just about in tears when I called Bob Brandt, my closest friend. We were together throughout our flight training. I hoped and prayed he'd be home. Thank God, he was.

He knew that Lil was due to arrive tomorrow. I told him of my confrontation with Captain Nation. I could tell by his voice that he was concerned. Good old Bob. He said he'd meet my family himself and work everything out with Father O'Callahan somehow. He told me not to worry.

Not to worry? How would that be possible? One thing I was sure of: I certainly was not in a frame of mind to command an R4D on an over-ocean flight that, with layovers, would take ten days at least.

We agreed that perhaps the best thing for him to do would be to send Lil and the boys back home. God only knew how long I'd be out there in the Admiralties.

I got little sleep that night.

The next morning, a Jeep pulled up at the BOQ. I piled on my gear and was transported to the Oakland Naval Air Station to take off for the Admiralties.

When I reported at Oakland I got a message to see the VR-13 operations officer, a Lieutenant Commander Sullivan, before checking in.

"Lieutenant," he said, "you don't want to go with this squadron, do you?"

"Commander, it isn't that I don't *want* to go. I'll go anywhere I'm ordered and do my best. That's why I'm here. But I'm facing a critical situation at this time."

I started to explain that Lil and the boys were arriving, but he interrupted me.

"No need to explain," he said. "I understand your situation. Captain Nation called me last night. He told me that

1955—"Today" cast shortly after Lee Meriwether joined our happy little troupe.

October 1952—New York. Dave Garroway, Jack Lescoulie, J. Fred Muggs, and me shortly after I became the regular newscaster on the show.

April 20, 1952—Washington, D.C. "Georgetown University Forum." Left to right, professor Stefan Possony, Ambassador William Bullitt, Senator Richard M. Nixon. Topic: "Can We Stop Russia?" *Photo by Harold Briegs.*

1954—RCA Exhibition Hall, "Today." Dave, Bob Hope, and me. Bob looks at me like that because Dave has just told him I am a father of seven children.

1954—"Today." Faye Emerson substitutes for Dave. It was a delightful experience.

1954—Jack Lescoulie, Dean Martin, Jerry Lewis, and me on the boardwalk at Atlantic City when "Today" originated (live) from there.

1955—Racquet Club, Miami, Florida. Interviewing Vic Seixas and Tony Trabert (tennis stars) for "Today."

1955—"Today." Easter with son Billy appearing as an Easter Bunny. In background is photo of President Eisenhower as he recuperates from his first heart attack in Denver.

1955—Lil at our home on Ardsley Terrace in Irvington-on-Hudson, New York.

1955—In front of the "Today" weather map. Lee, Jack, and me. We liked one another. We still do.

1955—"Today." Dave and I interviewing Leo Genn. Some people thought Leo and I looked alike. I don't think so. Do you?

1956—The family as guests on "The Ted Mack Hour" (an interview program on NBC). Our son John was in the Marine Corps at Parris Island, South Carolina. *Photo by Alexander Kerry.*

1956—"Today." Jack, Lee, and I playing tic-tac-toe on a horse's derrière at the Kansas City Livestock Show. Note one of Jack's famous facial expressions. *Photo by Warner Studio.*

January 16, 1957—"Today" from the RCA Exhibition Hall with Helen O'Connell, our "Today" girl, celebrating the fifth anniversary of the show. *Photo by Ralph I. Shockey.*

1957—Gerry Green, "Today" managing editor, and I en route to a "Today" origination. Gerry wrote on the photograph: "To good, old reliable, the oldest, established, permanent, floating (bigoted) newscaster in New York."

1958—Disneyland, in California. Lil, Theresa, Mary, Paul, Billy, and I are the guests of The Insurance Company of North America at their agents' convention. Mary says, "We rode on everything." Billy kept running away to visit with the Indians.

1961—John Chancellor and me. John was host on "Today." He and I liked working together. We are still good friends. *Photo by Raimondo Borea, ASMP.*

1961—"Today" originated from Tanglewood, the summer home of the Philadelphia Orchestra. I interviewed Norman Rockwell, whose studio was at nearby Stockbridge, Massachusetts.

1961—"Today." John Chancellor, Edwin Newman, and I. "See no evil, hear no evil, speak no evil." We thought we were a good trio, but our ratings told us differently. Changes were made.

when you reported here I was to have a conference with you and let you make the decision about whether you would go or not."

My spirits began to lift.

"If you decide against this assignment, Captain Nation asked that you return to VR-2. We have a substitute to take your place."

"Thank you, sir. If that's the way it can be then I have no choice under the circumstances but to return to VR-2. Thank you, sir."

I saluted and got out of there. I called Bob Brandt and told him. I got my gear together, climbed aboard the Jeep that had brought me, and started back to Alameda.

On the way I began thinking about what could happen to me.

Captain Nation had said he wanted me back if I chose not to go with VR-13. Brother! I thought. He's really going to throw the book at me.

I had to check back into the squadron. I had to report to administration, payroll, supply, every department including, of course, Captain Nation. I approached his office with trepidation.

I told the captain's aide I was checking back in, and I sat down to wait. I didn't wait long. The aide went into the CO's office and came back almost at once.

"The captain will see you now," he said.

I strode into Captain Nation's office, stood at rigid attention, and gave that man probably the sharpest salute in naval history. I expected the worst.

"Lieutenant Blair reporting for duty, sir," I said.

Captain Nation stood up and held out his hand and said, "Welcome back, Lieutenant."

I was taken aback. I swallowed heavily and managed to say,

"Thank you, sir. I'm sorry about my conduct of yesterday. I hope you appreciate the state of mind I was in. I appreciate your recalling my orders."

He studied my eyes. There wasn't a trace of a smile on his face.

"As a matter of fact," he said, "it's I who should be indebted to you, and I am. I think I have learned something from this experience—something I had lost sight of in my duties here."

He sat down again.

"Welcome back," he said. "Go about your duties. That is all."

I saluted and departed. I couldn't have had a better tour of duty than I had in VR-2 through the remaining period of the war.

I bummed a ride to Los Angeles on a Navy plane early that afternoon and arrived at the crowded Los Angeles railroad station with time to spare. I was standing on the platform when the train pulled in.

Lil never looked lovelier. She wore a purple dress, and her dark brown hair was almost at her shoulders. I took her in my arms and we kissed. There were tears in our eyes.

Mike tugged at my uniform.

"Hey, hon, we're here too."

I embraced my three sons.

"Hon," John said, "I'm hungry."

Lil and I smiled. Some things never change, even in war.

I had an upper and a lower berth reserved for our all-night trip back to Oakland. We put Mike and John in the upper, and Lil and Tommy and I took the lower.

Lil and I made beautiful love that night, and believe me it

wasn't easy with a four-year-old asleep beside us in a lower berth.

It was a bright, sunny morning when our cab pulled up in front of Charlie Curran's house. Thank God! Sunshine always makes things look better than they are. All the other houses on the block were presentable. Only Curran's was run down, like the old man himself.

Lil said, bravely, "This is it? Doesn't look too bad. We'll manage."

Curran seemed to like Lil and, in his abrupt, crotchety manner, he tried to be nice to the boys. He even said he sure was glad to see us.

We weren't sure how to address Curran. "Mr. Curran" would be too formal and "Charlie" would be disrespectful to a man of his age, especially coming from the boys. Mike solved the problem by saying:

"Uncle Charlie is a nice man to let us live in his house."

That was it. We would call him "Uncle Charlie."

When I announced I would go for groceries, Uncle Charlie brightened up and said I could use his car. That was a surprise; I didn't know he had a car. He said it was in a garage a half block away. He took me to it. There was a car there, all right. It was a 1927 Graham Paige sedan painted bright red, obviously a paint job he had done himself. The old man's eyes sparkled when he showed it to me. He climbed in and stepped on the starter and, to my amazement, after a little churning the thing started. He backed it out of the garage and turned it over to me. The boys piled into the back seat yelling, "Good-bye, Uncle Charlie!" Good-bye was right. I thought this was the end. The car had the old-fashioned stick floor shift, and when I tried to put it in first gear I damned near stripped the gears. There was grinding and chatter from the gear box. Uncle Charlie scowled. I tried again and made it, but as I let out the clutch the GP-27 lurched forward and stalled. I smiled at Uncle Charlie. He was still scowling. I started it up again and carefully got it under way with a smooth start.

Lil made us a great dinner that evening and Uncle Charlie really put the food away. There was obviously nothing wrong with the old man's appetite. He was in a good mood after dinner. He surprised us by saying:

"If you want to go out on an evening after the boys get to bed, I'll keep an eye on them."

We were overwhelmed.

Lil's first night out was a big success. Father O'Callahan was delighted to meet her, and he told her that she was all I said she was. She liked him too, and thanked him for taking such good care of me and helping her get there.

After dinner we were sitting around the officers' club having a drink when Father O'Callahan got a phone call. In a couple of minutes he was back and said that he'd have to leave us a few minutes to hear confessions.

There was a carrier at the dock getting ready to shove off for the war, and several men on board had expressed the desire to have their confessions heard; he had been requested to come down and lend a hand.

"Wait around," he said. "I'll be back in just a little while."

Lil and I had a few dances and soon Father O'Callahan returned with a bemused look on his face.

"Strange thing, or is it?" he said. "Everybody wants to go to confession at the last minute just before they shove off for parts unknown."

Another chaplain came to our table and joined us. He was

new to our base and I didn't know him very well. Father O'Shea, I think his name was.

Father O'Callahan restated what he had just said, and Father O'Shea agreed. Then he said he had a most unusual experience just before coming to Alameda.

"I heard the confessions of five brothers who were serving on the same ship."

"That's unusual," I said. "I thought the Navy didn't allow members of the same family to serve on the same ship."

"It's something the Navy rarely, if ever, does, for obvious reasons. They told me an exception had been made in their case. They had said that if they were going to fight, they wanted to fight side by side on the same vessel."

"What was their name?" Lil asked.

"Sullivan, from Waterloo, Iowa. George, Joseph, Albert, Madison, and Francis."

"What was the name of the ship, Father?" I asked.

"The *Juneau*. She's out in the Pacific somewhere now."

Just a few weeks later, in November, in the Battle of Guadalcanal, the *Juneau* was torpedoed. Her back was broken, she broke in two, and she disappeared in a matter of minutes. All five Sullivan brothers were lost.

A few weeks after Lil and I had had dinner with Father O'Callahan, he was ordered to the aircraft carrier *Franklin* to be ship's chaplain—duty, he had said, he really wanted. He really wanted to see action. He did.

The *Franklin* was attacked by a single Japanese plane in March of 1945 at a point about 50 miles off the Japanese mainland. A semiarmor-piercing bomb hit the ship and set off explosions in the carrier's ammunition supplies—724 men died. During the height of the fire and the continuing fighting, Father O'Callahan administered the last rites to these men. And he organized and directed rescue parties. And over and above that, he led men below decks to wet down magazines that threatened to explode. It was a feat of tremendous bravery. Father O'Callahan was awarded the Congressional Medal of Honor.

Although I wasn't anxious to go off on a trip and leave Lil and the kids, I was pleased, in checking the schedule board, to find that I had again been assigned to Tommy Tomberlin's crew, with a scheduled departure for September 13. Same crew: Tomberlin, Bean, Blair, and Billingsley. I hadn't seen any of them since Lil arrived, so I was, in a way, looking forward to being with them again.

Things were going along as well as could be expected at the Curran house. The old man had calmed down and, in his own way, he really tried to be civil.

Lil and I had scored a few points with him by driving him, in his 1927 Graham Paige, to the sanitarium on the outskirts of Oakland to see his wife, who was confined there.

Up to that point we weren't sure old Uncle Charlie really had a wife. The old boy got himself all dressed up for the occasion, and he looked pretty good. After that he was almost cheerful, even to our sons. This gave me some reassurance as I packed for the upcoming trip and left for the air station to meet the scheduled departure.

We never knew when we departed NAS, Alameda, where a particular tour would take us. The schedule board showed only departure time, the identification number of the plane we were assigned to, and HNL (NAS, Honolulu) as destination. At Honolulu either we would be turned around, after a layover of a couple of days, and sent back to the mainland, or rescheduled farther out into the Pacific. This trip turned out to be one of the latter. It took us farther than I'd ever been.

From Honolulu we were destined for Kwajalein atoll, and after a two-day layover there we were scheduled on to Manus in the Admiralties. Although we would lay over between legs of a trip, the plane went straight through after servicing, off-loading, loading, and gassing up. Another crew that had been laying over would take the plane on to its next destination and we'd have to wait our turn.

Ebeye, an island in the Kwajalein atoll where we laid over, had been denuded by the bombardment and shelling during the United States' taking of the atoll. There was only one palm tree left on the entire island. Someone had put a fence around it and it was declared sacred ground.

Manus, on the other hand, was lush with growth; it was like something in a Dorothy Lamour movie. It was a ship-repair base and a very busy place. They had a huge floating dry dock where smaller warships could be hauled for repairs. It was jointly occupied by the Australians and the Americans, and it was where VR-13, the squadron I almost got tangled up with, was based. The land-plane operation was on the other side of the island, so one day during our layover I hitched a ride on a supply truck and went over to see my good friend Bud Dyas. Unfortunately he wasn't there; he was away on a trip—island-hopping personnel and supplies.

The main thing I didn't like about the trips was that there was no way to communicate with home, and this worried me immensely, in case one of the boys got sick or something like that turned up. Lil was very good about using the mails, however, and almost always when I'd get back to Honolulu from a trip farther out there'd be a letter for me, but it was usually a week or more old. One other way of getting some news about home was through other squadron members, especially close friends. That way we could get messages a lot quicker: We could get them to call our wives if they returned before we did, and we rendered the same service to them. All of us had a lot in common in those days, and it bound us close and created lasting friendships.

Things went along fairly smoothly—or, at least, if they didn't, Lil never said anything about a mishap. She was very close to Kitty Yingling, from across the street, and she had made friends with some other women on our block. Apparently she and the boys spent as much time as possible away from the house.

We now referred to Tomberlin, Bean, Blair, and Billingsley as "our crew."

"Our crew" continued making trips that would keep us away from home about three weeks at a stretch, and so it worked out that we had about one trip a month.

Meantime, the presidential campaign was rolling along and I could see each time I was home that Uncle Charlie was getting closer and closer to the breaking point in his dislike for Roosevelt. We never let on that we didn't like Dewey; we avoided all conversation about politics. Lil followed the campaign by putting the radio under her pillow and keeping the volume low. I was almost hoping that FDR wouldn't win, even though I wanted him to, for fear of Uncle Charlie's repercussions.

On November 6, 1944, the Monday before Election Day, "our crew" headed out into the Pacific destined for, we thought, once again Manus in the Admiralties.

Of course, we followed the election returns in flight on the plane's radio. When it was determined that Roosevelt had won a fourth term (he had approximately twenty-six million votes to Dewey's twenty-two million) I really started to worry about what was happening back at Curran's house. When we got back to Honolulu from Manus, there was a letter from Lil awaiting me. What I read made me furious and even more anxious to get home. We had one more leg to fly, we thought, from Honolulu to Alameda, but it didn't work out that way, much to my bitter disappointment.

Lil's letter related that on the morning after the election (November 8), when she came out of our room to prepare breakfast and get Mike off to school, Curran approached her and threw the morning newspaper at her feet.

"ROOSEVELT WINS," the headline read.

"Look at that," he shouted. "Now you've really done it."

"But Uncle Charlie," Lil replied, "neither Frank nor I could vote."

"But you wanted this man to win," Curran scowled. "Well, your wishes came true. I hope you're satisfied."

Lil wrote that about that time the lady from next door came in, and Curran lit into her, too. He said he knew she was a Democrat and that she had voted and her vote had canceled his. Then he turned to Lil and said:

"You are not welcome in this house any longer. I want you to leave."

Lil got her dander up and told him:

"I have no intention of leaving. Our rent is paid and, furthermore, I can't go any place and don't intend to until Frank gets home. And if you want some breakfast you can fix it yourself." She took the boys and went over to the Yinglings' and spent the day.

I made up my mind then and there that as soon as I got back home, which I hoped would be in two days, that I'd get my little family out of Curran's house even if I had to take them to a hotel. But what happened to our crew almost sent me up a wall.

The U. S. Marines and Army had captured the islands of Saipan and Tinian in the Marianas during the month of July. Fighting and the "mopping up" process had been going on until October, at which time the islands were declared "se-cured." At that juncture, our squadron began operations into Tanapag Harbor at Saipan. But up until now our crew had never made the trip.

We returned to Alameda on the twenty-first of November and I hurried home. I made it pretty clear to old man Curran that I did not like his behavior and the concern he had caused Lil and me, that he should look for another tenant, and that we would be getting out of there just as soon as possible. He seemed to show some remorse, but I wasn't buying it.

That very afternoon Lil and I took the boys and went to see Trader Fred—L. B. Fredericks, the most advertised dealer in real estate in Oakland. He did a daily, five-minute radio program on a local Oakland station in which he told what properties he had listed for rent or sale. Lil had listened to him often, trying to get a lead on something that would be more suitable for us than Curran's place.

There was a sign in front of Fredericks' that read: "TRADER FRED, REALTOR. Servicemen welcome."

We entered a busy office and asked for Mr. Fredericks. Soon a gaunt man in his early sixties, I supposed, came to the counter where we were standing, and I was shocked seeing him approach. He was a dead ringer for Abraham Lincoln ex-cept for the beard and the mole on the right cheek. He walked slowly, deliberately as I imagined Lincoln must have walked, and he had the same strong, lined face I had remem-bered from Lincoln portraits. When he spoke the resem-blance was even more shocking: He spoke exactly like I imag-ined Lincoln must have spoken—slowly, almost a drawl. I liked him immediately. We started explaining our intolerable situation and he kept nodding his head as if he were appreci-ating our distress. Then suddenly he looked at me and said:

"Don't I know you from somewhere?"

"No, sir, I don't think we've ever met before."

"There's something very familiar about you."

We shook hands again. I could see we were going to be good friends. He told us he was a retired Navy chief petty officer and that's why he tried to be of help to servicemen, especially Navy people.

He said he didn't have anything at the moment that would interest us but that he was contemplating making a deal for a furnished house out on Ninety-first Street.

"It's pretty far out," he said, "but it would work well for you and your family."

He told us to get in touch with him the next day and he'd let us know more about it.

The next morning we were in his office early. Mr. Fredericks told us he made the deal on the house and that he'd take us out to see it, if we thought we'd be interested. Lil and the boys and I piled into his Packard and he drove to Ninety-first Street.

He was right: It was a long way out, but public transportation was close by. It was a fairly new house, completely furnished. It had three bedrooms and was just made to order for us. I asked about the rent and he said fifty dollars a month. I didn't bat an eye. I said:

"We'll take it."

Flying personnel in our squadron were on a per-diem allowance of seven dollars a day when we were flying in the Pacific, and although we had to pay for our meals wherever we stopped over, I figured we could make it easily.

In two days we were out of Curran's house and had moved into the house on Ninety-first Street. Mike was doing very well in second grade at St. Joseph's and we didn't want to transfer him to a school nearer Ninety-first Street, so one of the drawbacks was that Mike, at age eight, would have to take a streetcar to and from school each day—sixty-seven blocks. I took him and met him the first couple of days to make sure he knew what he was doing, and then after that he was on his own and did very well as a commuter. One nice thing about Ninety-first Street was that several of the fellows in the squadron lived in Brookfield Village, which wasn't very far away, so we had friends close by. I felt so much better about my little family being away from old Uncle Charlie. We never saw him after we moved out.

December arrived, according to the calendar, and Lil and I started shopping around for things for the boys. There wasn't much to be had. Steel for use in toys was banned, and the only things to be had were made of wood. We bought the best we could find and some games that would amuse Mike, John, and Tom.

We were all hoping we'd get an early flight in December so that we'd stand a chance of being home on Christmas. It meant a lot to Tomberlin and me particularly because of our kids. Bean's family was still in Minnesota, and to Tex Billingsley it really didn't matter—he had nobody nearby. We had planned a big Christmas feast and party to be held at Tomberlin's. But, damned, on December 19 we were on our way again. This time we really hoped for a turnaround at Honolulu but, no, we spent Christmas Day flying between Kwajalein and Saipan. It was a sad day. Lil said upon my return on December 29 that it was the worst Christmas of her life—she had cried because of loneliness, and all the wooden toys we had bought for the boys fell apart on Christmas Day. There was one cheery note, however. She said that Mike had taken the streetcar to St. Joseph's to go to confession on Christmas Eve and she expected him back fairly soon. Somehow he was delayed and it was getting dark and the fog was beginning to roll in and she was getting worried, and kept going to the front door, and looking down the street, hoping she could spot Mike coming home. She couldn't see more than a half block because the fog was so thick and then through the fog, she said, she heard somebody whistling "Silent Night, Holy Night," and out of the fog Mike appeared casually strolling along.

A very pleasant thing happened to me on that lonely Christmas trip.

On the twenty-third of December (east longitude date) we landed in Tanapag Harbor at Saipan. A crowd of GIs gathered around the ramp as our plane was being hauled ashore. They shouted things like, "Got any mail from the States?" or, "What movies did you bring this trip?"

In the midst of all that a Jeep pulled up and a young major got out and walked toward the ramp. I recognized him immediately: It was Steve McCormick, my very good friend from our WOL, Washington days together. I had lost track of Steve after I went into the Navy. I was sure glad to see him. He was now assistant intelligence officer and aide to Major General Jarman, Western Pacific Base commander.

After we had checked in at operations, Steve took us up to his quarters on what was referred to as "the hill." It was located in the general's complex, and Steve and another officer shared a small but very comfortable shack, considering it was wartime, and he had a supply of whiskey, which, he said, he kept on hand for "official purposes."

Steve also had a flush toilet in his quarters, one of the few on the island. How it was acquired, Steve explained, was that one of the guys on the general's staff was a liaison Navy officer who was a "great acquirer." He had gone aboard a

Navy ship that was anchored in the harbor and made a deal with some of the fellows on board and they literally unbolted and disconnected it from one of the ship's heads, got it ashore, put it in a Jeep, and brought it up to Steve's quarters. Then they got the Army Engineers to figure out how to get water to it so it would flush. It got to be a big, big project but they made it work and it became a very popular facility. Steve said they invited their friends to his quarters to enjoy the privilege of using a Stateside job for relief.

We had a helluva holiday party sponsored by Major Stephen McCormick. We met Steve's girlfriend, Theo, who was a Red Cross worker. A charming lady who was also "Saipan Ann" on Armed Forces Radio, Theo did a program that was broadcast through the OWI's half-million watts station to the forces in the Pacific to combat the "Tokyo Rose" propaganda broadcasts. Steve and Theo became engaged while serving on Saipan and they were married shortly after the war.

After that, each time I flew into Saipan I brought Steve a "care" package of fresh milk and vegetables which I could acquire at Honolulu en route.

On December 24, we headed back for "Charming Ebeye" and arrived there about midafternoon. We were all agreed that as soon as we had dropped our gear in our tents, we should head for the officers' club and prepare for a late afternoon of Christmas caroling, inasmuch as it was the festive season and actually was Christmas Eve on that side of the dateline.

It was also our intention to go to the base movie that night following supper. However, as we warmed up the chorus (joined by others on this "holiday" occasion), and as our harmony improved with each can of beer, supper faded farther and farther in the distance.

I did a lot of flying in the months that followed. We flew to Honolulu regularly, and then onward from Honolulu to such places as Manus in the Admiralties, Ebeye in Kwajalein, and Tanapag Harbor, Saipan. I am sure our crew made its small contribution to the war effort, but I think that on one of our flights out from Alameda to Honolulu, we may have carried the strangest cargo in all the history of war.

It was consigned to Admiral Chester Nimitz, commander-in-chief in the Pacific Theater. The admiral was either a dedicated gardener himself, or a gourmet who demanded garden-fresh vegetables for his table, or alternatively, a man with a household staff who felt he deserved the best. In any event, orders went out, and thus it was that my crewmates and I flew across the Pacific to Honolulu carrying one thousand pounds of good American sheep dung, for Admiral Nimitz' victory garden.

Early in April, I heard about a village of new homes that had been constructed by an enterprising developer named Bohannon. The houses were selling for sixty-five hundred dollars, with only five hundred dollars down. Bob Brandt and his wife and children and Lil and the boys all piled into my Ford Fourdoor and went to look.

The place was called San Lorenzo Village. It was a few miles north of Oakland near the city of San Leandro. Several of the pilots of VR-2 had already purchased homes there. A colony of Navy people was developing. There were schools within walking distance and there was a shopping center. There were neat rows of two-bedroom stucco houses—each slightly different and all painted in pastel colors. They would be more than adequate and, with others of our squadron moving out there, we'd have a special kind of security for our families when we were away on trips.

Brandt put a deposit on one immediately even though he had no furniture. But we not only didn't have furniture, we also didn't have the five hundred dollars for a deposit. Even so we selected one directly across the street from the Brandts' and told the salesman we'd be back with the money. God only knew where I was going to get it. Lil solved the problem. She suggested that I telephone Fulton Lewis, Jr., to see if he would advance us five hundred dollars. The money arrived the next morning by Western Union.

We moved in on May 7, 1945—VE Day, the day the war in Europe ended. We had opened a couple of revolving charge accounts and furnished the place inexpensively. The Brandts moved into their new house on the same day. They still had no furniture, except for one single bed and two baby cribs. Bob had arranged for the Navy to ship his furniture from storage in Chicago, his hometown. It was due any day. Meanwhile, the Brandts would get along. They would use orange crates to sit on, and Bob would drink his morning coffee out of a shaving mug.

The Brandts' furniture still hadn't arrived when the war in the Pacific ended three months later. It was still on the way—the Navy way.

By September 1945, I had made my last flight across the Pacific. I was now on duty as a test pilot—very good duty, indeed. It meant I was able to remain at home. Lil and I were spending much of our time in those days talking about our future. My discharge from the Navy could not be long in coming now, and with the war over I badly wanted out. I wanted to get back in the news business. At the same time, I nurtured a dream. As Lil put it, I wanted "my own little radio station up in the sky, with a picket fence around it."

Now, with the fighting behind us, we could afford to dream

again. The danger I had faced wasn't something that Lil and I talked much about, but obviously Lil was relieved that it was over. My work as a test pilot was not dangerous in itself. That, at least, was my appraisal of it before the flight I made early in the morning of October 4, 1945.

It was two o'clock that morning when the telephone awakened me. The maintenance duty officer was calling. He said there was a seaplane that had just been repaired and would have to be test-flown that night so it could be loaded and on a flight to Honolulu in the afternoon.

"A test flight at night?" I asked in disbelief.

"Yes, it's unusual, I know," he replied, "but that plane is badly needed, and the skipper would like to have the job done tonight."

"What was the nature of the repair job?" I asked him.

"Engine change. It's been tested on the ramp and it checks out okay."

"Oh boy, a new engine to run in, and on a night flight?"

"Yeah, it's unusual, but Lieutenant Commander Conley will be in command and he's requested you as his copilot."

I had flown with Conley on several test hops. I trusted his judgment and his ability as a pilot.

"If it's okay with Conley," I said, "it's all right with me. I'll be right there."

I dressed hurriedly and drove to the air station, where Conley was waiting. I picked up the necessary forms for the check list and we climbed aboard the PB2Y3R—No. 7232.

I got clearance from the control tower, and as we taxied into position, testing and running up the engines on the way, we noticed that the lights on the right side of the sealane were out. Especially at night those guidance lights are important in holding a heading for the takeoff run. I notified the tower.

"Yeah, we know. They're working on them and should be on any minute," was the reply.

The minutes ticked by and still there were no lights. I called the tower again and we were told that, under such conditions, takeoff was at the plane commander's discretion.

Conley and I conferred. We decided to go ahead and get the test over with.

We set our gyro compass to the indication given by the magnetic compass. We knew the compass heading of the sealane, and we planned to use the gyro compass and the lights on our port side to get us safely off the water and into the air.

We took a takeoff clearance from the tower and poured the coal on. The engines roared their full power. Our speed on the water increased to 90 knots (about 105 miles per hour). Then, just as we were about to lift off, we felt a jolt and heard a sound straight out of a nightmare. It sounded like two automobile fenders being crunched together in a collision.

"What in hell was that?" Conley yelled.

No one knew.

Conley kept his cool. As soon as I had retracted the wing floats and bled up the flaps, he leveled her off.

He instructed our flight engineer to go below and see what had happened.

"I felt it on the controls," he said.

The flight engineer shinnied down the ladder to Compartment K. He was back on the flight deck in seconds.

"There's a gash in the hull in K Compartment about three feet long and two inches wide," he said.

We had struck something upon leaving the water, probably some floating debris in the sealane, or perhaps we had gotten slightly off course and struck one of the unlit marker lights. Whatever it was, it was serious. We climbed on up to our assigned altitude of five thousand feet.

Conley told me to go below and have a look. My report was the same as the flight engineer's. When we were leveled off and trimmed up I took over, and Conley himself went below for a personal inspection. When he returned we radioed the maintenance shack and reported the damage.

There was no way to patch the tear in the hull while we were airborne.

Flying was no problem, but we knew when we landed and the hull settled on the surface we'd ship water through that gash.

It was decided that we would proceed with the engine check-out procedure and fly around over San Francisco Bay until daylight and then decide what was best. We had coffee and sandwiches and waited. Fortunately, when the sun came up it appeared to be one of those unusual clear days. That, at least, was something in our favor.

Conley and I decided to go down for a couple of touch-and-go landings and takeoffs in the bay to see what would happen. We stationed a man in Compartment K on the intercom to observe and report.

There was no problem when we first touched the water. But when we cut the throttles back and the plane slowed down and settled, there was a shout over the intercom:

"Shipping water! Shipping water!"

We poured the coal on and took off as quickly as we could. As we became airborne the water we had shipped got sucked out the hole.

Back in the air we reappraised our situation.

We could land with a launch standing by. We didn't feel

any lives would be lost, but certainly the plane would sink if she took on enough water.

Conley got an inspiration.

"What's the tide like right about now?" he asked me.

"I don't know, but I'll find out."

I radioed the tower. Mean low tide was at 0715.

"Good!" Conley said.

"What's the tide to do with our problem?" I asked.

"Well, you remember at low tide at ramp No. 2 there was always a strip of sand beach?"

"Yeah, it seemed to extend from the seawall about twenty-five yards."

"Right. How does this sound? We land as close to shore as we dare and try to beach the plane on that sand strip!"

"That's a big seawall and that strip of sand ain't much," I said.

"Yes, but if we land as close as we can and taxi with her up on the step as close as we dare and cut the throttles and you and I both pull back on the yokes, maybe we can raise her out of the water before she settles down and starts shipping any great amount of water. At least, if we can put her into shallow water, she'll sit on the bottom. It's better than trying to set her down out there in the deep stuff."

"Hey, you might have something there!"

"Willing to give it a try?"

"Okay with me."

We summoned the crew to the flight deck and informed them of our plan. They nodded assent.

Conley and I practiced the procedure out on the open water a couple of times.

When we touched the water and slowed down a little he yelled:

"NOW!"

I cut all four throttles and grabbed the yoke in front of me and helped him pull back. The big plane rose a little off the water with the momentum it still had and then immediately lost flying speed and plopped down. That was what we wanted to try to do.

We wanted to be in a full stall so there would be little or no forward momentum to smash us up against that seawall.

I told the control tower and our maintenance duty officer what we planned. As we were getting into position for our approach we saw fire trucks and ambulances pulling up near ramp No. 2.

"Okay," Conley said, "here we go—this is it!"

He set the big plane down and we were galloping over the water at ninety knots, heading straight for that strip of sand and the seawall.

Conley throttled back and the plane started to settle.

That seawall seemed to be coming toward us awfully fast.

"NOW!" Conley yelled.

I yanked the throttles closed, cut the ignition switches, grabbed the yoke, and pulled back with Conley.

No. 7232, with a gash in her belly, did just what she had done in our practice sessions. She came out of the water a few feet above the surface. Then she plopped in a full stall and skidded across that strip of sand. She came to rest about fifty feet from the seawall. No one was hurt. There was a yell of triumph from the crew.

It was eight-thirty that morning when Conley and I finally finished our reports. The hull was patched, the plane refloated, loaded, and en route to Honolulu that afternoon.

A thought occurred to me: It had been a long night, but while I was there I would drop by at the personnel office to see whether any of us had received orders for discharge.

There was a WAVE yeoman on duty in personnel.

"Ma'am," I said, "would you have any orders for discharge in the officer messenger mail this morning?"

"Yes, Lieutenant."

She smiled.

"Your own orders are here."

My heart leaped.

"According to your orders you are to be released any time. Any time at your discretion."

It was all over!

"And Lieutenant," the WAVE said, "your friend Lieutenant Brandt's discharge is here, too. Same deal."

I hurried out to a telephone and called Lil.

"It's over," I said. "My orders are here!"

She shrieked with joy.

Brandt and I went through our final physical examinations and collected our discharge papers the next day. The papers were dated October 6, three years to the day after I had been sworn in. I would return to Washington, and the Brandts would go back to Chicago to resume civilian life.

Brandt and I drove home to San Lorenzo Village, and as we turned into our street, we saw it—a moving van. It was parked in front of the Brandts' house. The movers were there from Chicago, ready to unload Bob's furniture. He told them to forget about it and take it back to Chicago.

XVII

WOL GAVE ME MY OLD JOB BACK and I was able to buy a small cottage at 521 Meadow Lane, in Falls Church, Virginia. It was exciting and stimulating, working again as a newsman and announcer in Washington, but somehow it left me unsatisfied. For a long time I had had a dream, and it was not being realized. When Lil had said that I dreamed of "my own little radio station up in the sky, with a picket fence around it," she was not far wrong. I dreamed of creating a radio station with a perfect sound. I yearned for the opportunity. The need to express myself, to implement my own ideas in radio programming became more important to me than almost anything other than my family. It was surely more important than my bank balance.

Then, too, there was something bothering me other than the need to create. There was some pride of craft involved, too. I wanted to be an "all around" man in my field. I wanted to be able to say to myself that there was nothing I could not do in radio. I wanted to demonstrate that I could run a radio station myself—the whole operation—and do it as well as, or better than, the next man. I liked the job at WOL, but I was eager to move on.

I had been back in Washington only a year and a half when the opportunity came. Radio station WARL in suburban Arlington, Virginia, was to go on the air soon, and the owners, Kilbourne Castell and Frank Fletcher, were looking for a manager.

Whoever was hired would have absolute control. The prospect was exciting. But obviously no suburban station could match the salary I was drawing from a major station in the capital. And I had a growing family. Lil was pregnant again—in fact, she was in the very last stages of her pregnancy. Our three boys, the youngest now seven years old, would soon have another brother or a sister, and it appeared that Lil and I might be starting a second, postwar family. In any event, there would be new demands on my income. On the other hand, the job at WARL could be a stepping-stone to bigger things.

Lil and I talked it over and her courage came through. She told me to go after the job. I did, and I got it, taking a substantial cut in income. I took over WARL the same month that our daughter, Mary, was born.

I wanted WARL to be a family station. We called it just that, "WARL, the family station," and our advertising logo was an artist's conception of an old-fashioned family clustered around a Gramophone. I set out to create programming that would interest, entertain, and inform the whole family.

I assembled the best announcing staff I could find, including an old-timer in Washington broadcasting, Harold Stepler from WMAL, and a little guy with a big voice and authoritative delivery, Richard Barr. All told we had four announcers including myself. Barr did most of our newscasts—every hour on the hour—although I did some, too. In the beginning, I programmed the station with good music. We made little shows out of every segment. There would be fifteen minutes of Bing Crosby, for example, and then fifteen minutes of

Frank Sinatra, or half-hour programs of big bands complete with theme songs. Stan Kenton was really big in those days, and when he and his band played the Capitol Theater I arranged with the theater's public-relations people to have him as a guest.

Whenever we could we'd get big-name guests.

I programmed a lot of news about Arlington County and northern Virginia, and I instituted "The Georgetown University Radio Forum," which permitted me to know and work with two of the finest men I've ever known, Father Francis Heyden and Father Daniel Power.

By accident I hit upon a type of programming that really paid off. I scheduled a fifteen-minute daily segment of Tex Ritter, cowboy singer, and it really caught on. I started programming more and more country-western stars.

I got lucky when I hired a skinny little guy with a real down-home, folksy manner, from Lizard Lick, North Carolina, named Connie B. Gay. I made a deal with Connie. He would get a small salary but a commission on everything he could sell. We scheduled a one-hour program of country-western music from noon to one o'clock. In a matter of weeks he had the entire program sold. He was a great salesman and on-air personality. When he began to click, I put him on in the early morning from sign-on to nine o'clock, opposite the big boys—Arthur Godfrey, Art Brown, and Mike Hunicutt—and it wasn't long before our morning program was sold out, too.

Connie started making personal appearances around the countryside with hillbilly musicians he'd hire. It was good promotion for the station, and Connie made a lot of money out of it. He was making more money than anybody at the station, including the owners themselves. Connie said to me one day that we should go into business together. I told him I was too busy running the station to do it.

Connie started booking big names from the country-western field into halls and auditoriums in the area: Ernest Tubb, Hank Williams, Tennessee Ernie Ford, Tex Ritter, and other stars from the Grand Ole Opry. He even put on a show at staid Constitution Hall, a black-tie affair featuring country-western stars. It was a big success. A few years later Connie owned an automobile dealership in Vienna, Virginia, and seven radio stations throughout the Southland. Yes, I sometimes wished I had gone into business with Connie, but I was too interested in running a radio station.

I had been managing WARL for only a few months when a man I had never heard of telephoned me, identified himself as one of our listeners, and said he would like to have a talk with me. His name was Gene Burke. He told me a little about himself.

He had been in the Navy during the war and he was still in the Naval Reserve, as I was. Now he was a lawyer practicing before the Federal Communications Commission. He also was a stockholder in a new radio station that was about to go on the air in Scranton, Pennsylvania, which at that time was a city of about a hundred thousand people. Scranton was the capital of the anthracite coal area in Pennsylvania. It is now a manufacturing and industrial center.

I had no idea what Gene Burke wanted when we sat down together at our first meeting. But I was flattered by his opening gambit. He said he had been listening to WARL and liked everything he had heard. Our station, he said, was fulfilling its public-service obligations; it was the sort of station that justified its franchise. It was what he hoped the new Scranton station would be.

I nodded, and he got to the point.

A majority of his fellow stockholders in Scranton were dissatisfied with the general manager, who was himself a stockholder and in fact the president of the company, the Lacka-wanna Valley Broadcasting Company. He operated a radio equipment supply company. He had set up the station and as-sembled a staff, but he had no experience in radio manage-ment and he was about to be dumped as general manager. He would stay on as president, but the actual management would be in other hands.

"Would you like the job?"

It sounded more than a little interesting. I agreed to go up to Scranton to look it over.

Transportation was no problem. I was in the Naval Re-serve, and the Navy wanted its reserve fliers to keep on flying. I was active in my reserve squadron at Anacostia. I was doing public-relations work there and I was very friendly with the commanding officer, Captain Fred Funke. Funke always held a plane in reserve for his personal use. It was maintained like no other plane on that base, and he had left instructions that anytime I wanted to fly I was to use his plane.

When I told Lil about Gene Burke and his offer, she saw the possibilities. Among other things, it could mean a better standard of living; costs presumably would be lower outside the capital area. With a newborn baby in the house and three growing boys to educate as well, money had to be a factor. I might do better in Scranton and still have the opportunity to do all the things I wanted to do in radio.

So I took a day off from WARL, Burke and I donned our Navy uniforms, and I flew him to Scranton in an SNJ, a sin-gle-engined plane used for training—a beauty of an airplane that I really loved.

When we put down at the Scranton airport, there was a welcoming delegation waiting to greet us. Our welcoming party drove us directly to the new Scranton radio station.

There I met the man I was to replace. His name was Dahl

Mack. The word had already reached him that he was on the way out. It was obvious to him that I, as the station manager of a radio station in Arlington, Virginia, could only be there because I might be on the way in. Dahl hated my guts from the first moment he saw me.

He showed me around, however, and as I studied the facilities and equipment of radio station WSCR, my enthusiasm grew. The station was operating on one thousand kilocycles and one thousand watts, which meant it would have a good signal audible over a considerable listening area. I got a thought that it should be called "the 'one-grand' station." Its equipment was new and in every case first class. It was a magnificent setup. That in fact turned out to be the problem.

The stockholders appeared divided into two factions, one supporting Dahl Mack and one supporting Gene Burke and Burke's father-in-law, James "Doc" Doherty, a painting contractor who had made a barrel of money. Burke's faction included three powerful local politicians—Judge Mike Egan, County Commissioner Mike Lawler, and Philip Mattes, all of them wheels in the local Democratic Party.

The Burke-Doherty faction took me to lunch, and it was at lunch that I got a clearer picture of WSCR's problems.

Dahl Mack had overspent. The Lackawanna Valley Broadcasting Company had a financial illness that could at any moment become terminal. The money had gone on equipment. There was practically no operating capital. But, as I listened, it seemed to me that there might be a cure, through radical surgery.

However, there were other aspects that had to cause me concern. There were ten deeply interested stockholders, which meant I would have ten bosses, and some of the stockholders would also be my employees if I took the job. The station's sales manager, Joe Dobbs, and the chief engineer,

Malcolm Macmillan, both owned shares, and Doc Doherty's daughter, Rose, would be on the staff as well. It could turn out to be too cozy.

All in all, however, the opportunity was irresistible. The Burke-Doherty faction, representing the majority of the shares, made me a firm offer, and I accepted. I think I needed my head examined.

But when I flew back and told Lil about it that evening, I was as excited as a child on Christmas Eve.

I turned in my resignation at WARL. I gave the owners two weeks to find a replacement.

It was while I was serving out my notice there that Dahl Mack telephoned me from Scranton. I took the call at my desk.

"Blair?" he asked, curtly. "This is Dahl Mack."

"Yes?"

"I'm calling to tell you that if you set one foot inside this radio station I'm going to throw you down the stairs."

Well, after all, the Blairs are of Irish heritage, and you can't say a thing like that to an Irishman without generating sparks.

"Mr. Mack," I said, struggling for self-control, "if I go down those stairs, you're going down with me!"

I slammed down the receiver.

Shortly thereafter, I traveled up to Scranton and took over station WSCR.

Dahl Mack's resentment persisted. It grew even more pronounced when I began weeding out the staff he had so carefully put together. I did a real hatchet job. I hated doing it, but it was evident that either some people would have to go or we all would.

All in all, I trimmed the staff down from fifteen people to ten, and I reassigned one of the most important staffers in the operation.

Anne Culkin was our good-will ambassador in Scranton society. She was doing a public-relations job for us and broadcasting a five-minute community calendar program called "The Society Editor of the Air."

I remember one day Anne had an announcement about a skeet shoot planned by the American Legion. She did a spoonerism on "skeet shoot." She started with "skoot sheet," then tried it again and it came out "sheet skoot," and then followed with a couple of other combinations. I was horrified. A four-letter word might come next. But Anne finally gave it up and went on to another item. I said silently, "Thank God."

Anne at one time had been an aspiring actress. She had been understudy for Jessica Tandy on Broadway. Anne was capable and a loyal employee and she seemed to know everyone in Scranton, but I couldn't see what she was doing here on a full-time job. However, I could see a big potential for her on the WSCR sales staff.

I called her in and told her she had a new assignment. She was going to sell the station in a different way. She would sell time. I asked her to take the rate card and go out into the street and drum up business. She did, and she turned out to be the best salesperson on the staff. She also became Lil's closest friend—still a friend after more than a quarter of a century.

Firing and reassigning people was a job I learned to abhor. I began thinking I was not cut out for management. I was no Bob Kintner, the hard-bitten newsman who became a hard-bitten president of NBC. Nor was I a Dick Wald, another tough-minded news executive who served as president of the

News Division of NBC during my last years with the "Today" program. These were men who seemed able to avoid any personal, emotional involvement as they did their job in handling personnel. On the face of it, at least, they agonized little over decisions that would change people's lives. When the well-being of the company demanded it, or seemed to in their eyes, they were able to fire a man with as little concern as I might have in sending back an overdone steak at a favorite restaurant. People like Kintner and Wald had the knack, but I simply was not built that way. Even so, I did what had to be done.

But with all my pruning, we were still operating right on the brink of financial disaster. We were finally saved by what, at first blush, looked like a catastrophe.

It was the middle of the night. The telephone rang at my bedside table. I struggled awake and answered.

"Yes?"

"Blair?"

"Yeah."

"It's Dahl Mack. Your radio station is on fire."

That really woke me up.

"What the hell are you talking about?"

"I'm telling you. Your radio station is on fire!"

"I'll be right there."

I pulled on my clothes and drove into town—and found fire trucks all over Adams Avenue in front of WCSR.

Fire had broken out in the storeroom adjoining the library of phonograph records.

When the fire was finally put out, the firemen allowed me to enter the building. I made my way to the damaged area, my nose wrinkling against the acrid smell, I made a quick inspection and found that the damage was not so bad and that we would be able to operate. We could get on the air, all right.

But our record library had been destroyed. Music was a mainstay of our programming, and the thousands of records in their wall-to-wall racks were in twisted ruins, devastated by both heat and water.

Without music, WSCR was not going to sound like WSCR. A sudden change in sound, even assuming we could get all-talk shows organized, could only hurt us competitively, and we were already being hurt by the stiff competition from the local CBS and ABC affiliates and the NBC affiliate in the neighboring city of Wilkes-Barre.

I borrowed records and got us on the air, and I got the insurance adjustors in a hurry.

The value of those records was self-evident. The insurance company came through.

I never did mention to the adjustor that most of those records had been outright gifts—no-strings-attached gifts from the record companies for promotional purposes. It was the insurance company's money that kept us in business.

I am not going to be bashful about saying that I knocked myself out to keep WSCR alive. I laid out the programs, supervised every phase of the operation, and, in addition, did newscasts. On top of all that, I was getting myself involved in community activities. I wanted to participate in community affairs not only as a citizen but also to win friends and build good will for the station, especially among the town's businessmen. I wanted to be out in the town talking about WSCR and letting the people themselves feel closely involved. It was my theory that this was the way a local radio station should operate. It would prosper if it rendered a community service and if the people felt it was *their* station and they were part of it. I wanted to get as many names on the air as I could, names of both people and organizations. In a sense I was following the dictum of the old-time country newspaper editors: Names make news.

Looking back on it now, I can see that, willy-nilly, I also set up a news format that was in its way a forerunner of the modern "eyewitness news" on local television stations. I did the hard news, Anne Culkin did the society news, and Jim Killian did sports. Had we had a local weatherman on the air, we would have matched the TV news programming of the 1970s, especially because I was doing occasional "actualities."

Actualities are what we call natural sound—the actual voice of a newsmaker. Actualities are commonplace now on radio news, of course; a newscast without one or two of these "inserts" is often judged to be a weak newscast. Actualities were made easy and popular with the development of the tape recorder. Nowadays a reporter can carry a small tape recorder directly to the scene of breaking news. It's a relatively simple job to record a voice, as anyone who owns a tape recorder can testify. In my Scranton days, however, a reporter could get actuality only with a *wire* recorder, and wire recorders were clumsy, unwieldy instruments that often yielded imperfect sound. They were rarely used in news operations. Even so, I made use of a wire recorder occasionally in covering fires and accidents, and WSCR listeners thus heard the real thing—what might be called "earwitness news." It was in a way a revolutionary technique in news gathering, and it excited and fascinated our listeners.

I was enjoying the job. But problems were developing. I found that Doc Doherty's daughter, working as my secretary, was carrying tales back to Doc about things in radio that she was not geared to understand and that appeared to reflect on my management.

Doc had led the faction that had hired me and I knew I had his support, but it was not comfortable to have distorted stories on management going behind my back to a major stockholder.

However, our balance sheet was finally looking good. Our audience was growing, and sales on the whole were strong. Our coverage gave many Scranton folks the WSCR listening habit. One of our drawing cards was sports coverage. Professional sports created a special problem. The days became shorter as the football season progressed, and of course our license obligated us to get off the air at sundown. If we ignored the rule, we would risk losing our license. We would interfere with the signal of an important and influential around-the-clock radio station. We shared our wavelength during daylight hours with the American Federation of Labor station in Chicago, station WCFL, a fifty-thousand-watt clear-channel operation.

But we could not risk going off the air before the last whistle sounded in a professional football game. Anything can happen in the last minutes of play, and we would have made a large audience of enemies had we stopped coverage just before a decisive play. In later years, the NBC Television Network was to cut a pro game off the air just before the losing team scored—and won. NBC was deluged with protests. There was a constant danger of something like that happening in Scranton when the games dragged on. It became practically a ritual for me to send telegrams to both WCFL in Chicago and the Federal Communications Commission in Washington asking permission to go on broadcasting until the game ended. Both WCFL and the FCC always obliged.

But I found myself working some man-killing hours. For one thing, I had begun broadcasting the early-morning show by remote control from my own home there on the side of a mountain in Chinchilla, a Scranton suburb. I went on the air at sunrise. It was a show that cut costs for WSCR, although it took its toll on me. Even so, I enjoyed it. It was, by design, a folksy, homey show. Our sons would stop by and say good-bye to me (with the mike open) as they left for school, and Mary, now just beginning to talk, would sit on my lap and gurgle over the air or say childish things in her small voice.

After a full day at the studio I was out often at night attending meetings of the community organizations. I was active in the Lions Club, the Junior Chamber of Commerce, the Chinchilla Civic Association, the Boy Scouts, the Community Chest, the Advertising Club, and the Lackawanna Industrial Fund Enterprise (LIFE), which raised money to bring industries to Scranton.

In addition, I was teaching journalism at the University of Scranton. This was a job that paid me forty dollars a week during the school year, and that was nice money to have. The job also tickled my vanity. The name on my mail slot there in the university administration office read "Prof. Frank Blair." I enjoyed the irony of that, because of course I had never earned even a bachelor's degree.

With all this going on, my time was no longer my own, and Lil was beginning to complain about my being so constantly away from home. She had made good friends there in Scranton, but she missed the more active and I guess more stimulating and glamorous social life of Washington, and she missed my company.

Both of us were feeling the strain—a lot of strain—when suddenly, on a Sunday afternoon two years after we had arrived in Scranton, our lives took a sudden and drastic turn for the worse.

Mary was two years old then, a healthy, happy, beautiful toddler who charmed the lady listeners on my early-morning radio show and who was a real delight to our boys as well as to Lil and me.

I took a Sunday afternoon off and Lil and I took her to the zoo. She stared in childish awe at the animals and giggled at the antics of the monkeys. She gave no hint whatever of any physical discomfort.

As we were leaving the zoo, I lifted her into the front seat of the car—she always rode standing beside me—and as I did so I noticed she seemed warm.

"I think Mary has a temperature," I said.

Lil put her hand on Mary's forehead. She, too, felt the warmth.

"Probably just a cold," she said.

But I thought she looked worried.

In spite of her temperature, Mary seemed her usual self as we rode home. When we got there, Lil took her in her arms and carried her indoors, and I went off to mow our lawn.

I had just gotten the lawn mower in position when I heard Lil scream. It was a scream that terrified me.

"Mary's having convulsions! Mary's having convulsions!"

I raced into the house.

Somewhere, in the far recesses of my memory, I was capturing a thought: I had heard somewhere that a child who had convulsions should be put in lukewarm water.

"Get some water in the tub!" I shouted. "Hurry!"

Every muscle in the child's body appeared to be twitching. There were bubbles of froth at her lips.

We immersed her in water, but the convulsions continued.

Lil and I were frantic.

I called our family doctor.

"Get her to the hospital! Quick!" he said. "I'll be there at once."

We drove Mary to Scranton Hospital. I drove so fast I very nearly killed us all.

When we got there, a nurse took Mary's temperature and gave us news that I'll never forget.

"She has a temperature of 106," she said.

"My God!" Lil said. "She's burning up."

Mary continued to convulse. She convulsed for eight hours. Finally the convulsions subsided, but our little girl was no longer the same. She could not stand up. And her right side was useless. We thought she was permanently paralyzed.

Mary stayed at the hospital for ten days, and Lil was there with her around the clock.

I tried to work. I had a family to support and I had responsibilities to the stockholders and staff as well as to the patrons of WSCR. But the worry was agonizing; it took enormous efforts of will to get my mind on the job and keep it there. I pictured Mary's life destroyed almost before it began. I saw her spending her days as an invalid, depending on others even to move her from one chair to another.

But the paralysis gradually wore off, and after ten days she was released from the hospital. It was then, however, that our doctor broke the news that left us devastated:

"Sorry. I have to tell you. Mary has epilepsy."

It was a shock. Neither Lil nor I knew much about epilepsy then; the doctor's words had the ring of doom.

I don't suppose there are many ailments that are more misunderstood, even today, although great progress has been made since those days in wiping away the people's ignorance. It used to be thought that an epileptic was "possessed of the devil." There were states in which an epileptic was actually forbidden to marry. And there have been times in our history when any male epileptic was castrated. Neither Lil nor I was guilty of quite such abysmal ignorance, but even so, the disease was beyond our ken; we didn't quite know what to expect.

Mary had occasional convulsions for years after that first seizure. We never knew when they would come. Every time she told us she felt sick, we expected the worst.

Our son John also had what looked like an epileptic seizure some years later. It terrified us. We were afraid that he, too, would have long years of suffering. His seizure, however, was traced to a football injury—a blow on the head—and he recovered after what he refers to as "seven years in hell."

Mary's recovery was long delayed, but she is in good health now, and the mother of two children.

Our experiences with Mary and John naturally gave Lil and me a strong interest in epilepsy. For many years now, I have been on the board of the Epilepsy Foundation of America, and whenever I make speeches in behalf of the foundation I try to preach a message of hope. Two of my children had a form of epilepsy, and both are in good health today.

The constant, nagging worry about Mary in those early days of her illness added greatly to the strains of life in Scranton. I was putting in impossible hours, and the tensions in the office seemed to be on the increase. Now it was not only Doc Doherty's daughter, Rose, but also his son, Jimmy, who was watching my work, carrying tales to Dad and in some cases trying to second-guess my decisions. Jimmy was not a shareholder, but I imagine he expected to inherit some or all of his father's shares, and he seemed to feel that he already had a vested interest in WSCR's affairs. He was in and out of my office frequently. His manner was officious. He was short on common courtesy. And his knowledge of radio was zero. His interference was eating into my time. I grew to dread seeing him walk through the door. And, not to put too fine a point on it, I grew to despise the guy.

In that atmosphere of stress and strain in the office and at home I began to feel, for the first time in my life, some concern about my health. I was having stomach trouble. I felt sure I was developing an ulcer. The pains were frequent and sometimes intense, and the only thing that would soothe them was milk. Finally I went to see our doctor, convinced that his diagnosis would be grim. He examined me and pronounced the verdict:

"No, you do not have an ulcer. The only thing that's bothering you is tension."

That, at least, was good news.

"But," the doctor went on, "you're right on the edge of something—an explosion of some kind. Something's bugging you. There's something in your craw that you've got to get out."

I nodded.

He wrote out a prescription.

"And in another ten days or so," the doctor said, "you're going to blow up. You're going to go higher than a kite. After that, you'll calm down and be all right."

That man must have had a hidden crystal ball.

Doc Doherty's son Jimmy had a wife, named Elinor, and she had lost her job at an insurance company.

Now, some companies wisely enforce rigid rules against nepotism. Not so WSCR.

Doc informed me that I would have to find a job for Elinor and, as Doc was a major shareholder, I had to oblige.

It was on a Monday morning two weeks after my visit to the doctor that Elinor and Doc's daughter, Rose, both failed to report for work at WSCR. Neither of them telephoned with an explanation. I could find no one who could tell me where they were.

Then, on Tuesday, they again failed to come in to work. My concern deepened but I couldn't reach Doc Doherty for an explanation.

On Wednesday morning, both Elinor and Rose appeared in the office at their usual reporting hour.

"I've been worried about you," I said. "Where have you been?"

They said they had simply decided to take a long weekend. They had gone off to Atlantic City.

"And you didn't bother to tell me?" I asked.

I could feel myself beginning to fume.

"We didn't think it was necessary."

That really teed me off. I could not see how I could run an important regional radio station and build it to financial stability if two of its employees—any two—could be allowed to maintain such a cavalier attitude toward their jobs. The effect on morale would be damaging. Furthermore, I felt personally victimized. I was beating my brains out for my shareholders, and two relatives of the biggest shareholder were taking a long, unannounced weekend in Atlantic City.

I told the Doherty ladies that they were through. I told them to collect their salaries and get out.

This was the episode that lighted the fuse for the Blair explosion.

I was at my desk studying a balance sheet. It looked pretty good.

The door of my office flew open. Jimmy Doherty burst in, scowling.

He planted himself in front of my desk, pointed his finger at me, and said in a voice just short of a shout:

"I want to talk to you!"

Obviously he was here to protest the dismissal of his wife and sister.

I leaned back in my chair and stared at him, and suddenly the thought hit me. This was the explanation. It was Doherty who was giving me pains in my stomach and probably, I thought, in another part of my anatomy as well.

If I had been a Hollywood director, I don't think I could have set up the scene that followed with any greater expertise.

"Blair . . ." Doherty said, and before he could go on, I blew.

I am not a high jumper, but I leaped over my desk—I literally leaped over. I grabbed Doherty by the seat of the pants and the scruff of the neck and I threw him out the door, straight into the outer office.

Every employee in the place was watching.

"Doherty," I said, "if you don't know the way out of this radio station, you'd better find it now. But quick. You go down one flight of stairs to the street. And don't ever come up those stairs again, because if you do, there's going to be one fewer heir to Doc Doherty's estate."

I went back to my office and slammed the door.

I sat down and relaxed, and I have never had a bellyache since.

The board of directors of the Lackawanna Valley Broadcasting Company met unexpectedly the following night. I did not immediately perceive the reason.

As the members arrived, I greeted them cordially.

"Gentlemen," I said, "use my office. By all means."

I personally found extra chairs. Their thanks, however, seemed perfunctory.

After their meeting was called to order I went back to the control room and dug out some of my favorite records. I put my feet on the control panel, lit a cigarette, and sat back to enjoy the music—and then it hit me.

"You silly ass," I told myself, "you know why they're meeting. They're meeting about you."

I made a snap decision.

I ground out my cigarette, switched off the music, and went back to my office. I tapped on the door, but I did not wait for anyone to ask me in. I opened the door and stepped inside.

"Gentlemen," I said, "I think I can save you some time. I have just reached a decision. Effective as of this moment, I quit."

I looked them over—this group of local politicians and lawyers and businessmen with their ignorance of radio, their nepotism, and their lack of understanding of how to run an organization—and I added a clincher.

"Gentlemen," I said, "you can take your radio station and shove it!"

I spent the rest of my time in Scranton working as the commercial manager, meaning sales manager, for another radio station, WQAN (now WEJL), owned by the Scranton *Times*. And I do mean working. We had a new baby, Theresa, born on February 10 of that year—1950—but I had almost no time for family life. I was immersed not only in selling but also in programming, and in the evenings I was still heavily involved in community activities. Among other things, I was president of the Advertising Club, president of the Junior Chamber of Commerce, and vice president of the Lions Club at one and the same time. I was rarely at home. Life was a whirlwind.

That went on until late on a summer day in 1950, when Lil lowered the boom.

Yes, I had been aware that something important had been missing in Lil's life. She was young and beautiful and very much alive, and now in a way she was beginning to die there on our mountaintop outside Scranton. It was not merely that she and I no longer had time to share our hopes and dreams and grouse at one another over life's little irritations and frustrations, although all this was in itself a void that caused her pain. It was something more than all this, because Lil and I were something more than husband and wife and something more than lovers. We were also friends. We had grown to rely on each other and trust each other, and now because of the pressures of life in Scranton we were growing apart.

The same pressures, growing out of the job and *its* frustrations, were to have their effect during my years on the "Today" program, and Lil would fight them again. But she bearded this lion for the first time in Scranton.

Apart from her own needs, she felt that our boys particularly needed me during their formative years and that my job and community activities were robbing them of time with their father that would be lost forever. Then too, Lil herself missed the feeling of being at the center of things, a feeling we had both experienced in Washington. She had had the intellectual stimulus of conversation and friendship with achievers on a national level, some of whom were people of great brilliance. Lil had made good friends in Scranton, but her life there had never been as rich and fulfilling as in Washington.

I can look back on it now and see that, in Scranton, Lil and I were in a situation that has led to the breakup of many other marriages. I can also see, and thank God for it, that Lil had the courage to act.

The time: dusk on a summer day.
The scene: our living room in Chinchilla.

Lil and I are alone at the picture window, looking out over the mountain.

There is tension between us. I had hardly been at home all through the week except to eat and sleep. Lil's patience is at an end. She turns to me.

"Hon," she says coolly, "I'm going to let you make a choice."

Her language is incisive.

"You can choose between Scranton and your family. I am not going to let us live like this. I don't want a husband who's a stranger in his own home and who puts his job and town ahead of his wife and kids."

I studied Lil's eyes. They were misty.

"So," she says, "it's your choice. Either we leave Scranton and get away from all this or I'm leaving you, and I'm taking the children with me."

I knew she meant it.

Her words put the kiss of death on my dreams of finding that little radio station up in the sky.

But I no longer cared.

I had long since concluded that my hours away from home, devoted to the job and the town, were unfair to Lil and the kids.

And, more important, I had long since recognized that management and selling, while they might be fun for a time, were really not for me. What I really enjoyed, and I could no longer delude myself, was handling the news.

XVIII

I WENT TO WORK for NBC through a fluke. After Scranton, I had returned to WOL in Washington as commercial manager and later as newscaster and host of a morning show, and had again taken over as moderator of "The Georgetown University Forum" both in radio and on the Dumont TV station, WTTG, of which Walter Compton was now general manager. All in all, I had managed to re-establish myself on the Washington scene in a relatively short time. Then came the first link in the chain of events that led me to NBC.

I owe it all to Bill Murdock of William D. Murdock, Advertising. I had met Bill before I left Washington to go into the Navy. He was then commercial manager of WJSV (now WTOP)—the CBS affiliate. Bill had mentioned to me on occasion that he liked my work on the air, and even though I didn't know him intimately, I considered him a friend. During the war or shortly thereafter Bill had left WJSV and started his own advertising agency.

It was in the spring of 1951, when one morning I got a phone call from Bill. He told me that he was conducting auditions that afternoon at the NBC-TV station (then WNBW-TV) for Peoples Drug Stores, his biggest account. The program would be on television, five days a week. It would consist of feature movies. It would be called "Peoples

Playhouse." Bill said he was looking for a spokesman for Peoples to handle the commercials. The job would pay one hundred dollars a week. It would be a competitive audition. There'd be ten other candidates. I assured him I would be there.

I'd had a raft of experience in announcing commercials on radio but none on TV. The only exposure I'd had in front of a camera had been in a couple of government documentary films for the Departments of Agriculture and Interior and as moderator of "The Georgetown University Forum" on the local Dumont television station, but I'd never done a stand-up commercial spokesman's job. However, I was eager to try, and I wanted that one hundred a week.

Bill had given me short notice. I had only a few hours before the audition time.

I went home to tell Lil about it and to put on my good suit. She was excited and reassuring. I reminded her I hadn't gotten the job yet. She felt sure I would. I wasn't so sure.

While I drove from our house in Arlington along Lee Boulevard (past where we had lived when we first came to Washington in 1938) and through Rock Creek Park, my mind was full of thoughts of what lay ahead.

I realized I was getting uptight. I was tense and nervous about going in front of the WNBW camera. I remembered something I had experienced way back in the days when I was an aspiring young actor with the Peruchi Players. I learned then that it is good to feel on edge before hearing your cue and going onstage. It means you really care about your performance. It helps you to concentrate, to leave yourself backstage and assume the character you are to be onstage.

"Be yourself," I said to myself. "That's it! Just be yourself. Don't force it or fake it. Just be convincing. Try to understand what you'll be saying and believe what you're saying. If *you* do, *they* will."

A young woman greeted me at the NBC studios. I told her my name and said I was there for the Peoples audition.

"Oh yes," she said.

I reassured myself that at least I'd gotten that far.

She said, "You will be No. 8."

She took a white jacket from a clothes rack and said:

"Here's your jacket. This should fit you."

"My jacket?"

"Yes," she said, "you will wear this instead of your suit coat. Please wait in the lobby until your number is called."

The jacket was one of those that doctors and pharmacists wear. It had a high neck collar and buttoned down the side. She handed me the script I would be asked to read.

I located a quiet spot in the lobby and proceeded to study the copy. I read it over and over again and recited it to myself several times until I felt I had it down pat. I found my memory wasn't as sharp as it had been when I was working on the stage several years before. There were no cueing devices such as we have today on TV. The job had to be done from memory.

While I sat there, Betty Bradley, with whom I worked occasionally at WOL, came into the lobby wearing a nurse's uniform. Betty told me she was there for the audition, too. Bill was looking for a man-and-woman team for the show. The woman would handle the commercials pertaining to cosmetics. The receptionist appeared and announced:

"No. 6 is next."

Betty said, "Whoops! That's my number. Here I go."

"Good luck," I said.

"Good luck to you, too," she said over her shoulder as she disappeared down a corridor leading to the studio.

Before I knew it, my number was called.

When I entered the studio I found myself in completely strange surroundings. The lights were bright and glaring, and it was difficult to see beyond a narrow perimeter. I did see that there were two cameras and a microphone suspended from a boom. As my eyes became accustomed to the light, I saw that there was a tinted plate-glass window at what I considered to be the back of the studio. I couldn't see through the glass to recognize anybody or anything. I saw only shadows. I didn't feel very comfortable, but there were encouraging and friendly notes.

Situated at one end of the studio, on which the lights and cameras were trained, was something that resembled a section of a Peoples Drug Store.

I was trying to get my bearing when a voice came over the intercom saying:

"No. 8. Take your time. Get the feel of the set, and let us know when you're ready to go. Okay?"

The stage manager led me to a position behind the counter and gave instructions.

"Here's the product. At one point you hold it up about so high toward camera 2."

"Camera 2?"

"On your left." One of the cameramen raised his hand to indicate his was camera 2.

I nodded and said, "Thank you."

I was too excited now to be nervous.

The stage manager said, "If you have to refer to the copy it will be all right for this. Why not put it on the counter in front of you."

I thought for a second and said, "I'd rather not. I might be tempted to look at it."

Everybody snickered, and the ice was broken.

I glanced at the copy to see where I was to hold up the product, and then I dropped the paper on the floor behind the counter.

I cleared my throat and said, "I guess I'm as ready as I'll ever be."

The crew snickered again.

The voice on the intercom said, "If you want to stop for any reason and start over, that's okay."

I nodded toward the voice.

The stage manager abruptly said, "Stand by. I'll cue you to start. Work the camera with the red light. Okay? Here we go. Stand by."

Then he pointed his finger at me.

I looked at the camera with the red light, shuddered a little, paused, and proceeded. I was able to go through it without muffing it. I even remembered to hold up the product and look at camera 2 as I did. I finished, and nothing happened for a few seconds. All was quiet. Then that disembodied voice said again, very casually, "That was fine. Would you do it just once more, please."

I nodded and stood by and did it all over again. The first try, I thought, was better than the second.

The voice said, "Now, No. 8, would you just forget the copy and ad-lib—make up a commercial about the product in your own words."

I nodded.

When I was cued I started talking again, using the salient points from the commercial copy but using my own language. I kept talking until the voice said, "CUT!"

I stopped and the voice said:

"Thank you very much, No. 8. If you'll just wait in the lobby a few minutes we'll appreciate it."

I thanked the voice, the cameramen, and the stage manager. One of the cameramen made a circle with his thumb and forefinger and waved it at me. I smiled and nodded and left the studio.

I sighed with relief when I got into the corridor. I was glad it was over. I didn't feel completely satisfied with myself. I went back to the lobby and met Betty Bradley.

"How'd you do?" Betty asked.

"I don't know," I replied. "Could have done better, I guess."

"It was my first time," Betty said.

"Mine too," I said.

If anyone had overheard us they might have thought we'd just had intercourse for the first time.

In moments, the receptionist reappeared.

"No. 6 and No. 8, will you come back to the studio, please?" she asked.

My heart was pounding. I hoped I wouldn't have to do the audition again. I thought I'd forgotten the copy.

As we entered, the voice said:

"No. 6 and No. 8, will you stand behind the counter together and face the cameras, please."

We stood there looking at the cameras and at each other. I tried to smile. I guess we were there about a minute when the voice said, "That's all, thank you."

We were just approaching the door when Bill Murdock burst in with his hand extended.

"Congratulations. You've done it," Bill said. "The show will start Monday. Any problems?"

Betty and I shook our heads and simultaneously said, "None."

Bill introduced me to Joe Browne, who would direct the show.

"Be here at ten Monday morning and we'll rehearse. Okay?" Joe said.

"Okay."

As soon as I could get out of there I dashed to a telephone booth, still wearing my pharmacist's jacket. I called Lil and told her the good news. She was bubbling over with joy, so much so that I thought she was going to cry.

I changed from the jacket back to my street clothes quickly and almost ran to my car. I was anxious to get home.

Television was in its adolescence. It was still not a full-time operation. The only thing telecast in the morning was the test pattern, for the benefit of repairmen and installers. Of course, it was all in black and white—living color television was still in General Sarnoff's dreams. These were the days of Milton Berle and "The Texaco Star Theater"; Sid Caesar and Imogene Coca and the Saturday night "Your Show of Shows"; "The Fred Waring Show"; Jerry Lester and "Broadway Open House" (the forerunner to the "Tonight" show); Howdy Doody; Kukla, Fran, and Ollie; and John Cameron Swayze's nightly newscasts at six forty-five for Camel cigarettes. On Sundays on NBC there was Lawrence Spivak's "Meet the Press" and Ted Granik's "American Forum of the Air," and Ted had another program on NBC, "Youth Wants to Know." Television was the baby of the communications industry. The people involved in it were willing to experiment, and daringly. It was an exciting field, and I wanted to be a part of it. The "Peoples Playhouse" job was the breakthrough I needed. I was already a very busy man. I was still doing the morning show from six to nine on WOL, and I was doing nightly newscasts for the Liberty network. On Liberty I also moderated "The Georgetown University Forum" on Sunday afternoons and a historical dramatic series that I produced and directed for the university titled "Prologue." Also, of course, I was still moderator of "The Georgetown University Forum" on the local Dumont television station on Sunday nights. The addition of "Peoples Playhouse" to my schedule meant that I would be tied up from ten to two every day, but I welcomed the opportunity. Among other things, it meant I'd be in daily contact with the people in television at NBC, and that's where the action was.

I walked into the NBC studios promptly at ten o'clock the following Monday to rehearse and start my career in commercial television.

I went first to the office of Joe Browne.

And in my first minutes with this man whose direction could make or break me, I found him churlish and sullen.

He didn't look up from his desk when I walked in.

"Sit down," he said, his eyes on the papers in front of him.

It wasn't quite like the command of a Marine Corps sergeant major. It was not quite that abrasive. It was like the cops say at a police lineup, "Step down!"

I sat. Still without looking at me, he handed me a set of scripts from the pile of papers on his desk.

"Look these over—I'll be with you in a minute," he said.

I found out later what he was doing—he was planning the camera shots for the commercials we would be doing. He made notes in the margins.

I became engrossed in the scripts. It was the first time I'd ever seen a complete commercial script for TV. There were directions on the left side and the announcer's words on the right:

VIDEO	AUDIO
OPEN ON ANNOUNCER	1. (*Announcer*) Should you take aspirin—or an aspirin substitute?
PULL BACK TO REVEAL ANNOUNCER AND PRODUCT	2. Well, for the overwhelming majority, etc. etc.
CUT IN CLOSER TO PRODUCT	
ANNOUNCER HOLDS UP PRODUCT	

Betty Bradley casually walked in, said "Hello," and Browne shoved a set of scripts toward her, again, without looking up.

"A little late, eh?"

Betty started to explain.

Browne interrupted: "Look them over. Be with you shortly."

Betty and I smiled at each other and went back to our scripts.

Suddenly Browne stood up, dropped his pencil on the desk, rubbed his hands together, and said:

"Shall we give it a go?"

I was anxious. Betty and I both nodded assent. We followed Browne into the studio and there in the quiet and in semidarkness was the Peoples Drug Store set. On the counter was the nurse's-type uniform for Betty. It was a light blue instead of white. My pharmacist's jacket was there, too. It had been dyed light gray. White was taboo because it reflected light into the lens of the camera and caused a blooming effect. That's why I wound up with a wardrobe of blue shirts as I progressed to other things in television.

Browne said, "There's your playhouse, kiddies, and there are your playsuits. Have fun!"

He went into the control room.

It was very quiet in the studio except for the low hum of the cameras. In the semidarkness Betty and I were studying our scripts when Bill Murdock and the Peoples Drug Store people came in. With them was Ralph Burgin, the program director of the station.

"All set?" Bill asked.

"We're working on it," I replied. Betty nodded.

Ralph Burgin said, "Glad to have you with us."

"Glad to be here," Betty and I said almost simultaneously.

"We'll leave you and let you get to work," Bill said. And with that they left the studio.

Suddenly the place came alive. Lights came on. Men came out of nowhere, exchanged greetings with Betty and me, and took up stations—some behind cameras, others adjusted lights, one adjusted the mike boom, and the stage manager put on his headphone.

Ed Lynch was the stage manager, an affable and accommodating man who came over and shook hands. He said that if there was anything he could do for us just let him know.

(Ed later became a teacher in the Communications Department of the University of Georgia. I still see him occasionally.)

Browne came into the studio.

"Let's go to work," he said.

He seemed mellower and friendlier now.

He led us to another part of the studio where there was a living-room set used on another program. We sat down on the sofa and he "ran down" the show: It would open with music and slide titles, I would read the opening announcement, and the movie would begin. We went through the entire program, step by step. I had a lot to learn.

Betty and I took up our positions before the camera, and

the rehearsal was under way. It went well. Each of us performed without a fluff. And that's the way it went when the show itself went on the air. It was a smooth performance, and Browne congratulated us both.

His manner had softened. I found myself beginning to like him. Later on this man whom I had at first disliked became one of my good friends and certainly one of the best directors I would ever encounter in television. I began to perceive that when he was churlish and sullen, as he sometimes was, he was putting on an act; it was a lighthearted pretense.

I've said that every time a new addition came into our growing family something good would come along as a bonus. It just seemed to work out that way for us.

Our son Paul had been born on April 22, 1951, and it was just a couple of weeks after Paul's arrival that I'd received that phone call from Bill Murdock inviting me to audition for "Peoples Playhouse." Had Paul arrived two weeks later, however, I would not have been able to take the audition and get the job.

I brought Lil and Paul home from the hospital and everything seemed to be going along fine when some minor female problem developed with Lil and she had to be put back in the hospital for a few days. We didn't have housekeeping help—we couldn't afford it—but we did have good neighbors and friends, thank God, or I couldn't have survived. I've tried for over forty years to be a good father, but I'd never tried being a mother, too.

I called WOL and described the situation and told them that under the circumstances I would just have to have a week off.

Well, there I was with Mike (fifteen), John (thirteen), Tom (eleven), Mary (four), Theresa (two), and new baby,

Paul. I soon found out that just taking care of a new baby was a full-time job, although Paul was a very good baby. He didn't demand much—just to be fed, burped, changed, and bathed—but the responsibility was awesome.

Things were going along as well as could be expected until one night when I was putting Mary to bed I noticed that she felt warm. I took her temperature. The thermometer read 102 degrees. I called Lil at the hospital and she told me to give her baby aspirin and lots of water to drink. I was up practically all of that night watching her. Normally a temperature of 102 in a small child is not too alarming, but in Mary's case it had been a high temperature that had triggered her first convulsion during our Scranton days. The next morning she seemed normal. Her temperature was down. But that afternoon her temperature started going up again. I tried to reach the pediatrician but couldn't get him. When I went back into her room to look at her I noticed that funny look in her eyes that I had seen before in Scranton. The next thing I knew she was in a convulsion.

I almost panicked. I immediately started doing everything I could think of. I rubbed her down with alcohol to try to bring her fever down and I rolled her on her side and tried to keep her from biting her tongue. I prayed. She just wouldn't come out of it. In desperation I phoned Mary Felker, who was Mary's godmother and an old and dear friend. Mary had been a trained nurse.

All I had to say was, "Mary's having a convulsion."

Mary Felker said she'd be right over. The Felkers lived about ten minutes from us, but believe me that was the longest ten minutes I think I've ever spent in my life.

When Mary Felker got there and saw our Mary's condition she suggested that I call an ambulance and get her to the hospital. The ambulance arrived within minutes. We wrapped

Mary in a blanket and I held her in my arms as the ambulance sped away.

She was taken immediately into the emergency room, and the doctors and nurses went to work on her. They wrapped her in wet sheets and rubbed her down with alcohol in an attempt to get her fever down. I was completely unnerved. I paced up and down and prayed harder than I'd ever prayed in my life. Soon the twitching calmed down and then it ceased entirely and she went into a deep sleep. The doctors decided that they'd keep her in the hospital for observation.

I dreaded leaving her but there was nothing I could do. I called a cab and went back home. I was dejected and exhausted. I decided it best not to tell Lil of the situation. I didn't get much sleep that night. I just couldn't get Mary off my mind, wondering how she was, and I prayed throughout that long and lonely night.

I didn't learn until several days later that Mary Felker had been preparing for a dinner party when she dropped everything to hurry to Mary's side and help.

I had been doing "Peoples Playhouse" about six weeks when Ralph Burgin, the program director of the TV station, came to the studio during rehearsal and asked me if I'd drop by his office after the show.

I hadn't the slightest idea what he wanted. Burgin's office was in another part of the building. The NBC studios at that time were located in the Wardman Park Hotel, which was more of a residential than a transient hotel. Many prominent Washingtonians, including senators and congressmen and Cabinet officers, lived there. Lawrence Spivak, producer of "Meet the Press," had an apartment there. It was a huge, spread-out building, built in wings, and it would be easy to get lost in it if you didn't know your way around. It is now the Sheraton Park Hotel, and it has been changed considerably.

The offices for NBC personnel and management were converted bedrooms. Each office had the convenience of a bathroom with a bathtub in it. I don't think anybody ever took a bath in those rooms, but one tub did come in handy in the newsroom area. With NBC's television news operation expanding, getting newsfilm processed and getting it on the air in a hurry became more and more important. One of the bathrooms off the newsroom was converted into a darkroom. A commonly heard question around NBC was "When will the film be out of the bathtub?"

There was a certain poetic license in that language, but not much, at that. The bathtub in that bathroom-darkroom was very important to the operation. NBC had taken its newsfilm processing problem to MIT, which developed a stainless-steel machine called a "portable" film processor. "Portable" it really wasn't. To lift one of them took four men, each of whom risked a hernia. Two of these machines were originally built— one for NBC New York and one for NBC Washington. The one in Washington was mounted over a bathtub.

Well, when I finished "Peoples Playhouse" that day, I immediately and anxiously made my way down the long corridor of what had become known as the NBC wing to Ralph Burgin's office.

"Sit down, Frank," Ralph said, indicating a chair opposite his desk.

I wondered, "What in hell is this all about?"

"What we have in mind hasn't really jelled yet," Ralph said, "but it looks good if we can get the budget approved in New York.

"We are proposing," he continued, "a one-hour network program as a summer replacement. It will be called 'Heritage' and it will originate at the National Gallery of Art on Wednesday nights. We will use the National Gallery Orchestra with Richard Bales conducting. We'll interview the curator and other guests of the gallery about the works of art on display there while we show them on camera. Rose D'Amour will comment on Bales' music and interview composers."

Rose D'Amour was the concert pianist whose program I had announced on WOL ten years before. I was getting excited about the idea. Then he said:

"And we'd like to have you consider being the host of the series."

Host of an NBC-TV network show!

I tried to remain calm but it wasn't easy. I wanted to jump up and down and yell, "Whoopee!" But I retained my dignity, such as it was.

"Would you consider doing the series?" Ralph asked.

"Most certainly," I replied.

"We feel it will be a beautiful show," Ralph said. "We'll get back to you when we get the approval to go ahead with it."

I heard no more about it until a few days later when I walked into Joe Browne's office.

"I hear we're going to do a network show together," Joe said.

"What?"

"Yeah, it's all approved. We start two weeks from Wednesday."

"You gotta be kidding."

"Nope. They'll tell you."

I said, "Joe, you shouldn't tell me things like that before I do this show today. I might forget my commercials."

"You do and I'll kill you."

"And you're going to direct the show?"

Joe nodded and said, "Yep. Guess you're stuck with me again."

I said, "Joe, I can't think of anybody I'd rather work with." And I meant it.

Burgin came to the studio during the "Peoples Playhouse" rehearsal and informed me that the deal was all set. We would meet the next day to start planning the programs. I was excited. "Heritage" became the kind of show I really liked to do. It was prestigious, and it was interesting and educational.

The critics were enthusiastic. The Washington *Evening Star* called it "evidence that Washington can produce something other than news and interview programs."

Dorothy Gilfert, writing in *TV Guide*, called it "television at its most promising." Ms. Gilfert said: "Frank Blair, the host of 'Heritage,' has been an announcer, newscaster, program director, and star. Each week before the program he takes what he terms 'a short art course' from a gallery lecturer. He listens, asks questions, and determines which are good questions and which are stupid. He studiously avoids patter."

Believe me, I was proud of the reviews and of Joe and Ralph and all the people who had anything to do with "Heritage."

It was a breakthrough for me and also, I think, for NBC and for television.

We hoped to acquire a prestige sponsor like one of the big steel companies or a car manufacturer or, with Frank Folsom's interest—RCA. But that never happened.

So, with costs mounting, the NBC executives in New York decided it was too expensive to produce as a summer replacement. "Heritage" was terminated after its eighth week. But we had demonstrated that television had scope . . . that it could go beyond comedy and talk.

During the first week of October 1951, Ted Granik was stricken with a heart attack, and Ralph Burgin notified me that Ted wanted me to take over for him as moderator of "The American Forum of the Air." Granik had transferred the program to NBC during my years in Scranton.

Ted also wanted me to handle his other program on NBC titled "Youth Wants to Know." The format called for high-school and college students to ask questions of a guest from Congress, from the Administration, or from labor, business, or industry. This program was televised on Saturday evenings, and "Forum" was on Sunday afternoons. I took on both shows, and thus I began a whole new career as a moderator on discussion programs. I moderated "The American Forum of the Air" and then rushed from NBC to Dumont Studios three miles away to moderate "The Georgetown University Forum." It was while moderating "The Georgetown University Forum" that I first met a rising young congressman from California, Richard Nixon.

On "American Forum" and "Youth Wants to Know" I met and came to know well the leading legislators of the time and leaders in other fields. The roster of prominent people who appeared on these two programs reads like a Who's Who of Washington.

It was a rewarding job and not a difficult one. Production details were handled by Ted's capable staff—Jay Royen, Ann Corrick, and Agnes Curran—and I had only to serve as moderator and appear to have no opinion on any topic. Another bonus I received was again having Joe Browne as director on both programs.

Occasionally too, at Lawrence Spivak's request, I sat in for him as moderator of "Meet the Press." Granik didn't like that too much. He considered Spivak a competitor.

Ted returned to "The American Forum of the Air" as moderator after a five-month absence, but he still called upon me to sit in for him when he didn't feel up to it. Ted was a great guy, but the heart condition he suffered had taken its toll, and he appeared more nervous than before. He often played on the "heart attack" theme and our sympathy to get his way with things. Ted had a habit of referring to everyone who worked with him or for him as "my boy" or "my girl."

Sometimes he would say:

"My boy, I don't feel very well today. You'd better stick close by."

Everything was going well for us now. Mary's health seemed to be well. Baby Paul was a fine, healthy youngster. Theresa was learning to talk, and Tom, John, and Mike were getting old enough to look after themselves. The only problem was that we were outgrowing our little house on Henderson Road in Arlington. On the few occasions when I had free time from my broadcasting schedule, we'd go scouting for a larger house. We found one that exactly suited our needs on Fulton Street, close to St. Mary's Church and School in Falls Church, Virginia. It was a little farther out from Washington, but it had the rooms and grounds we needed. It had five bedrooms and three baths; it was large and spacious. We wanted it the moment we saw it. Lil certainly deserved the freedom and roominess it provided.

By now I was getting to be recognized from my television appearances, and it amazed me how much that helped in making a deal. Being on television hardly meant that I was more honest or more deserving or a better risk than the next guy, but the people I dealt with thought of it that way. I found it fairly easy to conclude the deal on that Falls Church house and float a mortgage loan with a local bank.

We were able to get a quick sale on our Henderson Road house. That helped me to meet the down payment. We were able to move into the Falls Church house about three weeks after we'd found it. We were happy for as long as we lived there, which, as it turned out, was not very long.

Bill McAndrew didn't often come out to the TV studios, even though he was general manager for both NBC radio and TV in Washington. I had seen him a few times there during the planning stages of "Heritage," but usually he transacted his managerial duties by direct telephone line from his office in the Translux Building downtown, where the NBC radio studios were located.

One day in early September (1951), Ralph Burgin's secretary came to the TV studio just as I was signing off "Peoples Playhouse." She said Bill was in Ralph's office and they'd like to see me if I had time. I didn't even take off my pharmacist's jacket or my makeup. I walked back to Ralph's office at once. As always I was delighted to see Bill. I was fond of him as a person and I had great respect for his abilities as a broadcast executive.

Bill invited me to have a seat, and as he glanced at his watch he said, "What time do you have to be back at WOL?"

"Not till five o'clock," I replied.

"Good. Do you have a contract with WOL? Are you locked into any deal with them? In short, if we had something that might interest you, could you get free in two weeks?"

I was glad I was sitting down. Otherwise Bill's question would have floored me. Apparently I was being offered a job with NBC, the most prestigious of the networks at that time.

I managed to reply, "Yes, sir, no problem except for "The Georgetown University Forum."

"What's the problem there?" Ralph asked.

It was the first time he had spoken, except to say hello, since I had entered his office. I explained:

"Well, you see, I started the program five years ago and except for the time I was in Scranton I've been with it. I feel a strong loyalty to the university, that's all."

"It's on the Dumont network now, isn't it?" Bill asked.

"Yes, sir," I replied, "all eight stations."

Bill asked, "What about radio?"

"Well, it's presently on the Liberty Network."

Ralph said, "But Gordon McLendon's bubble has burst and Liberty is going out of business."

"Yes, Ralph, I know, but we have plans to make audio tapes and syndicate the program to stations that still want it. We've now got commitments from sixty-five stations."

"How much of your time does it take?" Bill asked.

"Only on Sundays. We do the radio in the afternoon and the TV version of the same show on Sunday evenings at eight o'clock."

Bill said, "Well, let me tell you what we have in mind and we'll see if we can work out something."

Then Bill began, and with almost every sentence he muttered my pulse rate quickened.

Bill said he was thinking of an early-morning TV program. It would be on the air from seven to nine. Washington, he said, was a news-conscious city and the program would be strongly news-oriented. It would consist of "hard" news, plus news interviews, plus weather reports, plus whatever else we might decide upon to lure an audience.

His idea, in the context of the times, was revolutionary. In 1951 the Washington TV stations did not even come on the air until noon. Bill and his associates would have to decide whether, once his morning news program was on the air, the station would plug the hole between 9 A.M. and noon with other programming or simply sign off at nine and return at noon.

Moreover, a strongly news-oriented program running for two hours was in itself a revolutionary concept. Newscasts were only an incidental part of the TV fare in those early days. Television was seen as an entertainment medium and little else. Only a few of us thought of news as having any real future on individual stations or on networks. What Bill was offering me was an opportunity to plow new ground. I could feel my heart pounding.

"What do you think?" Bill asked.

I was so excited that it took me a few seconds to reply. I was finally able to say:

"Great—just great!"

Bill and Ralph smiled and Bill said, "Want to think it over and get back to us in a day or two?"

"That won't be necessary. I can answer right now—yes!"

"Okay," Bill said, "we'll have to begin with staff salary scale until we get things under way."

I didn't know how much staff scale was, and it didn't matter in the least. I could see a whole new world in broadcasting opening up to me.

Bill said, "If it's okay with you we'll start drawing a contract."

I was slow in answering again. My thoughts were in the future. Imagine having a contract with NBC, being able to say: "I'm with the National Broadcasting Company." I remembered the days in South Carolina when I envied the network announcers I'd hear. I remembered my boyhood in Charleston when I read my history lessons aloud, pretending I was

Lowell Thomas, and dreaming of the day when I might have an important news program of my own. All that went through my mind in the split second before I answered Bill:

"Yes, sir, by all means—I mean, certainly that's all right with me."

I was so excited I walked out of the Wardman Park Hotel still wearing my pharmacist's jacket.

For the next two weeks we met every afternoon in Ralph Burgin's office, building a format for the new program.

I discovered that NBC was great for meetings, for brainstorming sessions. I assume there was some advantage to collective thinking, and also there was probably a feeling that no *one* person would have to take the blame for faulty decisions. In those days, television was not sure of itself, and the networks were very unsure of television. Television was costly, it was new, it was still in the experimental stage. What money was invested in it was a gamble. Would the public accept it? There weren't very many sets in use. George Y. Wheeler, who was assistant to Francis Marion "Scoop" Russell, once told me that in the early days the budget allotted for television in Washington was so limited that they had difficulty getting money to create scenery in the studio. George said at times he took money out of his own pocket, bought a couple of cases of beer, and told the staff there would be one helluva set building party at the Wardman Park the next Saturday afternoon. Staff men would come out with their own hammers and saws and spend the afternoon drinking beer and building flats for a set.

When we were planning TV's first morning news program it never occurred to us that the money would not be forthcoming for our start-up costs. We developed a format that would embrace not only news, sports, weather, and interviews, but also film clips of orchestras and singers.

One thing we developed was a contact with the weather bureau; we could telephone each morning and talk with one of the forecasters. We would have a blackboard showing the map of the area, and as the forecaster talked I would put the weather details on the map. My meteorological training as a naval aviator would be put to good use. The man we dealt with at the Bureau was Jimmy Fiddler.

The working title of the show was "Good Morning, Washington."

I was still at WOL, working out my two weeks' notice, when I walked into another planning meeting—our tenth, I think—and came upon a lot of glum faces.

Bill McAndrew and Gene Juster, Bill's assistant, were there. That was a little unusual. Up to that point the planning had been left mainly up to Ralph and Joe Browne and me.

Ralph broke the news as gently as he could.

"We got some bad news this morning," Ralph said. "New York turned down our budget."

Trying to remain calm I said, "Does that mean . . . ?" That's as far as I got.

Bill said, "It means we can't do the show."

My heart sank.

"And it means I'm out of a job even before I start."

"No," Bill said, "you've got a contract. We will find things for you to do around here. Welcome aboard."

I breathed easier but, like everyone in that room, my disappointment was showing.

The next Monday night I went to work at NBC-TV. I made station breaks, did commercials between network programs, and delivered a five-minute newscast at eleven o'clock. I introduced the late movie and put the station to bed, so to speak. I had embarked on a whole new career in broadcasting, one that was to lead to the busiest days of my life.

I had been on the NBC Washington staff only a few weeks when Bill McAndrew was transferred to New York to become manager of news and special events for NBC radio and television.

Shortly after Bill was transferred, the news broke in *Variety*, the show-biz newspaper, that the NBC network would soon produce an early-morning news and information program—almost precisely along the lines of the "Good Morning, Washington" program that we had planned for the network's Washington station. The new program would be called "Today," and the network was negotiating with Dave Garroway, a Chicago nighttime TV personality, to serve as the host.

It was more than coincidental, I think, that when the format for "Today" was finally laid out it contained many of the ideas we had discussed in our planning sessions in Ralph Burgin's office, even including Jimmy Fiddler's telephoned weather forecasts.

In time, through talks with most of the people concerned, I was able to piece together the story of how "Today" came into being.

The National Broadcasting Company had been a lusty, vigorous, highly profitable enterprise since the early days of commercial radio. It had embedded itself on the American scene. Its radio network had nurtured many of the great entertainers of the times: Bob Hope, Fred Allen, Jack Benny, Eddy Cantor, Fibber McGee and Molly, Amos and Andy, Edgar Bergen and Charlie McCarthy.

With radio reaching its peak, NBC executives in those

early days looked at television as a futuristic toy—something that might be developed in some future century. The technology was at hand. TV had had its roots in electronic discoveries made fifty years earlier. A device for transmitting pictures by telegraph had been patented in Germany as early as 1884. But it was taking decades to bring it to fruition, and the broadcast industry had a jaundiced view of its profit-making potential. Lowell Thomas has written that General David Sarnoff, the guiding genius of RCA, once advised him never to invest a penny in television. Sarnoff said the costs would far outweigh any revenue. What irony that Sarnoff's press aides would later proudly proclaim him "the father of American television."

Sarnoff's bleak appraisal of TV's profit potential underwent a dramatic change in the middle thirties. Under his direction, there were a few experimental telecasts, and Lowell Thomas himself made American television's first network newscast on CBS in 1940, just as he had made the first radio network newscast on NBC fifteen years before.

The outbreak of World War II interrupted television's development, but when peace came in 1945, NBC began investing in TV on a colossal scale. The company set up studios, control rooms, and facilities for developing and editing film. It created shops to make scenery and props. There had to be costumes and makeup and there had to be artists, technicians, and craftsmen—hordes of them.

NBC television's first big network shows, on a limited network because of transmission costs, went on the air in the late forties. All were prime-time programs. There was no morning television on the networks then. The chime ringers were Milton Berle's "Texaco Star Theater," "Philco Television Playhouse," "Goodyear Theater," Sid Caesar's "Your Show of Shows" with Imogene Coca, and "The Fred Waring Show."

It was an expensive experiment and it took NBC several years to get in the black.

By 1951, NBC was somewhat frantically looking for ways to bring in more money. One possible way was to open the network earlier in the day.

Sylvester "Pat" Weaver, the NBC program executive, conceived the idea of what he called a "national newspaper of the air"—a morning newspaper. In the context of those times, the concept was mind-boggling. Some of Weaver's colleagues thought he was crazy.

He wanted a "living" newspaper that would appeal to every section of America. He wanted live cameras on the scene wherever major news was breaking. He wanted sports reports, weather forecasts, book and movie and play reviews, reports from newsmen overseas, live interviews with newsmakers and theatrical figures. The host of the show would be a well-known personality, but the mainstay would be news of what was happening today. It would be a daring venture—enormously costly—but Sarnoff approved the plan, and Weaver appointed Mort Werner to work out the details and get the show on the air.

Mort, who later became the czar of all of NBC's network programming, had been in television less than one year. He had been part owner of a radio station in Ventura, California, and his wife, Marty Wilkerson, had been a Hollywood scriptwriter. Marty, incidentally, was the "GI Jill" heard on radio by hundreds of thousands of American servicemen in World War II.

Mort had come East to break into television, and when Weaver assigned him to organize the "Today" program he had already established himself as a creative executive. Among other things, Mort had been involved in the production of a Jerry Lester show called "Broadway Open House."

This incidentally was a show that brought hundreds of viewer complaints because of Lester's recurrent references to the ample bosom of his costar, Dagmar. In today's climate, Lester's observations would be regarded as either corny or unworthy of a raised eyebrow, or both.

Mort called on Dick Jackson when Mort faced the problem of setting up a budget. Dick had worked with Mort on the financial details of "Broadway Open House." Dick had joined NBC in 1949 after leaving the College of the Holy Cross.

Dick had a sharp, inquisitive mind that absorbed facts and figures like a computer. He had learned about all there was to know about the cost of getting a television show on the air; he understood the cost factors in carpentry, engineering, hair dressing, electrical work, all the crafts involved in TV.

But Dick, with all his expertise, found the job almost impossible when Mort Werner asked him to estimate the cost of putting on the morning news program that Pat Weaver had in mind.

Pat wanted live pictures—important events covered with mobile units.

But what would be considered an "important" event? How many of them would there be? Where would they take place? The cost of live coverage of a hotel fire in central Manhattan would differ greatly from the cost of live coverage of a child trapped in a well in central Idaho. Dick faced the problem that the business offices of major news organizations had faced since major news organizations came into being.

How do you budget for the coverage of news events that cannot be predicted? Furthermore, as his planning conferences with Weaver and Werner went on, it became evident to Dick that he, fresh out of college, knew more about some aspects of television than his own bosses. One of the things he sensed was that Weaver's concept simply could not be made to work—not, at least, on the scale envisaged. NBC, for example, had only a limited number of mobile camera units, and some of them were already committed to other shows. More could be bought and staffed, of course, but the costs would be staggering. Then too, when a big news story broke, it would take time to assemble a mobile unit crew and move the unit to the scene. Could people in government understand the freakish setup under which NBC newsmen would be performing for a show produced by another department?

The infighting was heated. Jobs were at stake, Mort Werner's among them. Mort would not have survived had the show been placed under News Division command.

"Today" planners felt instinctively that the show would need something more than a news staff behind it to make it a success. As they saw it, program ideas and development would not be forthcoming in the right way from within the News Division. Such things were not a hard newsman's cup of tea, and the feeling was that if newspeople took control the future of the show would be bleak.

In the end, General Sarnoff kept Pat Weaver, the Program Department remained in command, and Dick Jackson came up with a budget of three million dollars a year.

Pat Weaver's edict had been to get the show out of the studios and into the streets, out where people were. He wanted the show to be live and be alive. He wanted the viewer to see and hear real America and not show-biz America. How to provide the "feel" that Pat demanded? Mort and Dick Jackson pondered. Perhaps the show could be done from the windows of a New York department store. Perhaps a deal could be made with Saks or Altman's. Then it dawned on Pat and Mort that a perfect place was, in a way, right in front of their own eyes: the RCA Exhibition Hall opposite the RCA Building in Rockefeller Center. The Exhibition Hall had huge windows, adequate floor space, even a raised platform that could serve as a stage. It was in the very center of New York in a section that was in itself a tourist attraction drawing millions of sightseers every year from farms and cities and small towns all across America.

Mort and Dick called on Harry O'Brien, the tough-minded executive who served as manager of the Exhibition Hall. Harry ran the Exhibition Hall almost as if it were his own fiefdom. He demanded the absolute in cleanliness and tidiness. Like a drill sergeant, he held a daily inspection of his ushers, checking that shoes were polished, trousers creased, fingernails clipped and clean, faces freshly shaven. The exhibits themselves were dusted and waxed regularly. O'Brien was proud of that place and treated it like his home.

Mort and Dick took a long, hard look and liked everything they saw. There was space for a small control room on the lower level near the small private theater that General Sarnoff used for showings of first-run movies. They found an executive lounge that would be a perfect place to entertain "Today" guests waiting to go on the air. The lounge even had a built-in-the-wall television set that appeared and disappeared with a flick of a concealed switch. The guests could monitor the show as they stood by.

O'Brien beamed as he showed off his domain. But when he learned what Mort and Dick had in mind, he nearly collapsed of apoplexy. His precious baliwick to be invaded and vulgarized by a television show? He would not hear of it. This was a hall he controlled and operated for the purposes of displaying RCA's wares and dramatizing RCA's goals in a style and manner consistent with the dignity of a great corporation. It could not be bastardized by actors and newsmen and technicians and crowds of people peering in from the sidewalks of Forty-ninth Street. Never?

It's a rule of thumb in the corporate jungle that almost anyone can get almost anything he wants if he has enough clout. Pat Weaver had it. When Mort Werner and Dick Jackson told him about the Exhibition Hall and Harry O'Brien, Pat picked up his telephone and called General Sarnoff. O'Brien was overruled. The decision was that if the "Today" show ever actually got on the air it could originate in O'Brien's hall.

While preliminary planning for the show was taking shape, executives of NBC's Station Relations Department were out drumming up interest among the owners of affiliated stations. That phase of the campaign was led by Harry Bannister, vice president in charge of station relations, who himself had managed an NBC affiliate in Detroit. He had assists from other NBC executives, notably Don Mercer and Paul Rittenhouse, and their first responses from station owners were heartening. Some of the bigger, more prosperous affiliates made tentative commitments to clear time for the show if it came on the air. But many affiliate owners remained skeptical. The climactic moment came at a convention of affiliates at Boca Raton, Florida. Pat Weaver took the floor.

Like most good corporation executives, Pat was a master of the pitch. He described his ideas for the show in language that excited and inspired. The show would make history. It would not only reap profit, it would also add luster to television's image and set a new standard of public service. It would inform the country, stimulate thinking, and help to mold the varied people of the nation into a more homogenous whole.

Pat could touch only lightly on the catchy theme that this would be a morning newspaper of the air. Some of the affiliates were, themselves, owned by well-established morning newspapers. Many would be wary of competing with themselves, of weakening old and prosperous newspapers through a chancy venture in television. Pat emphasized that the show, while covering the news, would be anchored by a prominent person who could be counted upon to draw audiences on the strength of his own personality.

Before he sat down, Pat had cast a magic spell. What was left for station relations executives was almost a mopping-up operation. Holdouts remained, but soon after that meeting, twenty-one affiliates plus NBC's owned stations had committed themselves to carry the show if it came on the air.

That was around November 1, 1951, about the time our idea in Washington for an early-morning TV show had to be shelved on orders from New York. Mort Werner was told to aim for early January as a starting time. That left him hardly eight weeks. In that short period he would have to find talent, hire a staff, find office space, and settle production problems in endless detail.

Until then Dick Jackson had been in the role of an unofficial consultant, not officially attached to the developing "Today" unit. Now Mort made him a firm job offer, and he came aboard as "Today's" first business manager, or unit manager, as the job is defined in television.

Dick and Mort rolled up their sleeves and dug in. Sid Caesar's producer, Max Liebman, had vacated office space on the twenty-eighth floor of the RKO Building above Radio City Music Hall, and Mort took it over as "Today's" first office suite. Secretaries were hired and installed. Jack Hein was named as director of the feature parts of the program, and Mike Zeamer was engaged to direct-news segments. A Hollywood scriptwriter, Bill Stuart, joined the staff as a feature writer to help ensure a "show-biz" flavor. "Today" began growing out of its offices even before it went on the air. The

Kate Smith production staff was moved out of adjoining offices to make way for "Today's" growing staff.

An attractive young woman named Estelle Parsons was hired as a "gofer," a sort of errand girl and jack-of-all-trades, most of them menial. Her last job had been as a tomato picker on a farm. Estelle became the first "Today" girl and of course later became an award-winning Broadway and Hollywood actress.

The need for a strong news staff was self-evident, and the appropriate place to find the right newsman was in the NBC News Division, but the infighting between "Today" and the news executives had left relations strained. How to get top men away from Bill McAndrew? Mort took his problem to Pat Weaver.

The result: "Today" got Gerald Green, one of the sharpest writers in the business, as its managing editor. Gerry went on to become a popular novelist (*The Last Angry Man, Hostage Heart, Blockbuster, The Lotus Eaters,* and *Holocaust*).

One of the first people Gerry took aboard as a newswriter was a young Irish-American named Paul Cunningham, who had spent part of his teen years as a Depression-time hobo. Paul had been a merchant seaman in World War II, then a reporter on the Minneapolis *Star,* and then a one-man TV news operation in Minneapolis, shooting and editing his own newsfilm and doing the reporting as he went along. From "Today" newswriter, Paul went on to an exciting reportorial career in the tradition of the old trench-coat school of journalism.

Another of the first staffers was a gem of an Irish colleen named Marie Finnegan, who is still on the "Today" staff. Marie was hired to help in scheduling and organizing commercials, a job she still does.

There was Mary Kelly, a buxom young woman, eager, boisterous, a hard worker. When she was around everybody in the place was aware of it. I don't think her position had any real job classification. Mary was a doer, and when anything needed doing the cry went out, "Mary!"

As the behind-the-scenes staff grew, the search intensified for on-camera talent. The selection of a host would be critical. The right man could make the show. Pat Weaver and Mort Werner began looking hard at a personality that television itself had created. He was Dave Garroway. His show "Garroway at Large," which originated in Chicago, had been a huge success, and he had a relaxed, soft-sell approach that was considered right for an early-morning show. People just getting out of bed were not likely to want a brash, hard-sell performer on their TV screens.

Negotiations were opened for Dave's services. Unhappily for NBC, but I guess happily for Dave, he was represented by one of the toughest, shrewdest agents in a field that attracts only the tough and shrewd. Dave's manager was Biggie Levin, a nervous little man in chronic bad health. He had ulcers, hypertension, nervous rashes, and such a bad case of eczema on his hands that he wore gloves to conceal the infection. When the insensitive, of whom there were many, asked Biggie why he was wearing gloves, he would first become embarrassed, then angry. He was not an easy man to deal with, and for a long time negotiations were touch and go. Garroway was signed only a few weeks before the show was to go on the air. Dick Jackson helped supervise his move from Chicago and found him a small suite of offices in the RCA Building.

The show needed someone to backstop Dave on the air and to play foil for him. This also was a critical choice. The second man—"second banana," so-called—would have to complement Dave and not detract from him. Yet he would have to be strong enough to take over during Dave's vacations or if Dave fell ill.

Mort Werner recalled a big, toothy blond actor and announcer he had known in California, a performer of warmth and charm who also knew his way around in the broadcasting industry.

Jack Lescoulie had been stage-struck since his childhood in Sacramento. He had studied at the College of the Theater in Pasadena and then in 1937 joined the staff of radio station KFWB in Los Angeles as an announcer. He had served as a combat reporter with the United States Army Air Force during World War II, flying twenty-eight missions over Italy, and he had had a try at the Broadway stage, appearing with such stars as Walter Hampton and Melvin Douglas. When "Today" was being organized, Jack was a producer on CBS radio and yearning for a crack at television. He was relatively unknown on the national scene and that was a plus for him; he would not overshadow Garroway. When Mort offered Jack the No. 2 spot, he could only see it as a standout opportunity. He came aboard with high hopes. I don't think his hopes were ever fully realized. I think Dave himself, whether deliberately or not, saw to it that Jack would not outshine him on the air.

When they were casting the show, as I was later told, one of the toughest jobs that Weaver and Werner faced in the staffing was the choice of a newscaster. News would be a powerful selling point. There was a hope that many viewers would switch on for the news, then stay tuned out of curiosity to see what features might follow.

NBC considered trying to get Walter Cronkite away from CBS. Walter was already well established. Even before joining CBS he had developed a national reputation as a foreign correspondent for United Press (later United Press International). Another candidate for the job was Clifton Utley, one of NBC's best-known radio newsmen, and, incidentally, the father of Garrick Utley, who years later was to appear frequently on "Today" as an NBC foreign correspondent and occasional guest host. Every on-air newsman in the shop was considered. The problem loomed large. Some candidates demanded more money than "Today" could afford, and some the NBC News Division would not willingly release. The News Division accused "Today" of trying to steal its stars.

In the end the decision was to find a newsman with good potential who could be developed in "Today's" own image. The nod went to Jim Fleming.

Jim was a pro in radio news. Furthermore, he could ad-lib, and that was considered a must. The show intended to cover news as it happened, and the newscaster would have to extemporize. Jim was personable, witty, and erudite, and eager for the chance.

While Weaver and Werner were organizing the cast and staff, NBC salesmen were pounding the pavement of Madison Avenue trying to sell commercials.

Up until that time it had been standard procedure for a sponsor to buy a fifteen-minute, thirty-minute, or full-hour program or segment of a program and get exclusive use of all the commercial time allotted. But "Today" would not be programming in prime time, and the show was essentially experimental. It was too much to hope that a sponsor would take the gamble and buy a segment of the show. NBC was keenly aware of that, and it was the background of a major policy decision. Instead of trying to sell entire segments, "Today" would offer four one-minute commercial segments during each of four half hours. This was a new concept in television advertising. It meant that an advertiser could buy as few minutes as he wanted. To Pat Weaver, who conceived it, the idea seemed sound. He called it the magazine concept.

To George Frye, vice president of NBC in charge of sales, it sounded like madness. George threw up his hands. "Today" had one hundred separate minutes of programming to sell each week. The Sales Department, he said, simply did not have the manpower to undertake a selling project of such magnitude. Yet Dick Jackson had estimated that twenty-five of those hundred minutes would have to be sold merely to justify keeping the show on the air through its first thirteen weeks. On Dick's figures, forty commercial minutes would have to be committed before the show could show a profit.

When George said help would be needed, "Today" got the services of Joe Culligan, one of America's supersalesmen, who later became chairman of the board of Curtis Publishing Company. NBC hired Joe away from Hearst's *Good Housekeeping* magazine. He was a handsome man who cut a romantic figure; he wore a black patch over one eye, a reminder of World War II. Joe set up a spellbinding presentation for the Madison Avenue advertising men, and under his aegis the show began to sell. But it was a hard struggle. Some people later said the show was finally saved by a master stroke of salesmanship on the part of a man who was not a salesman at all. He was "Today's" first executive producer.

Mort Werner had been involved at the top level of planning for the "Today" show almost since the idea for it came into Pat Weaver's mind. Mort had worried and fretted over endless details and conceived innumerable programming ideas. But two weeks before "Today" went on the air, another executive was put in over him. Mort stayed on with the title of producer. In the developing situation, it was clear that he had been faulted on two counts. For one thing, he was not a newsman. Yet news would be all-important on the show. Second, he did not yet have a big name. A "name" would give the show prestige, it could influence press criticism, and it could help in the sale of advertising.

The man chosen for the top job was Abe Schechter, my old boss at Mutual.

Pat Weaver hired him away from Mutual for a variety of reasons, all of them obvious to us. First, of course, was his outstanding ability. Second, there was his prestigious name, which assuredly would influence the buyers of commercial time on Madison Avenue. And finally, there was the fact that Abe had worked with Dave Garroway. As head of NBC News and Special Events in the early days, Abe had sometimes used Dave as the talent for special events in broadcasts. They had maintained a smooth-working relationship that would be a plus for the "Today" show.

Abe took over as executive producer on January 1, 1952, two weeks before "Today" was to go on the air.

It was at about the same time that NBC asked me to serve as "Today's" first Washington correspondent. It would not be a full-time assignment. I would handle "Today's" Washington interviews and report some of the Washington news.

To me, at the time, it was just one more assignment, although I was well aware that I would be taking part in a history-making experimental program that, if it succeeded, might well transform the television industry. I was glad to be a part of it but, like others, I had private doubts about the prospects for survival. I was not too sure that people in sufficient numbers would watch television at seven o'clock in the morning. We would have to change the very lifestyle of millions of people if we were to succeed.

"This is 'Today,' the day you're going to live!"

Jack Lescoulie spoke those words on the first "Today" program at precisely 7:00 A.M. EST on January 14, 1952.

It was a busy set we saw on our TV screens that morning,

apparently designed to give the viewer the impression that he was watching an active communications center. It looked like something out of science fiction. An array of clocks behind Garroway's desk told the hour and minutes for every time zone in the world. There was a rack of newspapers fresh off the presses, flown in by the airlines from all over the country to dramatize the "immediacy" of the program, and there was a big circular sign announcing JANUARY 14. And there were apparently busy people all over the set.

Dave Garroway (horn-rimmed glasses and bow tie) in his mild, easygoing manner introduced Jim Fleming, the first newscaster, and Jack Lescoulie, who smiled his beautiful, toothy smile. Jim called in reports from NBC news correspondents overseas. The reports were audio only. This, of course, was before communications satellites made possible instant transmission of actuality news and newsfilm from faraway lands.

There were prerecorded telephone conversations of parents talking with their sons in Korea. The sons' reactions had been filmed by NBC news correspondent John Rich.

Occasionally, the cameras panned the huge plate-glass windows of the Exhibition Hall, showing the crowds watching from the sidewalks.

Garroway introduced the show's first guest, Fleur Cowles, who talked about her new book, *The Bloody Precedent*.

Garroway gave a national weather forecast. Just before air time, Estelle Parsons had telephoned the weather bureau, obtained weather information, and indicated it on a map on a blackboard. She used red chalk. Red would not show up on the black-and-white screens of those times. In giving the weather, Dave talked again with the weather bureau by direct line from Washington. As meteorologist Jimmy Fiddler passed on the information—for a second time—Dave traced Estelle's red lines in white chalk. It was an effective device.

After that, Dave called on me in Washington to begin a segment called "America Waking Up Today." Our Engineering Department had mounted a camera on the TV transmission tower at the Wardman Park Hotel. I was in the announce booth in the studios. There I watched the changing Washington scene on a monitor, as it was transmitted from the tower. I learned something about television that morning. There was no point in talking about something the viewer couldn't see.

I suppose the historians of television journalism will seize upon the irony that the "Today" show's first report from Washington, other than the weather, was not a news report at all. Instead, it was an effort to make maximum use of the live TV camera.

The camera showed and I talked about the nation's capital coming alive. The camera pictured streams of automobiles moving along roadways of Rock Creek Park and Connecticut Avenue and across Memorial Bridge from Virginia, bringing bureaucrats and office workers to their jobs. Through its zoom lens, the camera transmitted "beauty shots" of the Capitol, the Jefferson Memorial, the Washington Monument, and the Lincoln Memorial in the early-morning haze as the sun was rising, seemingly, out of the Potomac River.

When my assigned two minutes had elapsed I gave a cue to switch to Philadelphia, and we saw the City of Brotherly Love awakening to the new day; then the scene switched to Chicago, where from the roof of the Merchandise Mart we got a picture of the Windy City in the semidarkness. There, of course, it was one hour earlier than in our eastern cities. The concluding piece of the "Awakening Cities" segment was seen from still another live camera atop the seventy-story RCA Building in New York.

I couldn't help thinking it was all a waste of money and manpower. It could have been done for much less money on film. The scenes could have been filmed a few days earlier and at a time of the morning when the light could have been better. But this was an attempt to emphasize live, actuality television. Most viewers that first day saw scenes they had never seen before.

The program was available in only twenty-seven cities, all in the Eastern and Central time zones. But it occurred to me that in a small way it had contributed to the slow process of binding the disparate sections of our country together through sharper perception and understanding.

The next morning, critic Janet Kern of the Chicago *Herald American* described "Today" as "something without which TV can do very nicely."

Another critic, whose name I can't remember, said, "Why doesn't NBC roll over and go back to bed?"

Bernie Harrison of the Washington *Times Herald* again raised the question that had been on the minds of a lot of people responsible for "Today": "It was interesting, but who's going to watch television at seven o'clock in the morning?"

And John Crosby, the distinguished television critic of the New York *Herald Tribune*, suggested that "Today" could not possibly last more than thirteen weeks.

It's interesting to note that both the *Herald American* and the *Herald Tribune* have now gone out of business and the *Times Herald* has been absorbed by the Washington *Post*, while "Today" has become an American institution.

As the "Today" program progressed, so did my career. More and more I was being called upon to do "Today" interviews and report the news for "Today" from Washington. Fortunately for me, I did not have to set up the interviews myself. The arrangements were made through the office of Julian Goodman. Julian, who later became chairman of the board of NBC, was NBC Washington news director. He had joined the Washington news staff in 1945, just before VJ Day, after a period of training on a small newspaper in Kentucky. He started at NBC as a newswriter, working at night. His editor was a young man named David Brinkley. As David's on-air assignments increased, Julian replaced him on the night news desk. By the time I joined NBC in 1951, Julian had become director of news, the top news job in Washington. He was a handsome young man with a relaxed manner. As the top NBC newsman in Washington, it often fell to him to act as host to important Washington personages whom I would interview on "Today." Julian would have to arrive at the studios in the early morning. As a matter of common courtesy, he had to be on hand when an important interviewee arrived. The interviewees had to arrive early, too. The net result was that Julian sometimes had to sit there in that studio for two hours and more, drinking coffee and chatting with a guest waiting to go on the air. Years later, he told me the experience had often been harrowing. He said he had often been bored to tears by some of the most important people in America.

Sometimes, in those early days, I catnapped on the couch in Julian's office after the "Today" program signed off and while I waited for my next assignment. Julian never seemed to mind.

In Washington and other eastern cities, "Today" was on the air for three straight hours in those early days, from seven to ten, Eastern Standard Time. Stations in the Central time zone tuned in to us at eight our time—or seven theirs. We were seen for only two hours in the Midwest. For a time, we were not seen at all in the Mountain and Western time zones.

Eastern stations carrying "Today" until 10 A.M. faced a tricky decision: Should they sign off at ten and return to the air at noon, when other programs were already being broadcast? Or should they add new programs to fill the gap between ten and noon?

The Washington station chose to plug the gap. A search was on for fresh, new programs. I volunteered. I had to stay on in the studio anyway until 1 P.M. in order to do "Peoples Playhouse." I suggested that during part of those two hours I do a program angled toward women viewers. It would consist of general interviews, with emphasis on women's news. Ralph Burgin, in his role as program director, bore a primary responsibility in choosing programs. Ralph liked my proposal. He assigned Joe Browne to direct and also to take on some of the functions of a producer.

"What'll we call the program, Joe?" I asked. "How about 'Today in Washington'?"

"Hell, no," he said. "There's enough 'Today' in Washington already. Three hours of it."

He thought a moment, then smiled and said:

"We'll call it 'Blair's House.' "

"What?"

" 'Blair's House,' you dummy," Joe said. "It's a natural."

Blair House, of course, was the government house on Pennsylvania Avenue where official guests of the President were sheltered. Harry Truman had lived there himself during part of his presidency.

" 'Blair's House,' eh?" I said. "I like it."

"I thought you would."

"Blair's House" was on the air from 10 to 11 A.M. five days

a week. Ruth Lyon provided a program from WLW in Cincinnati to fill the 11 to 11:30 A.M. slot, and from 11:30 to 12:00 noon Ted McCrary and Jinx Falkenberg provided a talk show from New York. Inga Runvoldt filled out the schedule until "Peoples Playhouse," with another show designed for women audiences.

NBC Washington was a busy place for me in those days. I was caught up in it all and I loved it. I had no time to read my horoscope, but apparently my star was in the ascendency, at least in television and television journalism.

XIX

FINANCIAL TROUBLES dogged "Today" in its first days—indeed, in its first years.

However, the program had a competitive edge in the field of journalism that would help in ensuring its survival. That edge was dramatically demonstrated when the show was only three weeks old.

King George VI of England had had an operation for the removal of his cancerous right lung, but his recovery had appeared complete. He had resumed public appearances and even again taken up shooting, his favorite sport. The British people felt that all was well with their monarch.

Then on the morning of February 6, 1952, the King died in his sleep, apparently of coronary thrombosis. Buckingham Palace delayed the announcement of his death until 10:45 A.M. London time. That was 5:45 A.M. New York time, too late for American morning newspapers. When AP's bulletin cleared the wires in the NBC newsroom, less than an hour and fifteen minutes remained before "Today" would go on the air. Abe Schechter, Mort Werner, and Gerald Green remade the program. They scrapped planned segments and substituted detailed reports on the King's death and career and the automatic succession to the throne of his twenty-five-year-old daughter, Elizabeth, who was away on a ceremonial tour in Africa. I was alerted in Washington to round up reaction in the capital.

This was one of the most dramatic news stories of the decade, and while "Today" was pouring out the details on television and showing still pictures (this of course was before the time of the satellite), the newspapers on American breakfast tables bore such relatively prosaic headlines as "Secret Bombsight Shown to Senators" and "Reds Ask Parley on Korean Issues Left After Truce." The advantage the "Today" program had by reason of the speed of TV and the difference between European and American time was something we were to exploit with rewarding regularity in the years ahead. Often after I became the "Today" newscaster I was able to broadcast at 7 A.M. the news that would appear under big, page-one headlines in the evening newspapers or morning newspapers of the next day.

Despite "Today's" competitive advantage over newspapers, there was real doubt in those first days about whether the program could survive. The early fan mail looked good, but many potential sponsors were holding back. There was a waitsee attitude on Madison Avenue. People were taking bets that the show would die after the first thirteen weeks. It was in this atmosphere of anxiety that Abe Schechter turned salesman. Abe had been reading the mail.

Typical letters:

"Please tell Dave Garroway to ask the children to get ready for school and not to watch the TV all morning."

"I am a nurse and I live alone and get home at eight o'clock in the morning. It's wonderful to have someone at breakfast with you."

Abe ordered the secretaries not to open the next thousand letters. Then NBC set up a big breakfast meeting at the old Park Lane Hotel on Park Avenue for ad agency executives and the advertising directors of potential sponsors. Garroway and Pat Weaver gave some pep talks about the show and then Abe took the floor.

"Obviously," he said, "we are trying to sell this show, but you don't have to take our word for it. Why don't you just see for yourselves how the public likes us?"

That was the cue for half a dozen uniformed NBC page boys to enter the breakfast room bearing stacks of unopened mail. They dumped the letters on the tables and passed out "Today" embossed openers to the guests.

For the next twenty minutes the Madison Avenue people sat there slicing open envelopes and reading "Today's" fan mail. A few weeks later "Today" had sold out about half of the show. That was enough to keep it on the air, at least for a while longer.

It was understandable that in this uncertain atmosphere tempers would flare. Abe stood between the staff and Pat Weaver, whose career was riding on the success or failure of the show. Pat was in there every day with criticism, ideas, and orders, many of which the staff found impossible to implement. I imagine Abe was buffeted every day. His position was made the more awkward by the differences between his own finely honed news judgment and Pat Weaver's conception of what news stories should be covered and just how they should be presented. Abe, as one of the big names in broadcast journalism, had no tolerance for any excessive interference from above. He and Pat came to a parting of the ways in a few short weeks.

Abe left the show and went on to establish a public-relations agency that was still thriving twenty-five years later, with Schechter still at its helm.

His successor as "Today's" executive producer was Dick Pinkham—Richard A. R. Pinkham, later chairman of the ex-

ecutive committee of Ted Bates & Company, a big Madison
Avenue advertising agency. When he took over "Today,"
Dick was Weaver's most trusted deputy. It is a measure of
Pat's concern that he moved him from broader network responsibilities to handle one show. Dick had come to NBC
after a stint as circulation manager and member of the board
of the New York *Herald Tribune*. Earlier he had been a
writer for *Time* magazine. He was tough and imaginative.

However, I don't think it was Dick or any one individual or
group of individuals who saved the show from extinction. I
think this longest running daytime TV program, which became so much a part of the fabric of American life, was saved
not by people—but by a chimpanzee.

Paul Cunningham, having finished an overnight writing
stint, and Len Safire, associate producer, sat at Toots Shor's
bar worrying about the show's future. The ratings were down
again. Sales were bad. Talk persisted that "Today" would
soon go off the air. There was a crisis atmosphere in the executive suite. Dick Pinkham was calling urgently for suggestions. Cunningham and Safire had been racking their brains
for an idea that would get the country talking about the show
and watching it.

"What we need is a gimmick," Len said, tapping his fingers
nervously on the bar.

Paul nodded.

"Something to liven the show. We need humor."

When Paul mentioned humor, Len recalled having seen a
newspaper cartoon in which a gorilla had been depicted as a
newscaster. The gorilla was seen walking away from a
broadcasting desk and turning the microphone over to a
human newscaster. The caption read: "And now for the
human side of the news!"

An idea began building in Len's mind. How about a monkey on the show? He paid his bill and hurried back to the "Today" offices. There, he mentioned his idea to a number of writers and production people. It was seen more as a gag than a serious suggestion.

Charles Speer, a "Today" writer, poked his head in at Len's office door.

"You looking for a monkey?"

"Yes."

"Come on!"

Charles led Len out into the corridor of the building, and there, just about to get on the elevator, was a year-old chimpanzee in the arms of one of his owners. The owners were Ray Waldron and Buddy Minella, both former NBC page boys whom Len knew well. They operated a pet shop in New Jersey, and they had brought the chimp in to appear on a medical program.

"Hold it!" Len shouted.

He led a strange procession of chimp and people into Dick Pinkham's office.

"Here's an idea for you," he said.

Dick studied the little beast. He was captivated.

"Great!" he said. "Let's put him on the show tomorrow morning."

"No," Len said, "put him on *every* morning."

Pat Weaver had demanded "a New York *Times* of the air," and as a result the show had been too solemn and serious.

Dick agreed, and thus it was that a chimpanzee became a television star.

The chimp joined "Today's" cast in a blaze of nation-wide publicity. A chimp makes it to big-time. TV contracts were signed in a ceremony that looked like a Hollywood takeoff on some of the more bizarre aspects of show biz. Flash bulbs flashed, TV cameras and reporters watched and recorded every angle.

That chimp went on to serve much the same purpose for "Today" that a comic strip serves for a newspaper.

Children flicking their TV dials in the early-morning hours were attracted by the horseplay of a tiny, adorable, mischievous, half-human little chimpanzee on NBC. They stayed tuned. Soon their parents were watching, too. Then the parents discovered that NBC not only had a chimp but also a good, morning news program. "Today's" audience grew dramatically. The chimp was a success almost overnight.

The chimp was named J. Fred Muggs. That was judged the best name among thousands suggested in a contest among the viewers. J. Fred Muggs went on to become a national figure. He made the cover of national magazines. He went on a tour of the big cities. He was deluged with invitations to make public appearances. Later, for a few ugly days, he would become more than a national figure; he would become the principal in an international incident that soured relations between two great nations.

Muggs was one smart chimp. Sally Quinn, after she goofed as hostess of CBS's morning show, complained that no one had ever told her what those little red lights meant at the top of the TV cameras, the lights that indicate the camera is alive and watching. Well, no one ever told J. Fred Muggs, either. Muggs figured it out for himself. He learned quickly that if those lights were on, no one was going to reprimand him for his mischievous deeds.

Anyone seen scolding that little imp on national television would have been buried the next morning under a deluge of angry protesting letters, and we could be sure that the protest would not come from children alone.

When the lights were on and Muggs was on camera, he

would work himself loose, leap off his chair, scurry over to Jack Lescoulie's desk and grab it and shake it, meanwhile stomping on the floor and looking up at Jack with what to most viewers was a look suggesting one part mischief and one part adoration. Or he would escape and snatch Dave Garroway's glasses off his nose. Or scamper to a perch on top of a TV monitor to study Dave quizzically and make sour faces. In 1957 we had a fifth anniversary party with a huge cake on the set. Muggs leaped out of Dave's arms while Dave was crooning "Happy Birthday." Muggs landed in the middle of the cake and immediately spewed gooey gobs of it high in the air. This sort of thing, of course, the viewers loved. The cast didn't, although it was understood all too clearly that this was good television. All in all, I cannot say that J. Fred Muggs was excessively popular with the staff of "Today" or with some of the guests. Muggs liked to tease stars who were making guest appearances. Once he pinched Kim Novak's left breast.

It's incredible, perhaps, but in the end NBC actually had to keep a studio "hot" with overtime for the crew, at enormous added expense, in order to break Muggs' confidence in those little red lights.

During these sessions, which of course never went out on the air, the crew would switch on the red lights, wait for Muggs' antics, and then someone would scold him severely. In time, the poor chimp got confused. He found that the red lights were a strictly unreliable signal. He couldn't really be sure of getting away with mischief while they were visible.

I suspect that Dave Garroway resented Muggs, although of course Dave tried never to show it on the air. Perhaps there was just a trace there of professional jealousy? However, I don't think Muggs liked Dave much, either, or Jack Lescoulie, for that matter. The little imp did have his favorites.

He used to stop at Paul Cunningham's desk regularly, for example, and rather solemnly shake Paul's hand. I developed a reasonable relationship with Muggs. Perhaps this was because he and I kept a respectful distance. We had a sort of unspoken "live and let live" arrangement, but always at the back of my mind was the nagging question: What in hell is a chimpanzee doing on a news program, anyway?

I first met Muggs when Lil and I and the kids—all six of them, at that point—were summoned to New York from Washington for a mass appearance on the show. I was a fairly well-known figure around Washington by then, and a local department store had used a picture of Lil, myself, and the kids to promote a Father's Day sale. I sent a clipping along to Gerry Green, just as a matter of personal interest.

Gerry immediately telephoned and asked if the family would do a fashion show for "Today," featuring back-to-school clothes. It was a major logistical problem, of course, getting all those kids ready for a trip to New York and then getting them there, but Lil managed. Estelle Parsons handled the New York details for us. We did the show (the kids, incidentally, got to keep the clothes they modeled—a big boon for Lil and me and our bank balance). In doing the show, we came face to face with J. Fred Muggs. The kids were overjoyed.

If Muggs left me cool, there came a time when he left Dick Pinkham frigid.

Against a background of hoopla and big-time publicity, the show arranged for the chimp to pay a visit to the Chicago Zoo, which was run by Marlin Perkins. The story line was that J. Fred would make a social call on some of his cousins there in Chicago. Naturally TV cameramen, still photographers, and journalists would record this momentous event for posterity; it would be worth thousands of column inches of feature-story coverage in the press, and that of course could mean still more viewers.

On the morning of the trip a fleet of Cadillacs and a convoy of reporters stood by in Rockefeller Plaza waiting to accompany Muggs and friends in a motorcade to the airport for the much-heralded flight to Chicago.

Just at the last minute as Muggs & Company were about to leave the "Today" offices, the telephone rang on Dick Pinkham's desk. Chicago calling. Marlin Perkins at the Chicago Zoo.

"Just checking," he said, "but has Muggs been wormed?"

"What?" Dick asked.

"Because if he hasn't been wormed, he can't come. He might infect the other chimps."

Dick turned to Muggs' keepers. Had he in fact been wormed? They weren't sure.

Dick relayed that information to Perkins.

"But," Dick said, "we can't stop now. The momentum is too great! The publicity apparatus has built up the trip too much."

Perkins was adamant. No worming, no trip.

Dick shrugged his shoulders.

"Well," he said, sighing, "how do I worm a chimp?"

Perkins began instructing him over the telephone.

"Put the chimp face down on your desk. Spread his buttocks. . . ."

Dick paled. He laid down the telephone, stricken, and said aloud, in what I have always thought of as one of man's classic protests against the workings of fate:

"My God! I'm a graduate of Yale University in English composition! What am I doing talking about a thing like this?"

January 1962—"Today." Garroway, Chancellor, and I on the tenth-anniversay program of "Today." All former producers of the show also appeared. It was another milestone.

1962—"Today." Chancellor and I talking with Jackie Robinson, who was the first black ballplayer in the major leagues. *Photo by Raimondo Borea, ASMP.*

1962—"Today" originating from Los Angeles. Poolside interview with Johnny Weissmuller, a former Tarzan. Johnny insisted on being in the pool because he didn't want to show the weight he had gained. We concluded with his well-known jungle yell.

1963—Another day of "Today" in the Florida Showcase. Jack Lescoulie, Pat Fontaine, Hugh Downs, and I. Jack and I were kidding each other in those days, but Al Morgan changed that.

1965—A change in the cast of characters. Barbara Walters became the "Today" woman, and Joe Garagiola brought his great sense of humor to the program. Ratings improved. Hugh Downs remained host. *Photo by Raimondo Borea, ASMP.*

1965—The "Today" cast with "Today" guest Ethel Merman. Delightful. *Photo by Raimondo Borea, ASMP.*

1968—"Today." Broadcasting the news of an unpopular war. I didn't like it. *Photo by Raimondo Borea, ASMP.*

1968—Thanksgiving Day. Lil again. You'd never know she was the mother of eight children.

1968—The day I had the privilege of introducing Pope Paul when he broadcast (by satellite) his congratulations to Georgetown University on its two-hundredth anniversary. I had a hand in arranging the telecast.

1968—Thanksgiving Day, Stamford, Connecticut. Our eight children, left to right, Tom, Mike, Billy, Patty, Mary, John, Paul, and Theresa.

1968—Thanksgiving Day, Stamford, Connecticut. Four generations of Frank Blairs—Junior, Senior, III, IV.

July 16, 1969—"Today" takes its stint during the ordeal of the Apollo-Saturn 11 first lunar landing (Neil Armstrong, Edwin Aldrin, Michael Collins). "A small step for man, a giant step for mankind."

1970—Naval Air Station, Corpus Christi, Texas. My last flight as a pilot in a Navy plane. I had been master of ceremonies at a Navy relief benefit and was invited to fly in a practice flight with the Navy's Blue Angels. One of my big thrills and ambitions realized.

October 1971—The day that Frank McGee took over from Hugh Downs as "man in charge on air" of "Today." *Photo by Raimondo Borea, ASMP.*

1971—Joe Garagiola and I have a chat. He's probably telling me about the "spitball," which was his favorite topic as a big-league catcher in baseball. *Photo by Raimondo Borea, ASMP.*

1974—Greeting Bette Davis, the great motion-picture star. She said to me as we embraced: "I've watched you every morning for years!" I was a great admirer of her, and this was a great tribute from a great lady.

1974—The weather forecasts were an integral part of "Today." I've often had airline pilots thank us for our comprehensive forecasts. (Mark Davison was our meteorologist.) *Photo by Raimondo Borea, ASMP.*

March 13, 1975—A great day in my life. Julian Goodman, chairman of the board of NBC, presents me with a gold watch inscribed: "NBC—Frank Blair—For long and faithful service—National Broadcasting Company —1975" (twenty-five years). *Photo by Raimondo Borea, ASMP.*

January 15, 1977—The twenty-fifth anniversary of "Today"—the SIGN-OFF! *Photo by Raimondo Borea, ASMP.*

March 14, 1975—The End. Lil sheds a tear, and so do I as I wave good-bye to a job I loved and tried to devote myself to.

Dick did not want to hear the next instructions. He picked up the telephone and said as much to Perkins.

Finally, Perkins relented.

"Oh hell," he said, "forget it."

The trip became an enormous public-relations success.

In the first year of "Today" I made occasional trips to New York to appear on the program from there and of course I was doing the Washington interviews regularly, but the bulk of my time was devoted to other activities.

I was the moderator of the Gulf Oil Company program "We, the People," which originally was designed to depict the hobbies and vocations of Americans in all walks of life. But for thirteen weeks I would cover the presidential scene. I was the second choice of Gulf's ad agency, Young & Rubicam, for the moderator's role. The agency tried first to engage David Brinkley. NBC would not permit David to do the job.

I also anchored NBC's coverage of the McCarthy hearings in which Senator Joseph McCarthy engaged in his witch-hunt for Communists in the government. I watched the hearings on a monitor and, by pressing a button, I was able to impose my own voice over the sounds of the proceedings to identify witnesses, clarify procedures, and do occasional recaps. Julian Goodman referred to me jokingly as NBC's "hearing aide."

McCarthy was so interested in TV coverage that he, personally, developed some of the skills of a television professional. We wanted to end our coverage precisely at noon. Our director would advise McCarthy at one minute and thirty seconds before noon, and McCarthy then would wind up the session smoothly, leaving me just enough time for the signoff.

Also in that period I was one of the stable of NBC newsmen assigned to the coverage of Dwight Eisenhower's inaugural. It was the first presidential inauguration to be covered by television on a large scale, and in a sense it was a break-through for both NBC and me. We were instructed to talk about what the viewer would be seeing, but not to insult him by describing too closely what he could see for himself. I was assigned to work in a structure that looked much like a tree house. It was on stilts on the south side of Lafayette Park, directly in front of the presidential reviewing stand.

Johnny Batchelder worked with me. Other correspondents were stationed at other vantage points along the parade route. Johnny and I were there all through that cold, damp, and cloudy day. NBC sent us an urn of coffee and a small electric space heater to help us keep warm. When that long day ended, I went back to the NBC studios in the Wardman Park for another assignment, and as I was passing through the hotel lobby I saw Bill McAndrew and Julian Goodman in an adjoining cocktail lounge with Gene Juster, one of Bill's assistants in New York; Carlton Smith, general manager of NBC Washington; and Bud Barry, network programming executive. Bill motioned to me to join them.

"Nice work," he said. "You did exactly what we wanted you to do."

I thanked him.

"Would you like to work in New York?" Bill asked.

I told him that was every announcer's ambition.

We dropped the subject, and I finished my scotch and left.

Bill, I thought, had made it clear that I might anticipate a new offer.

The word came a few weeks later. I was ordered to New York to anchor the news on the "Today" show during the week of the coronation of Queen Elizabeth II. By now, Merrill Mueller had replaced Jim Fleming as "Today's" newscaster, and Merrill, as a former London correspondent, was needed in London for the on-the-spot coronation coverage.

It would be a critical week for TV and for "Today." American interest in the coronation was intense. Millions of words had been written and broadcast about the preparations. Journalistic competition on the story was fierce. It would amount to a transoceanic race among the networks. There was much at stake. Great prestige would accrue to whichever network managed to broadcast the film first here in America.

What happened to NBC's Canberra jet bomber on coronation day confirmed what I have long argued about television news: There are too many people involved and too many opportunities for human error.

Planning for the coverage of the coronation had been under way in the networks and in all other major news organizations for more than a year. Millions of dollars had been invested, and uncounted man-hours of newsmen's time had been invested. Howard K. Smith, as president of the Association of American Correspondents in London, represented the American media in planning sessions with the British authorities, and Howard was so deeply involved that CBS, his employer at the time, had to send in another correspondent to handle the day-by-day news. Both Howard and Romney Wheeler, NBC's London correspondent, had leased jet bombers to fly their film to New York. It would shape up as a transatlantic race. NBC made elaborate technical and studio arrangements to broadcast from the Boston airport, because Boston, geographically, was closer to London than New York. The minutes saved would be precious.

On the day of the coronation, with the film safely on board, the NBC jet had flown a third of the way to New York when the pilot, Binky Beaumont, tested his belly tanks. He found a bug. The pump for the tanks was inoperative. The fuel could not be fed to the engines. Beaumont suspected an air lock. He checked his altimeter.

He was flying at forty thousand feet. He lowered the plane's nose and went into a steep dive, hoping to break the lock and free the fuel he would need to get to Boston. When he came out of that dive at twenty thousand feet, nothing had happened. The air lock held.

The question for him now was not whether he could make it to Boston nonstop. It was whether, with the available fuel only from the wing tanks, he could make it even to Gander, the nearest North American airport where he could refuel. He worked it out with a slide rule. He could, in fact, make it to Gander—just. But he would have fuel enough to make only one approach, and Gander was fogged in. The risk was too great. He radioed his decision to London: He was turning back.

When he landed in Britain that afternoon, the ground crew discovered what had gone wrong. Someone stowing the crew's luggage before takeoff had carelessly tossed aboard a suitcase—and the suitcase had broken a tiny wire that activated the pump on the belly tanks. One fleeting moment of carelessness (could it even be called that?) had befouled all of NBC's elaborate and costly planning.

As it turned out, however, NBC was not beaten, in spite of it all.

Another Canberra bomber had made it to Montreal with film for the Canadian Broadcasting Corporation. The Canadian film was fed to NBC on a co-operative agreement between the two networks. We beat CBS. But it was a hollow victory. For we had *not* beaten ABC. ABC had made none of the immensely costly coverage arrangements made by NBC and CBS. But that third network *had* made other arrangements for a feed of the Canadian film from Montreal. So when the feed went out to NBC, it went—simultaneously—to the American Broadcasting Company.

As the relief newscaster on the "Today" show, I carried out my own role in the coronation coverage without undue difficulty, but there was one aspect of our program that disturbed me deeply. It disturbed the British Government, too.

As most Americans know, the reigning monarch is a focal point for the patriotic emotions of the British people. She is what the American flag is to Americans, only perhaps more so. She is also the titular head of the Church of England. Thus the coronation of Elizabeth II was both a religious event and a milestone in British national history.

Well, on that morning of the ceremony, the "Today" cameras seemed to cut between still pictures transmitted by radio and cable of the coronation and the antics of a mischievous chimpanzee, J. Fred Muggs. British correspondents in the United States reported this travesty in all its detail. There were cries of anguish from British editorialists.

Romney Wheeler was summoned to Buckingham Palace and scolded by the Queen's press secretary, Lieutenant Commander Richard Colville, who was also a friend and confidant of the royal family. A number of American newspapers were as appalled as Commander Colville. "Today" was accused of bad taste and an offense against the national dignity of an ally. I am bound to say I thought the charges were justified.

With the coronation story behind us, and Merrill Mueller back on the job in New York, I went back to Washington feeling pretty good about myself. I hadn't goofed. I had not dropped any great clangers, and people on the staff had had some nice things to say about my work.

Moreover, I had an intuitive feeling that I had been given

the job partly as a tryout—that Pat Weaver and Dick Pinkham and Mort Werner and Gerry Green had wanted to see how I would handle myself as "Today's" newscaster with a big story breaking. It was well known in New York that Merrill Mueller wanted to leave the job—he hated the hours—and that NBC for its part, while recognizing Merrill's considerable talents, did not consider him quite right for an early-morning program.

It was about a month later that Bill McAndrew and Dick Pinkham offered me the job. The salary would be $750 a week. That was more money than I had ever dreamed of for a single program. But accepting would mean a big upheaval for the family—and a risky assignment. "Today's" future was still uncertain.

I talked it over with Lil. As she had so many times in the past, she closed our conversation with the words: ". . . if that's what you want to do."

Well, of course, I wanted to do it. I telephoned Pinkham and accepted. I spent the next two weeks arranging to move and closing out my Washington commitments. On the Friday before I went to New York, I closed my local TV show, "Blair's House," by hanging a "For Rent" sign on a house on the set and walking off into the darkness. That, I thought, might be an omen of things to come for me in real life.

I found a house for us in Irvington-on-Hudson, a beautiful Westchester suburb in Washington Irving's Sleepy Hollow country. The house in which Irving wrote *The Headless Horseman* and other classics was close by. The house I wanted was a red-brick colonial on a dead-end street called Ardsley Terrace. At the entrance to Ardsley Terrace there was a sign reading "Slow—Children Playing." That augured well for the children in the big Blair family. The house had been owned by a radiologist, Dr. Cort Headland, who some time before had made an X ray of his own body and knew he was a dying man. His widow was offering it for sale and in fact would take a small second mortgage. Lil came up to take a look. She liked what she saw, and we closed the deal.

In November of 1952 our seventh child arrived—a boy. We named him William Pinckney for his great-grandfather.

It was on the Labor Day weekend of 1953 that I had a difficult little encounter with the Maryland State Police.

We were moving. There was a "For Sale" sign on the lawn of our house at Falls Church. The moving van had pulled away with our furniture, and Lil and I had stuffed our seven children into our station wagon, among suitcases and boxes of belongings, and set out for New York. Lil had put a cooler on board with little Billy's bottle and two cans of beer for me.

Along the highway I began rediscovering two basic truths about the American way of life. The first was that traffic can be heavy on Labor Day weekend. Another was that while a station wagon may appear to be roomy enough for two adults and seven children, a better choice would be a fifty-foot boxcar, with one section partitioned off and soundproofed.

As we sped through Maryland, with small children hanging out of windows, a service station appeared ahead of us and the first wail pierced my ears.

"Daddy! I gotta go! Can we stop at that gas station?"

"There's a better one just ahead!" I said.

I drove on. I was reluctant to get out of the stream of traffic. Anyway, these kids couldn't fool me. The plea I had just heard was more a plea for a break in the monotony of the trip.

It was hot. My throat was parched. I drank a can of beer.

"I'll keep the can!" Lil said. She stuffed the empty can into a paper bag and put it under the seat.

"Dadeee!"

This time it was little Billy. Nearly a year old, potty trained, and hardly incontinent.

I ignored him. I felt he could hold out for at least a few more miles.

There was an outbreak of free-style wrestling in the rear of the wagon, which Lil stopped with a sharp command, before the cry came again.

"Da-DEEE!"

This time Billy's appeal carried a ring of desperation. Lil's maternal heart melted. She reached under the seat, retrieved the empty beer can, and passed it back to an older son with appropriate instructions about how to assist Billy. It was an operation that required a steady hand because of the sway of the station wagon as we rounded a curve.

However, only a short time passed before the older children began protesting the presence of the well-filled can. Then one of the older boys, without consulting Lil or me, rolled down a window and sent the can sailing onto the green alongside the highway. As it went clattering down an embankment I heard the wail of a siren and saw, in my rear-view mirror, the flashing lights of a highway patrol car. A policeman was after us.

I pulled over. The patrol car pulled up behind me. A huge police officer got out and approached my window, glowering.

"Do you realize you're littering?" he asked. "You just threw a can out the window!"

"Officer! I didn't know! I just didn't know what was going on back there."

The patrolman glanced into the rear of the station wagon, into the sea of small faces, and when he turned back to me I thought I saw a look of compassion in his eyes.

"Okay," he said. "All right this time. But don't let it happen again!"

We knew when we moved to Irvington that Lil would need help. My peculiar hours and my commuting and the very size of the house and our family made assistance in the household almost mandatory, and with my new income I was able to afford it. We got lucky. We found Virginia and Jack Owens, a live-in couple. Virginia was a middle-aged black woman who had left her six children with her mother in Albemarle, North Carolina, and come North with her husband, Jack, to try to scratch out enough money for their support. She was an efficient housekeeper and surrogate mother and a warm and loving human being. She would become one of our dearest friends. Jack was a big, strapping man who reminded me of Othello. He had a daytime job in a garage. In the evenings and on weekends he would help with the yard work and do handyman chores. He and Virginia would share rooms on the third floor of our house, and it would be comforting to think of him, a giant of a man, there with my family when I would leave home in the very early hours of the morning.

In Ardsley Terrace I began a personal regimen that would last for years. In the evenings, while my older children were doing homework or watching television, I would excuse myself, go to my bedroom, lay out my clothes for the next morning, and hit the sack.

At three-thirty the next morning the clock would ring—a ghastly sound at that hour—and I would haul myself out of bed, bleary-eyed, while saner people were sound asleep. I could not allow Lil to get up and see me off as a regular thing —not when she had that big house and kids to concern herself with. I would switch on the coffee, take a few gulps, and take off for New York. There was no conveniently scheduled transportation between Irvington-on-Hudson and New York City in those early-morning hours. I had to drive, often under dangerous conditions. As the months passed, I would make that trip through rain, sleet, fog, and snow, and always in the darkness of night. I would make it when the rain was so heavy I could scarcely see the road. I would make it when ice coated the highways and the only other people abroad were sanding crews and policemen in patrol cars. I would be out there in the night inching along through thick fog when that same thick fog had forced the highway authorities to shut off all traffic on a nearby turnpike. And I would drive those lonely miles behind snow plows when the snow drifts around me were higher than my car.

Actually, in a way, the commuting would be easier when the driving was hazardous. In those conditions there would never be a problem about staying awake. The danger of an accident would be too real. The trips that would really have me worried would be those that I would make in clear, dry weather in spring and summer when the night air was balmy and the suburbs were asleep. On those trips my eyes would grow heavy and it would be a struggle to keep from nodding off to sleep at the wheel.

I managed by saying "Hail, Marys" and fingering my rosary as I drove.

But once in the "Today" studios there in Exhibition Hall, I would come wide awake, because the job ahead of me was always exhilarating.

The work of preparing a newscast for television was less complex then. There was no videotape, and the networks' newsfilm departments were still small, their product relatively sparse. That meant less newsfilm to be edited and scripted for "voice-over." The logistics were such that I could do more of my own writing. There was a news staff, of course, headed by

Paul Cunningham, who went on to become "Today" reporter at large, and there were three capable writers, but I was able to write at least part of the "Today" newsscripts myself in those early years. I felt very much involved and deeply conscious of my responsibility as the man whose words could carry the news into countless American homes.

Then, too, I was doing many of the feature interviews on the program, sometimes with Dave Garroway and sometimes alone. One of my early interviewees, incidentally, was General Mark Clark, who had just returned from Korea. I had not met him before then, but as a consequence of that interview he and I developed a friendship that would last for more than a quarter of a century and lead to my appointment to the board of advisers of The Citadel, the South Carolina military college that the general would take over as president.

Everyday on "Today" was unpredictable, and always there were lighter moments.

"Your Highness," I asked the Sheik of Kuwait while the cameras rolled in his suite in the Waldorf-Astoria Towers, "what is the biggest problem your small country faces today?"

"Mr. Blair," the Sheik replied, "the answer is simple. We need water in Kuwait and every time we drill for water, we strike oil."

In the studio, Garroway and Lescoulie and I thought of ourselves as a team. We enjoyed working together. We liked one another, and it was easy for us to co-operate. Mort Werner said that what made "Today" tick was the right "chemistry" and our ability to relate to one another. Jack and I loved to poke fun at each other, and the audience seemed to enjoy our jibes. There were suggestions that it was undignified for a newsman to engage in such horseplay. The argument was that it lessened my credibility as a serious journalist. The dominant view, however, was that it showed a human quality that could not weaken me in my role as anchorman of the news segments.

Jack used to do a thing he called his "Fearless Forecast." Every Friday before the big weekend football games and at other times before big sporting events, Jack would pick the winners. I wasn't knowledgeable in sports but I would stand alongside him and heckle as he checked his choices on a blackboard. At times when I'd wisecrack about Jack's track record, he'd look at me with a hurt stare. Jac Hein, our director, always seemed to be prepared. He would catch Jack's face, and then show J. Fred Muggs covering his eyes with one paw, as if he couldn't stand the ignominy of it all. Of course, the payoff would come on Monday mornings when Jack would have to give an account of his successes and failures as a picker of winners. The viewers apparently loved it all. The mail was very favorable.

Garroway was our undisputed star. He was a superb showman, one of the truly great on-air personalities. He sparkled, and at the same time he was, on camera, a neighborly human being, who sounded like a man chatting with an old friend. He was so relaxed that he once actually dozed off in the middle of an interview. He awakened only when the voice of the man he was interviewing went silent. Coming awake, he glanced at the script in front of him and asked the interviewee the same question he had asked before he dozed off.

"But Mr. Garroway," the interviewee protested, "you just asked me that."

Dave was master of the instant recovery.

"Yes," he said, "I know, but I thought you might like to elaborate on your answer."

Jack had been hired as Dave's "second banana," and I think Dave went to great pains to ensure that Jack would remain just that—second banana, never in a position to challenge Dave's supremacy. Dave's vanity demanded that he dominate the show, and indeed he did. I had known Dave only a short time when the thought occurred to me that a live camera was, in a strange way, his closest friend. On camera, Dave was as at ease as your sleepy old hound dog. But off camera, he was a very private person. He eschewed parties. He once told me he would pay five hundred dollars to get out of a cocktail party. He rarely attended the parties that other "Today" people gave for their coworkers, although he always came to parties that Lil and I would give. With us he was as relaxed and charming as with the viewers on camera.

Dave's office at 30 Rockefeller Plaza was hardly an office at all. It was more an apartment. There was a bed there, where Dave napped, and there was a refrigerator, which the unit managers kept well stocked with snacks. Dave kept himself secluded there. I don't think he even had a telephone to disturb him.

In some ways, I suppose he was a strange man. Among other things, he believed in ghosts—genuinely. He was convinced there were poltergeists abroad in the old house he bought on East Sixty-third Street, one of New York's row houses on a fashionable residential street. Yet he lived there, and I think he was content. The poltergeists did not frighten him.

We did a series of shows from Kansas City. We were booked into the Muehlbach Hotel, but accommodations were scarce. Dave would have the bridal suite, but he would have to share it with someone. He chose me. The suite had a large living room and two private bedrooms, each with a bath. The larger of the bedrooms was assigned to Dave, as the star. It was a huge room, painted white. We had gone to our separate bedrooms to unpack when there was a gentle knock on my door. It was Dave. He said he was uncomfortable in that big white room, and he had noted that my room was decorated in yellow, and yellow was his favorite color. Would I swap bedrooms? We swapped.

If Dave normally kept himself at a distance, there was a rare camaraderie among the rest of the "Today" staff. I thought the explanation could be found in two things. First, there was a feeling that we were together in a venture of no small importance to the television industry and perhaps even to the country at large. If the show succeeded, we would be adding a new dimension—early-morning viewing—to TV, and we would be changing the habits of millions of Americans. Second, I think, the camaraderie was there partly because of the man-killing hours we shared.

I think most of us experienced the fear of oversleeping in the early-morning hours. In my years on the show I was victim of it only a very few times, but the danger was ever-present.

I recall one time when I took an afternoon nap, which was something I didn't like to do and seldom did. I preferred to enjoy the afternoon at home, visiting or reading or working around the yard or, occasionally, playing golf.

That afternoon I discovered I was very tired, and I succumbed to the temptation to take a snooze. That was one of those days, I guess, when I'd stayed too long at Toots Shor's.

When I woke up it was daylight outside.

"Oh my God," I thought immediately, "I've done it. I've overslept!"

I looked at the clock. It was six o'clock.

We lived in Stamford, Connecticut, at the time, and I knew I couldn't get dressed and drive to New York in time for the show.

I grabbed the phone by the bed and dialed NBC as quickly as I could.

"Give me the 'Today' news desk quickly, please," I pleaded.

Bernie Brown was what we called our overnight editor. He came to work at two in the afternoon and worked to midnight arranging for film coverage and live pickups of news stories and getting the logistics out of the way before the others came in to start putting the pieces together as newscasts.

"'Today' news desk," a voice answered.

"Say, this is Frank. I'm sorry I overslept. It's six o'clock, and I can't possibly get there in time for the show. Please find somebody to present the news until I can get there."

There was a pause followed by a chuckle.

"Frank, this is Bernie Brown. It's six o'clock in the evening. You're okay. Go back to sleep."

"Oh thank God!" I said. "Sorry, Bernie, I thought it was morning. Thanks a lot. Good night."

I went downstairs and made cocktails for Lil and me and we had a good laugh over my boo-boo.

We had a good dinner and visited with the family and I went back to bed and slept until 3:00 A.M., in time for me to get ready, drive to the Stamford Station, and catch the three fifty-three New Haven mail train to Grand Central Station. I got to work on time, and everybody in the newsroom thought the incident was funny. I didn't!

Our writers and craftsmen and technicians rarely goofed. But goofs, when they occurred, were likely to be dillies. Take the case of Burroughs "Buck" Prince.

When I went to "Today" I was delighted to discover that Buck was the supervising news editor because it was Buck who, years before, had befriended me in Columbia when I was with WIS and he was city editor of the Columbia *Record*. I had lost track of him when I left South Carolina. Now he was one of my coworkers in a key assignment. His hours, however, were ghastly. He reported for work at one in the morning.

Early one morning, Buck sat down at his desk and yawned. He picked up the "Today" routine sheet, a typed form summarizing the segments of the program planned for the day. It was Buck's responsibility to go over the summary and double-check the details, especially the arrangements for any portions of the program that would originate from locations other than the Exhibition Hall.

Buck read down the routine. He came to an entry for 8:14 A.M. That segment was one that would need checking. He made a note of it:

"8:14 remote from Cleveland Armory. Check traffic and engineering"—is the way Buck saw it.

Later, he dialed the NBC traffic supervisor.

"All okay for the Cleveland Armory remote?" he asked. "Lines ordered and confirmed?"

"*What* Cleveland Armory remote?" the supervisor asked. "No record of anything like that here."

"Damn it! We're coming out of the armory in Cleveland at 8:14 A.M. If you haven't got the lines in, better get them ordered right away."

"Okay."

"And call me back and confirm when done."

Buck replaced the telephone, and his worries deepened. If the lines had not been ordered, were arrangements in hand in Cleveland?

He telephoned the NBC station there.

"All set for the Cleveland Armory remote? Crew ordered? Mobile unit set up?"

"What remote?"

"Damn it! From the Cleveland Armory. At 8:14 A.M."

"Sorry. Don't know a thing about it here. Nothing's been ordered."

"Okay. Get on it right away. Get the crew up and out, alert a correspondent, and we'll need a field producer."

The Cleveland supervisor routed half a dozen staffers from their beds. They hurried to Cleveland Armory. The mobile unit was put in position and the technicians began warming up the equipment.

The supervisor called Buck.

"Okay," he said. "We're set. What's the story?"

"Damned if I know. But thanks. Stand by. We'll be in touch."

By now Buck was fuming. He muttered unkind things about his daytime colleagues for failing to order facilities and follow through on the plans.

When Mort Werner came in at five that morning, Buck pounced:

"What the hell's going on in Cleveland? Why wasn't I briefed? Why didn't you guys order up facilities?"

"What do you mean, 'What's going on in Cleveland?'?"

"Look at the routine, damn it!"

Buck picked up his routine to show Mort. His eye ran down the list again to the eight-fourteen entry.

Then he blanched.

The eight-fourteen entry read—not Cleveland Armory, but Cleveland Amory. Cleveland Amory, the author, was appearing on the show at eight-fourteen to talk about his book *The Proper Bostonians*.

The cost of Buck's goof, of getting out a crew and activating a mobile unit at 3 A.M.: twenty-one hundred dollars.

I suppose the "Today" unit managers wrote that off as part

of the cost of trying to do business at 3 A.M., when people really ought to be asleep.

I goofed, too. Not every day, perhaps, but often enough to make me constantly aware of how easy it would be to do.

The show was coming out of a remote location, an outdoor spot in Chicago, with Gerry Green in the role of managing editor. I got to the set long before air time and in that state of exhaustion that "Today" staffers are prone to at 5 A.M. I settled down next to Gerry and began writing the opening blurb for the show. The words came slowly and sluggishly, and between sentences I stared out toward Lake Michigan. When the first page was done, I passed it to Gerry to edit and approve. My lead sentence began like this:

"Here we are on the shores of beautiful Lake *Erie* . . ."

Green to Blair:

"Frank, Buddy, if your lead is true, we've got the biggest damn news story of the year."

It was exhausting work for all of us. There were emotional as well as physical strains. Muggs had helped us to build the audience, but even so, we could not be sure the show would survive. Profits still were not great, and any day Pat Weaver or someone else could give birth to another idea for early-morning programming, perhaps a show that could cost less to produce but have at least equal or nearly equal audience appeal. Among most of us there was a constant struggle to do better, and there was a seemingly endless stream of program ideas flowing from the staff to the producers. After every morning show there was a staff meeting in which Mort Werner or Gerry Green would point out the good and the bad in the program we had just aired and run down the plans for the program for the morrow.

And after that meeting we went to Toots Shor's.

Toots' clientele read something like a Who's Who of sports and show-biz celebrities and out-of-town politicians. I once ran into Richard Nixon having lunch there. Jonathan Winters dropped in often and regaled us with his impressions. Jackie Gleason came by occasionally to exchange insults with Toots. Pat O'Brien, the actor, was there whenever he was in New York, and Bob Considine was as much a regular customer as the "Today" show people. Dave and Gerry Green only rarely joined us, but for many others on the staff, going to Toots Shor's became part of the daily routine.

Toots' place was on West Fifty-first Street, only a block from 30 Rock. Theoretically, his huge circular bar opened at noon, but most of us were admitted earlier, almost immediately after our morning staff meeting. It was a way to release the tensions after our working day and to overcome the letdown feeling that often followed a show.

It was in that first year, I think, that I began developing what we now politely call a drinking problem. Oh, I wasn't alone. Others among us fell victim, too. It happened so slowly and pleasantly that I and a lot of my friends failed to recognize it. It was just fun—pleasant and refreshing.

But even in that first year, our lunches became longer and longer, lasting sometimes until late afternoon. Occasionally I would avoid going to Toots' after the show, just to prove that I could. On those days, I would go directly home, hurrying past the bars.

A few weeks after I began working in New York, a postscript developed to the story of J. Fred Muggs and the British royal family. It was a postscript that said something about brash American television and also the blows that sometimes befall American correspondents.

It had taken Romney Wheeler weeks to patch up NBC's relations with Her Majesty's Government after the appearance of Muggs on the coronation "Today" program.

The Palace press secretary had given Romney to understand that the Queen herself was displeased. He had suggested that Romney would find himself ostracized from polite society in Britain and excluded from any future functions under royal aegis unless he could promise a more seemly and dignified handling of royal news by NBC. The secretary was only casually interested when Romney tried to explain that he personally had no control over the "Today" show and could not be held accountable for programming decisions. The secretary said that such organizational details were not relevant and what he wanted was assurance that thereafter every member of the British royal family would be treated on NBC television with the dignity that befits royalty. In short, there was to be no more tomfoolery, no more links between royalty and that chimp.

Romney had only just managed to assuage the flaming tempers at Buckingham Palace when he received a cablegram from the "Today" show. The cable said:

"PLANNING WORLD TOUR FOR J. FRED MUGGS INCLUDING CEREMONIAL STOPOVER IN LONDON. PLEASE ARRANGE FOR MUGGS TO BE RECEIVED FORMALLY BY PRINCESS MARGARET."

Romney, when he recovered, replied—truthfully—that British law would require Muggs to be quarantined at port of entry for six months, just as a precaution against rabies. Britain was written off Muggs' itinerary.

The chimp did, however, go on a world tour. "Today" viewers saw him dining at a gourmet restaurant in Paris and throwing food all over the place. They saw him riding a camel in Egypt and an elephant in darkest Africa, and they saw him sleeping like a baby in his first-class seat aboard an airliner.

Even now, I don't really like to think about all this. I kept asking myself, "What in hell is a chimp doing on a news program?"

During my first spring in New York, I was given an assignment that would turn out to be as tricky as any I would ever have in forty years of broadcast journalism. I was assigned to handle the Army-McCarthy hearings.

A Senate subcommittee was investigating charges by the Army that McCarthy had tried to get special treatment for his assistant, David Schine, after Schine had been inducted into the Army. The testimony aroused intense passions all across America. Some Americans felt that the motive was to "get" McCarthy because of his campaign against "Communists" in government. Others, of course, felt that McCarthy was finally being shown up for what he truly was. The hearings were televised in their entirety, mornings and afternoons, and many a man came from work to a TV dinner because his wife had been glued to the TV screen all through the day.

It was my job to capsulize each day's hearings on the next morning's "Today" show. We used film clips to highlight the main points. Overall, I had only a few minutes to report the proceedings of an entire day.

My mail poured in like an avalanche as the hearings progressed. Many viewers praised our objectivity. But many castigated me. Some accused me of pro-McCarthy bias, and some of bias in favor of the Army. The mail had to be answered, and answering all those letters would be a nearly impossible chore.

So I devised an easy way. I put the pro-McCarthy letters in one pile and the pro-Army letters in another. I took a letter from one pile, and I wrote across it, "one of you must be wrong," and attached it to a letter from the opposing pile. I stuffed the two in an envelope for mailing, and that was that.

Generally speaking, there were about the same number of complaints in one pile as in the other. I think the lesson I learned was that some people, when they become emotionally involved in a public controversy, are going to lambaste the reporter no matter what he says.

Speaking of mail, it was ever on the increase as the years wore on, and sometimes it was difficult to keep up with it, but I was diligent in trying. I felt that anyone who wrote to me, with either a gripe or a compliment, deserved the courtesy of a reply. Also, it seemed to me that to answer a letter personally was to help create or cultivate a faithful viewer. A lot of the principals on the show didn't feel that way about it, and in later years people were hired just to answer the mail. I preferred to do it myself, and my concern about it, my determination to answer every letter I got—good or bad—became something of an office joke.

When we finished broadcasting the three hours each morning I went directly to my desk in the little cubbyhole I shared with Jack and handled my mail until we were all called into the staff meeting to criticize that day's show and get a rundown on the next day and what was coming up in the future.

One morning I was at my desk reading the mail and awaiting bumptious Mary Kelly's clarion call, "Meeting, everybody. Everybody come to the damned meeting!"

I looked up from my desk and there was Gerry Green staring over the five-foot glass partition that separated me from a hallway. Gerry has a great sense of humor, as evidenced in the many books he has written over the years—*Portofino PTA* is one that comes to mind instantly. From the first day I came on the show as a regular, Gerry always referred to me as "Reliable" or "Good Old Reliable." He said he called me that because I operated "the oldest, reliable, *floating* newsroom in all New York"—a line from *Guys and Dolls*.

He saw I was working through a pile of mail.

"Reliable," he said, "give it up. You're wasting your time. You keep this up every day and you'll miss getting to Toots Shor's when the doors open." Gerry seldom went to Toots' with the rest of us. He couldn't stand the place and didn't care much for Toots as a host. But that's another story.

I replied, "Get lost, Gerry. I'm trying to win friends and influence people, and it ain't easy sometimes with the junk you schedule for us to do."

He just laughed and went into his cubbyhole. The meeting was called, and after it I returned to my mail chores. I picked up a letter with a return address of some outlandish religious cult and signed Rev. Long Pedigree. I didn't think anything about the peculiar signature, but when I read the letter I was furious. The virulent letter berated me as a biased Roman Catholic. It said my pro-Catholic prejudice and imbecilic attempt to cover it up showed through every morning in my handling of the news. Well, if there was one thing I tried to contribute to electronic journalism it was to keep my own feelings out of my coverage of any news event—religious, political, or otherwise.

I immediately went to work on a reply.

"Yes, I was reared in the Roman Catholic faith and I try to bring up my children in that faith. Religion is important in my life, as I am sure it is in yours, but there is no place in my heart for bigotry and prejudice, and I do not allow my religious convictions or, indeed, my beliefs in other areas to influence my handling of the news. I hope you don't allow your own prejudices to influence you to a point of view that is twisted or distorted."

I was about to pull the paper out of my typewriter and sign

the letter when I became aware of Gerry again peering over my glass partition with a twinkle in his eye and a big grin on his face. I knew immediately what had happened.

"You dirty, phony bastard, Gerry Green. You wrote that letter and slipped it onto the mail pile before you came to the meeting."

He burst out laughing. "Reliable," he said, "I told you it was a waste of time."

By now, thanks largely to the exposure I was getting on the "Today" show, my name was becoming better known, and no doubt because of that, I was asked to take on another job, this one on a new NBC radio network program to be called "Monitor." It would be primarily a news and information program to be aired on Saturdays and Sundays.

Jim Fleming, the first "Today" show newscaster and editor, was named the first "Monitor" producer. NBC designed and built an elaborate studio, which they labeled "Radio Central," assembled a staff of technicians and writers, and laid out thousands of dollars for a big promotional campaign. They came up with a fancy new title for broadcasters who would anchor the shows. They would be called "communicators." Jim asked me to become a "communicator." The job would carry a big, fat fee.

I would hold forth on Saturday mornings from 8:00 A.M. to noon—kicking off the program for the weekend. That would mean a sixth day of early rising and commuting to New York from Ardsley Terrace. It would mean the best part of another day away from Lil and the kids. That disturbed me. I had the gnawing worry that I was becoming a part-time husband and father, just as I had had to be when I was in the Navy. I wondered about my sense of values. Did I have a greater obligation to the job and my bank balance than to Lil and our family, especially the boys, whom I thought needed more time with their father? The job would interfere with our weekend boating adventures, which all of us loved and I looked forward to.

Lil and I talked it over, and again her unselfishness came through. She told me to take the job if I wanted it.

Well, radio had always had a special appeal for me. It still does. I am not alone among broadcast newsmen in feeling this emotional pull. Garroway felt it; Frank McGee felt it, and his successor on "Today," Jim Hartz, who is of a newer generation, also felt it. It is not so much that most of us, even Jim, grew up in radio. I think radio's particular appeal lies in the greater freedom it allows the man on the air.

The format of a radio show is likely to be less rigid than that of a TV show. There is likely to be more scope for ad-libbing, and in some ways more opportunity for creativity. Yes, I wanted the "Monitor" job, and when Lil raised no objections, my decision was made. I told Jim Fleming I was ready to join him.

But a complication developed. The broadcasting of commercials would be a vital part of the work, and my contract with NBC at that time stipulated that I was not to do commercials anyplace, for anyone. The theory, of course, was that a newsman's image would be tarnished if he went on the air to tout a product. This was a rationale that I have never been able to accept. Did NBC or the listeners really think I would suppress or distort the news of, say, the recall of thousands of automobiles for a safety check because I was paid to broadcast the manufacturer's commercials? Would I refuse to report a drop in the Dow Jones industrial average because I owned industrial shares? Was there anyone who did not understand that broadcasting is a business and that the money for newsmen's salaries originates with the manufacturer whose products are promoted on the air? I wondered if the broadcast executives who insisted, so publicly and sanctimoniously, on separating newsmen and commercials are not insulting the intelligence of the viewers.

I was not about to promote a product I had no confidence in. But it seemed irrelevant to me whether it was I who read a commercial or someone seated at my side, waiting to interrupt me midway in the news.

There was something beautifully absurd about the dilemma that Jim Fleming and I faced when I told him I would take the "Monitor" assignment. NBC badly wanted me to do the "Monitor" commercials, but also NBC couldn't let me. The issue was resolved by bringing in a second communicator, Don Russell, who was not contractually committed as I was.

So I became one of "Monitor's" first "communicators." I broadcast the first in the series of "Monitor" programs that would go on for almost two decades.

At noon each Saturday I was relieved by a bright, likable young man who had just come to New York from Chicago to do NBC-TV's "Home Show" with Arlene Francis. His name was Hugh Downs.

By 1954, the "Today" show was over the hump and showing a profit. It seemed incredible to some of us, but there were actually people out there—millions of them—who would and did watch television at seven in the morning. Our audience was growing, our commercial rates were going up, and we were now a show that the money men in other networks might look upon with envy.

It was at this time that CBS tried to break into the field. The CBS executives put Jack Paar on opposite "Today." I never got to see the show myself. I was too busy doing my own air work. However, others told me it was a light, fast-moving show, glib in the Paar manner. Charles Collingwood handled the newscasts. That, at least, spoke well for the program. Charles was one of the most talented newsmen in the field. Carol Reed, a local TV personality, did the weather forecasts. A lot of money and a lot of planning obviously went into that show, but somehow it never took off. We were too firmly entrenched. A year or so later, CBS would go another route with Walter Cronkite hosting "The Morning Show," whose format would be much closer to "Today's." And then in 1956, CBS would change its approach again with the "The Good Morning Show," starring Will Rogers, Jr., who had once subbed for Garroway on "Today" when Dave went on a vacation. That, too, would go off the air after little more than a year.

We had mixed feelings about our opposition. We enjoyed our own successes, but we welcomed any rival program that would get more people into the habit of tuning in between seven and nine.

The only opposition program that would ever really concern us was "Captain Kangaroo," which would later come on CBS from 8 to 9 A.M. The captain became a baby sitter to much of the nation, easing the morning rush for many overworked young mothers.

We too always tried to fashion programs that would appeal to the very young as well as to their parents. Sometimes we made these efforts with the help of our own children.

In 1954, when the Christmas season was approaching, the show needed a fresh idea for a Christmas morning program—something "warm and human, with a strong Christmas slant."

"Frank," Gerry Green said, "let's do a live remote from

your living room. You and Lil and the kids around the tree opening presents."

Lil agreed, and the plans were laid. The word spread through our neighborhood. Ardsley Terrace and the entire Blair family would be on television on Christmas morning! Even some of the adults were excited.

In the early-morning darkness of December 25, the big NBC mobile unit rolled up in front of our house with lights blazing. Stagehands, audio engineers, and lighting engineers poured into the street. Inside, a technician nursed the generator and a deep hum reverberated through the neighborhood. All along Ardsley Terrace, lights blinked on in bedrooms. Adults and children appeared at windows to watch.

The horde poured into Lil's living room, tracking mud. Jac Hein, the director, stood back and studied the furniture arrangement, and then he had everything there moved to allow for better camera shots.

At 5:30 A.M., one and a half hours before the show would go on the air, the Blair children were summoned from their bedrooms.

Jac stopped them outside the living room. He kept them huddled on the stairway in the center hall, all seven of them. He planned his opening shot.

Six o'clock came. One hour to air.

"Better stay right there, kids," he told the children.

Jac was an imaginative director with a lightning-fast mind, but he believed in playing it safe when he could. He had those kids where he wanted them, and he wanted them to stay there. Above all, he wanted to be sure they got no premature glimpse of the Christmas presents in the living room. One of his best shots would be the look of excitement on their faces when they first saw the tree and the presents. A premature look could rob their faces of the glow he wanted at air time. It was a shot he could not risk spoiling.

The kids sat there on the steps fidgeting for another sixty minutes. There was much to watch—lights being set up, cables laid, microphones tested—but even so, they built up a lot of impatience.

The show came on the air.

"Cue the children!" Jac ordered from the mobile unit.

There were some superb shots as the kids dashed into the living room and began opening their presents.

Our ratings could not have been better in Ardsley Terrace that morning. Every television set on the street was tuned to the "Today" show and the Blairs' living room.

When it was all over, someone switched off the generator in the mobile unit and we served breakfast for all hands, children included.

Sometimes even an old trooper, as I was now getting to be, can feel a flicker of embarrassment in front of a live television camera. I had such a moment when Lee Meriwether first came on the "Today" show. Lee was not then the TV star she is now. She was a guest on "Today" because she had just won the Miss America beauty contest. This was in 1954.

Lee captivated us all. She was beautiful and charming, her manners were impeccable, and she had a sort of childlike naïveté.

Dave Garroway interviewed her, and as the interview progressed, Dave got to the inevitable question.

"Are you planning to marry?"

"Someday."

"Anyone in mind?"

"No. But . . ."

She paused. There was just a moment of suspense. Then she went on:

"But when I do marry, I hope it will be to someone like Frank Blair."

The camera panned to me alongside the news desk, and I stood there with a silly grin on my face.

Later, I found that Mary Kelly in her role as associate producer had planted the question and briefed Lee on the answer.

Lee carried it off beautifully. In fact, her performance was so expert all through the show that, when it was over, she was quietly offered a job as our "Today" girl.

The following summer, NBC spent a small fortune on a publicity buildup about a mystery girl who would soon join the "Today" cast.

In the newspaper ads and press releases she was billed as "The Girl in the Gray Flannel Suit," a takeoff on Sloan Wilson's best-selling novel of that era, *The Man in the Gray Flannel Suit*. She was shown only in silhouette. No one could possibly recognize her. The publicity campaign created a buzz of excitement around the country. Our ratings must have been at a peak on the morning she was finally introduced to "Today" viewers.

Lee came very close to stardom on "Today." There was something magic about her and her innocence that the viewers loved. I adored her, too, and so did the rest of the cast and the crew. Inside the studio in the early-morning hours before the show would go on the air, Lee worked around as many as forty-two men, some of them short-tempered and many of them crude and temperamental. But I don't think any of them ever uttered a vulgar or profane word while she was around, and insofar as I am aware, none ever made a pass at her.

Her innocence and modesty were classic.

We did a show at a country club in Westchester County, just outside New York. It was basically a fashion show of summer styles. A swimming pool would be the backdrop for the modeling of swimwear. The minibikini had not yet appeared. If it had, it would not have been shown on television.

Gerry Green asked Lee to pose in a bathing suit.

A faint blush spread over her cheeks.

"I won't do it," she said.

Gerry accepted her edict. He had to.

Jane Mansfield—she of the legendary bosom—was a guest on the show with us that day.

"Jane," Gerry said, "would you wear a swimsuit for us?"

"Why, of course."

Lee was already in the ladies' room when Jane arrived to change.

Jane disrobed and, in the nude, bent over to step into her swimsuit.

Years later, Lee confessed:

"I looked at her, those great bosoms dangling, and I was afraid she would lose her balance and topple over!"

When Lee finally left the show, there was a farewell party for her, and it was one of the few occasions that brought Dave Garroway to Toots Shor's. Dave proposed the toast:

"To a lady."

Lee certainly was that—a beautiful lady.

She went to California and married Frank Aletter, a young actor. I received an announcement when she had her first baby, and on it Lee, as naïve as ever, had penned a personal note:

"While I was in the hospital, nursing the baby and watching the show on TV, I had pleasant thoughts of you. Love, Lee."

Lil read it and asked:

"What did she mean by that?"

"I have no idea," I said.

Four o'clock in the morning is one lousy time to go on the air with a live television show. Especially the "Today" show.

Ordinarily, the celebrities you want to interview—politicians, authors, entertainers—are more than eager for the exposure on national TV, but I have yet to meet one who wasn't momentarily taken aback at the thought of rising before 4:00 A.M. Furthermore, it's hard to be bright at that unearthly hour, even when you have a nationwide audience and a rare opportunity to promote your book or your career.

The "Today" show broadcast started at 4:00 A.M. during the Republican National Convention in San Francisco in 1956. There was still no videotape then. We had to go live. We had to be on the air at seven in the morning Eastern Daylight Savings Time, and of course seven in the East was four in San Francisco—a time when most people are bleary-eyed.

I walked into the "Today" show office in the Fairmont Hotel on the opening day of the convention—it looked like a newspaper city room, with writers pounding at typewriters, messengers scurrying, telephones ringing. Gerry Green, now our producer, looked up from his cluttered desk.

"Hello, Reliable," he said, and without pausing for breath he went on:

"I want you to get Dick Nixon in here to go on the air with us tomorrow morning at four-ten."

I stared at him.

Dick Nixon was the Vice President of the United States.

"Gerry! You're asking me to get the Vice President out of bed at three-thirty in the morning?"

Gerry gave me a questioning look.

"Yes. So?"

Sometimes I think producers and editors are men without hearts and souls.

"So," I said, "that's one hell of an assignment."

Gerry wasn't much interested. He had other problems.

"Yeah," he said.

He turned back to his work. He was editing copy.

Nixon was up for renomination, but he had it in the bag. He had no immediate, compelling reason to appear on the "Today" show.

"Gerry," I said, "we've got to be realistic about this. I'll be lucky if I can even get Nixon on film."

By now, Gerry had turned his attention to the routine sheet for our next program.

"Okay," he said absently. "Okay, get him on film."

It was five o'clock in the afternoon. Gerry was giving me only a few hours to get next to the Vice President of the United States and induce him to find time for an exclusive interview. Eleven hours remained before the interview would be aired, but in that time frame I would also have to get the film developed and edited.

As I left the office, Gerry looked up. He called out:

"Remember, Reliable, I'm slotting the Nixon interview for the first half hour. Right after the news."

I nodded and left. I hadn't much hope.

Nixon, I knew, was across the street at the Mark Hopkins Hotel right at that moment. He was speaking at a rally of young Republicans.

I walked over. As I entered, the Vice President was in the midst of a fiery speech, and his audience was interrupting him every few moments with bursts of applause.

I wormed my way through the crowd to the front row. I stood just under the podium, waiting.

Nixon glanced my way and recognized me. He had a politician's memory for names and faces and a politician's appreciation of the power of the media. He paused in his speech.

"Hi, Frank," he said. "How are you?"

I smiled, and Nixon went on with his remarks.

I had arranged for Richard Nixon to appear on "The Georgetown Forum" frequently during his years as a young congressman and senator, and I am sure that, as any ambitious politician would, he had appreciated the exposure. Since those days he had made it a point to be friendly with me. Lil and I had often met him and Mrs. Nixon at cocktail parties and embassy receptions in Washington.

When he finished haranguing the young Republicans, I did not wait for the applause to subside. I stepped up to the podium and grabbed him. I suppose the Secret Service could have opened fire! However, the agents had heard Nixon interrupt his speech to say hello, and presumably they had recognized me, anyway, as a newsman with due accreditation.

The ovation was still thundering through the hall. I had to shout in Nixon's ear.

"Mr. Vice President," I said, "I'm in a hell of a spot. I've got to interview you, and I've got to have the film ready for broadcast at four o'clock in the morning!"

"Well, I'd like to do it for you, but—"

Sometimes one must interrupt even a Vice President of the United States. I hoped that, in the din, Nixon would think I hadn't heard his "but."

"You're my big assignment," I shouted, "and I've got to pull this thing off or my name is gonna be mud!"

I thought I saw a genuine concern in his eyes.

But he shook his head.

"When I leave here I've got a dinner to go to," he said, "and Pat and I will have to be back at the hotel to change our clothes and go on to a couple more affairs. My whole evening is tied up. I honestly don't know what I can do for you."

The Secret Service agents were beginning discreetly to clear a path for him to the door.

"Well," I said, "how long do you figure it's going to take you to change clothes?"

"Oh, maybe thirty minutes."

"Look, if I can have a camera crew at your suite, all set up and ready to roll, and you've got your tux on and Mrs. Nixon is still dressing—hell, women are always slower than men—would you sit down with me for five minutes? Ten at the most?"

He thought for a moment.

"Well, I won't promise. But you have a crew there and ready and I'll do what I can."

We shook hands and parted, and I sent out an emergency call for a camera crew.

The cameramen and I were seated in the lavish splendor of the vice-presidential suite in the Mark Hopkins Hotel, with lights blazing and the camera ready to roll, when the Nixons got back from their formal dinner. Nixon, of course, was in white tie and tails, and Mrs. Nixon was in a long, formal dress.

We exchanged greetings. I was on edge. I hurried through the formalities. I didn't want to detain them even for a moment. Nixon sensed my anxieties.

"Frank," he said, "I'll hurry. I really will."

They went on to their bedrooms and I sat there, sweating it out. If Nixon could give me only a few minutes, it would be a coup. If he couldn't oblige, I would look like something less than a resourceful newsman. And if I *did* goof on this assignment, there would be a big hole in the routine for the next morning's show.

The minutes ticked away and finally Nixon came out of his bedroom.

"Okay, Frank," he said. "Ten minutes? No more!"

"I promise," I said.

We sat down in front of the camera.

"Roll it!" I said, and Nixon began answering my questions.

He was in a mood to talk. My ten minutes passed, and he went on talking. He wouldn't shut up. We were still chatting and the camera was still whirring when Mrs. Nixon came out of her bedroom.

To me, Pat Nixon has always been an attractive woman. Now she looked positively glamorous. I thought how good it would be to have her on film along with the VP.

We stopped the camera and I stood up.

"Ma'am," I said, "you look lovely."

"Thank you, Frank."

"Wouldn't you sit down for just a moment and answer a question or two for me?"

"Why, yes, Frank," she said. "Of course."

She took a seat next to her husband. The camera rolled again and we talked of many things—the excitement of the convention, the Nixons' children, her life as the Vice President's wife. I had far exceeded my allotted time, but neither of the Nixons seemed in any hurry to stop talking.

When the interview finally ended, I had twenty minutes of film in the can—more than enough for Gerry's program hole.

"Thank you, ma'am," I said, "and thank you, Mr. Vice President."

Those were not empty words. My gratitude was very real.

We shook hands and the Nixons left.

And, while the crew was packing up, I personally delivered that can of film to Gerry Green.

Gerry was at his desk, still working. I tossed the can in front of him.

"There's your damned interview with Richard Nixon!"

Gerry looked up, startled.

"And," I went on, "there's an interview there with Pat Nixon, too, for good measure!"

Sure I was gloating. He had asked for the impossible and gotten it.

"And," I said, "if that doesn't get on the air tomorrow morning right on schedule, if you squeeze it out in some silly, last-minute programming change, you're going to have my resignation!"

I turned and walked toward the door.

"Reliable!" Gerry called out.

I looked back. He was smiling.

"Nice work. That's why I call you 'Reliable.'"

I felt good.

I had a rare privilege in those times with former President Harry Truman.

The show was in Kansas City. Our regional correspondent there, Randall Jessee, and his wife invited the Trumans to dinner along with Gerry Green, Dave Garroway, and me. Thomas Hart Benton, the mural artist, was there as well with Mrs. Benton. The men of the party left the ladies in the living room and went off to Randall's den for drinks. The former President liked Bourbon on the rocks with a splash of water, and he had several.

When we sat down to dinner I was seated at the President's left, Mrs. Truman at his right.

We asked him many questions, all off the record, and he gave candid answers. At one point I said:

"Mr. President, one of the great controversies that was raised during your Administration was the firing of General MacArthur. If you had to do it over again, would you go through with it?"

"Frank," he said, "yes, I would. I felt that MacArthur had overstepped his authority and had created a dynasty for himself in Japan, and I thought he'd been away long enough and he ought to come home so he could see what us Democrats had been doing while he was away."

When dinner was over and the evening was drawing to an end, the former President announced that he'd have to be leaving, that he had to drive back to Independence. I think he, too, had enjoyed the evening.

Randall asked him if he wouldn't like one drink for the road.

Truman replied, "Randall, my boy, there are still a lot of people in this country who would like to pick up their morning newspapers and read where Harry Truman had driven up a telephone pole and had been charged with 'driving while drunk.' Bess, let's be going. Good night and thank you."

Later I learned that the reason he knew my name so well was that the man who loaned him the money to start his haberdashery store in Kansas City was named Frank Balir, and a few weeks later I received a copy of his *Memoirs* autographed to me:

With kindest regards to Frank Blair, whose name reminds me of the greatest country banker I ever knew.

HARRY TRUMAN

I was honored and flattered, indeed.

Helen O'Connell joined our "Today" troupe when Lee Meriwether left and, in her, all of us on the show gained a new drinking companion, although hardly one with a problem.

I had first met Helen in 1941, when she and Bob Eberle were singing with Jimmy Dorsey's Orchestra, and it fell to me to announce the program, as a Coca-Cola Spotlight Band, to Mutual radio audiences from the stage of the Earle Theater in Washington. When I had first met her, I was smitten. She was adorable. I don't think any man of my generation ever saw Helen on the stage without feeling that same thrill of admiration. I went home to Lil after that evening at the Earle and told her, teasingly, that I had just met the only girl in the world who was as beautiful as she. I next saw Helen again when she became our "Today" girl, fifteen years later.

Helen moved to New York from Hollywood with her three daughters—Jackie, who was then twelve, Joanie, nine, and Jenny, eight. She put the girls into Marymount School on Fifth Avenue and rented a house in New Hyde Park on Long Island. Later, finding the early-morning drive to New York too tedious, she took an apartment on East Sixty-sixth Street in the city.

On her first day on the show, Jack Lescoulie and I took Helen to lunch at Toots Shor's, and that started a lasting relationship. I am frank to say that I developed a crush on Helen. It was hard not to. I worked with her every day, breakfasted with her often, lunched with her often, frequently traveled with her, and sometimes Lil and I entertained her at home. There were people on the show who suggested that the relationship between Helen and me was something more than a friendly one. That, however, was a scurrilous rumor of the kind that I suppose is inevitable when an attractive woman is seen often in the company of the same man. Lil liked Helen as much as I did. They became good friends.

Someone—a brash reporter, I think—once asked Lil if she was concerned about Helen and her friendship with me. Her reply was one I shall never forget. It warmed my heart and enhanced my admiration, if that is possible, for a great human being confident of herself and the enduring love of her family. She replied, and without rancor: "No. I am always proud when an attractive woman is drawn to Frank. If other women didn't find him attractive, why would I?" I don't know if Helen found *me* attractive, but certainly we spent a lot of time together, and she gave me memories that I cherish.

Just after she joined the "Today" cast, she and Jack Lescoulie and I were having breakfast after a particularly difficult three-hour session of the show that originated from the Americana Hotel in Miami Beach. The waitress appeared to take our order.

"Coffee, please," Helen said. "And with brandy."

Jack turned to me.

"I think we've found the right girl!" he said.

Helen, thank goodness, was with me in front of the cameras on the morning of my most difficult "Today" show assignment.

The story began when Lil and I traded in our small boat, *Honey B*, for a thirty-six-foot Wheeler twin-screw, with two heads, a shower, and a complete galley. We called it *Pax*, for peace, and that summer during my vacation we cruised up the Hudson River and through the thirteen locks on the New York State Canal to Lake Champlain.

While we were tied up at an abandoned pier on an estuary of the lake, we took a walk through the woods along the deserted shore. It was a beautiful summer afternoon and a romantic setting. We made love there under the trees along the shoreline. And Lil became pregnant.

It was just nine months later that I was to make my debut as host of the "Today" show. Dave had taken over as communicator of a new Pat Weaver show called "Wide Wide World," which aired on Sunday afternoons, and he had written into his new contract a stipulation that because of his work on Sundays he would be free from duty on "Today" on Monday mornings. Meanwhile, Jack Lescoulie had left "Today" entirely, to replace Steve Allen as host of another program called "America After Dark." On my own suggestion, Jack, too, had had a special clause written into his revised NBC contract: If "America After Dark" failed, he could return to the "Today" show.

My own contract was amended so I could do commercials on Monday mornings, and on other mornings as well, and arrangements were made for Dick McCutcheon and others in the stable of NBC newsmen to handle the Monday-morning newscasts.

The morning of Monday, April 29, 1957, would be my first day as host. Helen would be in the role of second banana. I had hosted innumerable morning radio programs, of course, in South Carolina and Washington, and I was still doing my four-hour stint on Saturday mornings as "communicator" on "Monitor" on the NBC radio network. But still I had never handled an entire "Today" show as host, and I wanted to prove to myself and NBC that I could do the job successfully.

I slept fitfully on the night of April 28. My alarm rang at three o'clock in the morning. I wanted to be early that day, to run down the routine again and study any last-minute programming changes.

I was shaving and steeling myself for the drive to New York when Lil called to me from our bedroom.

Her labor pains had begun.

Well, I had gone through the business of childbirth seven times, the first time twenty years before, and one might have expected me to be a steel-nerved veteran by now, a casual, carefree father who, when informed that labor had started, would smile benignly and place a tender, loving kiss on his wife's forehead.

Instead, I dropped my shaving brush.

Lil was in labor on the morning of my debut! How could I sit there in front of a microphone and concentrate on my job, not knowing what was going on in a maternity ward?

I got to the telephone and called the doctor.

"Better get her to the hospital right away," he said. "After all, it's her eighth child. The baby could come quickly."

My God!

Lil got herself ready to leave. We were careful not to disturb the sleeping household.

I drove Lil to Phelps Memorial Hospital in Tarrytown, the next town north of Irvington.

Her pains were still well spaced. After the nurses settled her in the maternity ward, Lil insisted that I hurry to my job. The show had to go on. Neither Dave nor Jack would be there, and it would be unfair to Helen to ask her to handle an entire program without help. Among other things, she lacked the experience. At that time, the role of "Today" girls was strictly limited. In any event, as Lil said, smiling, there was not much I could do at Phelps Memorial, and I could keep in touch with her and the doctor by telephone.

I broke the speed limit getting to 30 Rockefeller Plaza. I wanted time to study the material and, if possible, steady my nerves.

Helen greeted me on the set. When I told her the news, she calmed me with assurances that all would be well.

We had been on the air about half an hour, and I think I had successfully hidden my anxieties, when Freddy Lights, our stage manager, slipped me a message that someone had taken down by telephone from the Phelps Memorial delivery room.

"Your wife has given birth to a daughter. Mother and little girl doing well."

What a relief!

The word spread throughout the studio and Freddy came up during a commercial and handed me a big cigar. I never smoke cigars—but I lit up then, there on the set, and proudly announced the birth of our new daughter.

Back in Irvington, life was only just beginning to stir. Virginia, our maid, came downstairs, made a pot of coffee, and switched on the "Today" program.

She had missed my announcement, but she saw me smoking a cigar.

"My Lordee!" she squealed with delight.

She ran to Lil's bedroom and peeked in and found it empty, and that confirmed Virginia's guess. She ran from bedroom to bedroom awakening children and shouting:

"Baby's come! Baby's come!"

"Is it a boy or a girl?" an older child asked.

Virginia didn't know. She had to call Phelps Memorial to find out.

That was the longest "Today" show I was ever on, but thanks to Helen O'Connell and the discipline developed through the years, I got through it, finally, and then hurried to the hospital to see Lil and meet our new daughter, whom we named Patricia.

Shortly thereafter life changed for Helen.

Tom Chamales, a young author, appeared on the show. He had just written a best-selling war novel, *Never So Few*, which later was made into a successful motion picture. After the show, it was Tom who took Helen to breakfast at Hurley's. And later in the day, when I stopped by at Toots Shor's, Tom and Helen were there having lunch.

Three weeks later I went to their wedding. The union was not blessed by the Church. It was in the penthouse of one of the plush hotels on Central Park South. James Jones, whose war novels Tom had admired, was his best man.

After that, Helen was never quite the same on the "Today" show. Problems developed. Tom was insanely jealous, and her old friendships had to be dropped. Then she became pregnant, and the NBC brass chose to replace her. Later, Tom died in a fire in his apartment. Helen has never remarried. She went back to her career, one of the great popular singers and a favorite still after more than thirty-five years.

In radio, as in television, one never knows. Well-received shows can be taken off the air on a moment's notice, and sometimes without notice to the on-air personalities. Edwin Newman once went to the NBC studios to do another program in one of his long-running series, and learned only then that the series had been canceled. Other people had learned of the cancellation of their shows by a casual reading of *Variety*, the show-business newspaper.

One day Al Capstaff, vice president for radio, invited Don Russell, my sidekick, and me to a luncheon in the Rainbow Grill, atop the RCA Building.

"I like your 'Monitor,'" he said, when we were seated. "I like it very, very much!"

What beautiful language!

I was still waiting for Al's "but." It never came.

"I like your show enough," Al went on, "to ask you to produce a show of your own. You produce it together and of course you host it together."

So we're not getting fired.

"What we want you to do," Al said, "is to put on a radio show five days a week, from noon to two o'clock in the afternoon."

We waited.

"Frank," he said, "it need not interfere with the 'Today' show, and of course we cannot let it interfere with your work on 'Monitor.'"

I sipped my martini.

"Of course not," I said. "Of course not."

The show would be a combination of talk—of Don and I ad-libbing on subjects of our choice—and celebrity interviews and music. It would be called "Network Time."

I was not eager for the job until Al mentioned the money.

We were to get $6,500 a week to produce the show, and NBC would throw in, at no cost to us, Skitch Henderson and the NBC Orchestra.

Sixty-five hundred dollars a week, from which we would meet only production, talent, and staff costs.

For once in my life I did not consult Lil before making a major decision.

I told Al, and Don did too, that we found his offer challenging—and entirely acceptable.

"Network Time" was a success from the day it went on the air. A principal reason, I think, was a young lady named Lenny Epstein.

I don't know what the "Lenny" stood for, and I don't know what ever happened to her, but if I were ever again asked to produce a show along the lines of "Network Time" I would search the world for Lenny Epstein. Her job was to get celebrities who would come to the studio and be interviewed. The list of "Network Time" guests came to read like a Who's Who of the entertainment and literary world. Lenny could turn up almost anyone at any time. We had the great stars of the time.

Early in the life of "Network Time" Don and I began taking notice of a young trumpet player in the NBC Orchestra. He was a witty and personable young man who affected a country-cousin accent and who constantly came through with entertainingly funny wisecracks. He couldn't be heard on "Network Time"—he was off-mike. But Don and I concluded that he should have a mike while we were on air. His cracks were too good to be lost. We ordered a mike for him and paid him AFTRA scale—thirty-two dollars a show, as I recall it—to wisecrack when the mood struck him. His thirty-two dollars was not much, perhaps, but it was "Network Time" that helped start Doc Severinsen on the road to fame.

We hired vocalists, too—Jack Haskell, June Valli, and Pat Suzuki, among others. Don and I were especially impressed by one young singer who sometimes came aboard. He had a fine voice and a beautifully relaxed and amiable personality. His name was Merv Griffin.

Merv, too, began chattering with us while we were on the air, and a brand-new theme appeared in our fan mail. The listeners wanted more of him. He became a regular on the show, and when I went off on a two-week vacation, I arranged for Merv to sit in for me. There came a time when I almost wished I hadn't.

Lil and I spent that vacation on our boat, and we were far out on Long Island Sound, near Montauk Point. I was stretched out in a lounge chair on deck with a drink in my hand and a radio set at my side. I was tuned in to WNBC, and "Network Time" was on the air. Don and Merv were chattering.

The sun was warm, the drink was good, and some of the tensions were flowing out of my body. My thoughts were of the beauty of the Sound and the delicious sirloin steak we were to have for dinner. I was listening to Don and Merv, but only with half an ear.

But as the show progressed, extraneous thoughts flowed right out of my mind. I sat up and began listening closely.

The reason was Merv.

As a substitute for Blair, Griffin was brilliant. He was too damned brilliant. Too glib, too personable.

I wondered if I would still have a job on network radio when I got back. I thought NBC would be silly not to fire me and hire this personable young singer.

As it happened, I need not have worried. Al Capstaff telephoned one day and advised that "Network Time" would be taken off the air after its thirty-ninth week.

The reason was that the affiliates were saying there was too much talk on the show and not enough music. I think history has shown how wrong they were. In the years that followed, great numbers of listeners would complain that "radio doesn't talk to me anymore." Talk shows would grow in popularity, and shows like "Network Time," with a mixed format, would be hits in many localities. Arthur Godfrey's show on the CBS radio network, also a combination of talk and music, would remain on the air for years.

Perhaps the real, underlying reason for "Network Time's" short life was the deep change that was taking place in the radio industry. The movement away from the networks was growing. More and more stations were assuming that a good local disc jockey and some good phonograph records could produce better profits than network shows. Perhaps those sixty-five hundred dollars a week we had been drawing to produce "Network Time" was symptomatic of something wrong in the networks; perhaps it was more than the traffic could bear. Perhaps, also, Don Russell and I were simply not as good as we thought.

On October 9, 1958, word was flashed around the world that Pope Pius XII had died at his summer residence at Castel Gandolfo, outside of Rome.

Bob Bendick, who had returned from California and had again become producer of "Today" his second time around, dispatched "Today" writer Maury Robinson and me to Rome to cover the funeral and the election of the new Pope. We would be working with Joe Michaels, "Today's" reporter at large for several years, who was now the NBC correspondent in Rome.

We checked in at the Majestic Hotel on the Via Veneto, and when we went on to the Vatican, we ran into a major problem. We were told our movements would be restricted— we were to have access only to the public rooms, and, incredible to us, we would not be permitted to use our own camera crews. Any film we wanted would have to be bought through the official Vatican cameraman.

I got on the telephone and called the man in charge, Count Pietro Enrico Galeazzi. Luckily for me, the count spoke English. He agreed to see me.

The count's office was in a building that had the aura of a big-city police station in America. I felt ill at ease as soon as I entered. The building, also, was the barracks for the Swiss Guard, and guardsmen dressed in historic costume of orange and blue pantaloons and *conquistador*-type headgear were coming and going, carrying spears and jabbering in Italian, which of course I could not understand.

In Galeazzi's private office, the atmosphere was totally different. The room was like something out of a museum. Galeazzi was seated behind a huge carved mahogany desk.

I was instantly aware that I would be dealing with a hard and unbending human being. He was austere and haughty, and his eyes were as cold as his smile. I decided on a frontal attack.

"Sir," I said, after a perfunctory exchange of greetings, "is it true that you're proposing to ban independent camera crews?"

"Yes."

"But I can't do my job without film. I don't speak Italian, and I can't work with a cameraman when I can't even communicate with him. I can't operate like that."

The count mumbled something about the Vatican cameramen being very "efficient."

"But I have to have quality coverage, and I simply cannot work with a crew that doesn't understand our specific needs and desires."

It was like talking to a stone wall.

I think I spent twenty minutes talking to that scoundrel, and I got nowhere at all. He wouldn't budge. He insisted that only official Vatican film could be shot, and he said I could have it—at a price.

I had heard stories about the Vatican press office. There were rumors that some of the laypeople handling press arrangements for the Vatican were money-hungry and sometimes even on the take.

I told the count I would be in touch.

I went back to the Majestic deflated and demoralized.

I had been sent to Rome to cover a major story, and now I

was being told, in effect, that I couldn't cover it properly. "Today" people back in New York would have only a casual interest in my explanation. Their interest would be in results, not excuses.

The telephone rang in my hotel room while I sat there brooding. It was Monsignor (later Bishop) Edwin Broderick, aide to Cardinal Spellman. The cardinal, of course, was in Rome for the funeral and the election, and Monsignor Broderick was with him. I had known Broderick in the past. I had called on him occasionally for information about news stories, and we had a rapport.

"Frank," he said, "I've got a problem, and maybe you can help me solve it."

"What's the problem?"

"Well, His Eminence was supposed to make a speech at a big Knights of Columbus rally in Yankee Stadium. But he has to be here. He can't make it. Is there anything that can be done?"

Obviously, he wanted to know whether somehow the cardinal's speech could be taped or perhaps broadcast live in some way.

"Sure," I told him. "I'll come over with my tape recorder. We'll record the cardinal's message. I'll ship the tape back to NBC in New York, and I'll call first to be sure that it's properly handled when it arrives. It can be put on the public-address system at Yankee Stadium."

"Great, Frank! I'll call you back. I'll talk to His Eminence right away."

A few minutes later, Monsignor Broderick called back. The cardinal had set aside a time for the taping.

I checked over my tape recorder to make sure I had plenty of tape, and I reported to the cardinal's suite in the North American College precisely at the appointed hour.

The cardinal, very gracious and charming, rose to greet me. When he was ready, I started the tape recorder, and His Eminence made his speech. When he finished, I played it back for him. It was obvious that he liked what he had said. He seemed proud of himself. He acted, for a moment, more like a child than a prince of the Church.

I assured him I would make iron-clad arrangements with NBC to accept the shipment of tape and deliver it to the right people in the cardinal's office at St. Patrick's.

"Thank you, Frank," he said.

He waited for a fraction of a moment, and then added:

"And now, is there anything I can do for you?"

I seized my opportunity.

"Your Eminence," I said, "there *is* something you may wish to do. These people here at the Vatican press office are giving me a hard time. I wanted to send back to our country film stories that catch the full meaning of the death of a Pope and the choice of his successor. I wanted to capture the flavor and mystique of the Vatican and the importance of the change in the papacy. But I have to do it my way. I can't rely on handout film. I can't even communicate with the Vatican cameraman. He doesn't speak my language. Furthermore, I am being told that I can have only limited access to the Vatican. If I'm going to do this job right, I've got to have some freedom of movement here. Is there anything you can do?"

The cardinal smiled.

"Is that all you want?" he asked.

"I think I'm asking a lot."

"It is not a problem."

He reached for his stationery, with his crest printed at the top, and he wrote out a message—I forget the precise language. It was just a short note, but to me it became a precious possession.

It specified that I as a representative of the National Broadcasting Company was to be granted every privilege at the Vatican and allowed to do what I wanted to do and go where I wanted to go.

I thanked the cardinal and left.

That note became a thing of magic for Maury and me. It opened every Vatican door. When I flashed it at the gates, the Swiss Guard always waved us on. It won us a regular parking space for our rented car. It got us into the Sistine Chapel to do a film story on the carpenters erecting the thrones the cardinals would occupy during the papal election. It got me a front seat at the papal funeral itself. And it even got my camera crew and me into the labyrinths of the cathedral, to the tomb of St. Peter, where we filmed a spot for "Today."

We were sorely disappointed when, just after the funeral, we were called back to New York. The powers on "Today" sent commendations for our work, but they said we were more needed in the studio. Joe Michaels, Merrill Mueller, and Joseph C. Harsch would cover the election itself.

When the white smoke issued from the Vatican chimney signaling to the world that the College of Cardinals had elected a new Pope, John XXIII, I was back in New York anchoring the "Today" news from 30 Rockefeller Plaza. I saw it on television.

XX

In THOSE EARLY DAYS we often had guest hosts who would sit in when Dave was away, and some of them were women. I don't mean to sound chauvinistic, but in one or two cases, that was a problem. They were women.

There were many exceptions, of course. Arlene Francis, a good and gracious hostess, did the job admirably. Faye Emerson, an early TV star and a former wife of Elliot Roosevelt, did well. She was charming and beautiful. She had one failing, if it was a failing, and it was a weird one for anyone doing a live television show. She had a tendency toward "spoonerisms"—that is, the inadvertent transposing of consonants in a word or phrase. When Faye introduced me, she sometimes said:

"Now, here's Flank Brair with the news."

"Thank you, May Femerson," I would reply.

Actress Robin Chandler was with us frequently, too. She was then the wife of Geoffrey Lynn, the actor. Later she married Angier Biddle Duke, who was head of protocol for the State Department.

Betsy Palmer replaced Helen O'Connell. Betsy in a way was like Lee Meriwether. There was a touch of delightful naïveté about her.

One morning on the show she asked Lescoulie, after his

Fearless Forecast of weekend sports results, whether he himself had taken part in any sports when in college.

"Yes, Betsy, I played some football and some basketball."

Betsy replied, "That's strange. I always thought of you as a broad jumper."

Her inflection was unfortunate. Her accent was on "broad."

Jack did one of his famous double takes, and there was some uncontrolled laughter from the studio crew.

Betsy stayed with us only a short time. She felt the hours interfered with her marriage. Her husband was a well-known obstetrician.

After Betsy, our "Today" girl was Florence Henderson, who brought a rare sparkle and a considerable singing talent to the show. Florence, too, however, was happily married and rather more interested in her home life than in the "Today" program. We didn't know it at the time, but when she joined us she was pregnant. It seems almost unbelievable now, but pregnancy was not something we talked much about on television in those days.

As time passed, and Florence's pregnancy began to show, the "Today" directors went to great lengths to conceal her tummy from the viewers. Always she was kept behind a table or a desk. On one outdoor remote, she was posed behind a hedge wall. Florence was proud and happy in her pregnancy, and she didn't like being camouflaged. She was also at times a very outspoken human being.

There came a morning when she had had enough.

While our millions of viewers watched, she stood up, walked out in front of her desk, and displayed her swollen figure.

"Look," she said, "I'm pregnant, and I'm very happy about it."

She may have been the first woman to use the word "pregnant" on American television.

She left the show at the end of May 1960, and her son Joseph arrived on June 27. Weeks later we had her back on the show as a guest, and she looked positively radiant.

A few short weeks before Dave left the show, I had received an ultimatum from NBC.

I had been quietly forewarned about it by John Ghilain who was to be given the imposing title, "senior administrator of new talent and program negotiations." Simplified, that meant that John was the chief negotiator of contracts with "talent," as we were called—the newsmen and other people actually seen on the air. John, of course, was very much a company man, but he was also one of the best friends I ever had at NBC. He was fair and honest, as well as tough in his periodic negotiations with me and my agent.

John took me to lunch and tipped me—no doubt at the request of his superiors—that NBC was disturbed about one aspect of my work. With the earlier revision of my contract, to permit me to do commercials needed on the show, I had been freed to appear in commercial telecasts on other networks as well. I was handling commercial announcements for a number of major accounts—Pall Mall cigarettes, Crest, and American Motors, among others. It was lucrative work.

Now, John said, it upset NBC to see my face popping up on other networks. Moreover, it was felt that commercial work damaged my credibility and dignity as a newsman. John told me I could expect to be asked to choose between one career or the other—between handling the news on "Today" or working as a commercial announcer.

Giving up the commercials would mean losing a gross annual income in the neighborhood of $150,000 a year. But newscasting was my first love.

As always when I had to make a major decision, I talked it over with Lil, and as always she told me to do what I wanted and what I thought best.

What I wanted, of course, was to remain a newsman.

For a time in 1961, "Today" was not entirely a live show. The theory was that it would be more convenient for our guests to tape in the afternoon, and of course it would be easier for Dave and Jack and the rest of the crew. Only new newscasts remained live. That meant that the news segments had to be timed to the precise second. This was not especially difficult, either for me or the writers. Like most newscasters, I had been timing to the second almost since I got my first job in radio. Taping, however, did bring an especially ugly complication one morning, in circumstances that were shockingly tragic.

A few days later, when Carl Lindemann, a vice president of NBC, asked me to choose between news and commercials— "we just don't want our newsmen doing commercial work"— my answer was ready. I gave up nearly three thousand dollars a week to stay on as the "Today" newscaster.

It was barely six weeks later that the decision backfired on NBC.

Robert Kintner, who was then the NBC president, had chosen John Chancellor to replace Dave Garroway, and John had refused to handle commercials. That left the commercial work in the hands of Jack Lescoulie and Robin Bain, our "Today" girl. But then, on July 14, less than a month after John took over, Lescoulie left "Today" again. He resigned to costar in "1-2-3-Go," an educational program for children, and that left no one to do our live commercials.

After the taping on the afternoon of April 28, 1961, Dave took his son, David, who was then three years old, to his house on the beach at West Hampton, Long Island, to spend the night. That was something he often did. He liked being alone with David and he loved to drive out and back in his Jaguar roadster. When he left on April 28, his wife, Pam, who was under treatment for a nervous disorder, remained behind in their home on East Sixty-third Street.

Very early the next morning, Pam telephoned her personal physician. She seemed unusually nervous. The doctor was worried. After their conversation, he called the Garroways' housekeeper and asked her to go to Pam's bedroom and confirm that she was all right.

The housekeeper found Pam dead in her bathroom. She had died of an overdose of barbiturates.

I heard the news that morning when I arrived at the studio, and I had to report it. Moreover, I had to explain to our viewers why they would be seeing Dave through the morning looking relaxed as ever, in spite of that appalling tragedy. The features of the show were on tape, and there was nothing we could do about it.

For several miserable days, Jack and I carried the show until Dave returned. He came back a changed man. All of us did what we could to comfort him. Bernie Florman, our property man, did much more than a little. Bernie assembled a crew of carpenters and painters. Then he redesigned the entire Garroway home. He moved walls, switched rooms, painted, and papered, hoping to make such drastic changes that Dave would no longer find the house a constant reminder of his deceased wife.

But early in June, with Pam dead only a month, Dave concluded that the spark was gone and he could no longer carry on in the manner that had made him one of the great stars of American television. He resigned and left us on June 16. In later years, he did try to make a comeback on TV, but he never quite carried it off. He became, at least to a degree, an embittered man. Years later, an interviewer quoted him as saying the networks were managed by right-wingers and that was why he, a liberal-minded man, was no longer welcome as a regular on television.

The "Today" show has always suffered from a mild case of schizophrenia. It has never been determined for sure whether it's a news program or an entertainment program. On one or two occasions the disease has gone into an acute phase, with one phase of the show's personality overwhelming the other. We suffered such a relapse during John Chancellor's reign as host, and it was so severe that the show nearly died. I was part of the cause.

The show's personality split has always been what has given the show its high ratings. We gave people what they wanted at an unearthly hour of the morning when wage earners were getting ready for work and harried housewives were getting their children off to school, when traveling men were killing time in motel rooms and when the sick and lonely were tuning in for the companionship of the host and a glimpse of the big world outside the familiar places where they were shut in. Few people want to be deluged with news or serious talk about the state of the nation at seven o'clock in the morning. A few minutes of that, for most people, is enough when they have just struggled out of bed and are facing the problems of the day. I think one of the reasons for the success of our news segments was the rigid time limit imposed. A newscast simply did not run beyond eight or nine minutes unless the news itself was transcendent. Among the majority of viewers, we maintained interest about as long as interest could be maintained. I think similar limits helped our feature segments. Few people will sit for an hour or two at the start of the day while a rock singer perforates the eardrums or an actress talks about life in Hollywood. A good mix of news, information, and entertainment is what made "Today" a fixture on the national scene. If ABC's "Good Morning, America" has begun creeping up on "Today" in the ratings battle, I think the reason is that it offered a somewhat better mix, with more emphasis on lighter, early-morning fare. Obviously, "Today's" mix was right during the Garroway days. We went wrong right after Dave left the show.

It fell to Robert Kintner to choose Dave's replacement. Bob was president of NBC. However, he was a journalist first. He had gotten his basic training on the *Wall Street Journal*. His first interest, I think, was news. When Garroway resigned he called on John Chancellor to take over. John was not a show-biz personality. At the time, he was an NBC foreign correspondent based in Moscow, covering the Kremlin in the Cold War. He was a newsman of unusual experience and erudition, a front-line correspondent with an impressive base of knowledge and wisdom. I thought Bob Kintner had made a superb choice.

The Sales Department insisted that sales would slump unless a male member of the cast, someone with a recognized name and a strong "Today" identity, could share the commercial duties. Much of "Today's" success had been attributed to the fact that the personalities themselves would tout a sponsor's product. There was something compelling about a Garroway or a Lescoulie suggesting that Alpo was the best food for dogs. Madison Avenue's conviction was that a member of the cast could outsell any unknown commercial announcer, even though the cast member's work might actually be inferior.

So Carl Lindemann, then VP in charge of "Today," called on me. Would I mind giving up the news and taking on a new role, replacing Lescoulie as second banana to Chancellor? Thus, no longer in the role of newsman, I would take on the commercials again.

My first reaction was one of anger. I had just given up a big fat income in order to accommodate NBC. Now I was being asked to give up the job I loved and go back to doing the work that NBC had demanded I give up.

I was about to tell Carl Lindemann to find himself a new boy when John Ghilain telephoned me again. He told me NBC was now prepared to make me a new offer, and he thought I should listen to the details.

John and I met with my agent, Leon Schinasi, on my boat, *The Patsy*, on a sunny July afternoon out in Stamford Harbor, and John spelled it out. I would have a sizable increase in base salary. In addition, I would have a fee for every commercial I did. And NBC would give me a full-time secretary. (I had been paying Lucille Casey, a "Today" secretary, fifty dollars a week to type my letters.) Moreover, I would have a private office—and a chauffeur-driven limousine to pick me up at Stamford every morning at four and drive me to 30 Rockefeller Plaza. I could continue on "Monitor" on NBC radio, and I could continue to do news-on-the-hour radio newscasts.

"But," I asked John, "what if I fail as second banana? What happens to me then? I'm not Jack Lescoulie, remember?"

John smiled. He had obviously come armed with all the answers.

"In the first place," he said, "you won't fail. But in any event, your contract will provide that if something goes wrong, you'll go back to the news."

Meanwhile, I would do the sports reports on "Today" and the weather forecasts, and I would handle some news-oriented interviews.

Edwin Newman joined us as "Today's" newscaster. He had had rich experience in America and abroad and he was one of the most versatile journalists I had ever known. He was as much at home covering a boxing match as a presidential news conference. He could review a Broadway musical and compose a brilliant essay. When Ed joined us, I thought we would be an unbeatable team. But it was that combination—Chancellor, Newman, and Blair—that very nearly put "Today" out of business.

We had some help from Robert "Shad" Northshield, our producer at that time, and a fine producer, too. Shad, also, was strongly news-oriented. He had worked with John on the Chicago *Sun-Times* before the two had joined NBC.

We were not aware of it, but we apparently began losing audience almost from the day our new three-man team took over. Our first interest was in the news. The lighter side of the program began to suffer. The old mix was lacking, and the old chemistry was gone. We simply were not quite right for an early-morning show. The ratings slipped, and advertisers began to complain. This was not the show they had bought into. Until that time it had been a program with show-biz personalities and a single newsman, and a lot of emphasis on fun and hijinks on the set. Now it was a program with three newsmen, and little of the lighter, show-biz aspects remained. John himself, I suspected, was not entirely happy in the role that Kintner had thrust upon him. I think John feared he was losing his identity as a reporter. He was doing close-to-the-news interviews, of course, but he was not reporting the news himself. My own feelings were much like John's. I had always done some of the "show-biz" work that I was now doing almost exclusively—the horseplay between Lescoulie and me, however corny it may have seemed to some, had always been accepted among most viewers, according to our mail count, and accordingly I was somewhat more experienced and more relaxed than John in what was essentially a job away from the mainstream of the news. But even so, I missed doing the newscasts, and no doubt my own feelings about it all showed through. Whatever the case, a complex and potentially dangerous personnel and business situation was developing for "Today," and there were many interests in conflict with one another.

After a few months, Ed Newman was informed he was being taken off the show. When Ed left, John took over the newscasts while continuing to perform as the show's host. That removed one person from the equation. We were now two newsmen instead of three. But in another way it sharpened the image of "Today" as a strongly news-oriented program. The slip in the ratings continued.

In the end, the show had gone so far downhill that the NBC board of directors met to decide whether it should be taken off the air. We survived, but by only one vote. However, the pressure was on us for drastic change.

Al Morgan, the novelist, took over as "Today" producer early in 1962. Al had written several well-received books, including *The Great Man* and *The Whole World Is Watching*, both built around the communications industry, and he was an able producer. In his first months the show was almost totally revamped.

First, we went back on the street, so to speak. A major factor in "Today's" early successes had been the crowds that gathered outside the big windows of the RCA Exhibition Hall every morning to watch. We had lost something important when, with the move into the NBC studio, the directors found themselves no longer able to cut to live "reaction" shots of spectators. Al put the show back on Forty-ninth

Street. He made a deal with the Florida Development Commission, which had a store-front location in the RCA Building. A complete studio was installed there, with permanent camera installations. Once again, the directors were able to show the crowds at the windows.

Second, with Morgan in command, Jack Lescoulie was brought back to the show, and I went back to the news desk. Jack's Fearless Forecast was reinstated as a weekly feature, and Jack and I resumed our on-air horseplay.

Then, in September, John stepped down as "Today" host.

Hugh Downs took over. Hugh came to us with a record of successes in both radio and TV. He had been a radio disc jockey, an announcer, newscaster, narrator, interviewer, and comedian's straight man. He had grown up on NBC's radio station WMAQ in Chicago and had come to New York to appear with Arlene Francis on the "Home Show." Later he became Jack Paar's announcer and foil on "Tonight" and also the host of NBC's highest-rated daytime program, "Concentration." Hugh was a man with a great range of interests. He read a lot and appeared to enjoy everything. He was a skin diver, a hi-fi fan, and an amateur astronomer. He built his own hi-fi equipment and his own telescope. He took flying lessons and earned a pilot's license. He rode motorcycles, and he leased a boat and sailed it to Tahiti, then wrote a book about the trip, which he called A *Shoal of Stars*.

He was a remarkable man with remarkable self-discipline. He had one or two strange little habits that appeared intended to exercise and strengthen his own will power. He refused anesthesia when he went to the dentist, and although he liked to smoke, he permitted himself to light up only when he was outside the United States. Years before, he had made a resolution that he would never smoke in his own country. On the air, he was a gentle human being. He talked

with and not *to* his interviewees, and he handled interviews
with grace and good manners. He had a peculiar knack for
making run-of-the-mill things seem interesting.

With Hugh aboard and the show looking and sounding
lighter and more relaxed, the ratings began climbing again,
and once again we were out of the woods. However, although
we did not know it, we were nurturing the seeds of our own
destruction.

I was only vaguely aware of the strains and tensions that
were building up on the show during the early Downs-Mor-
gan years. Too many nice things were happening to me. One
of those nice things, incidentally, was Lois Moran.

When Garroway and Lescoulie and I had had a minute or
two to fill on the show before a commercial, we played
"whatever happened to . . ." I had done my bit by asking
an idle little question intended to get a conversation started.

"Whatever happened to Lois Moran?" I asked.

Who?

I mentioned that Lois Moran had been the love of my
youth—the movie star of the early 1930s whose very presence
on the screen had induced me to hire out as a theater usher so
I could see and hear her and dream of knowing her.

It was only a quick moment on the show—but one morning
twelve years later, when I walked into my office, my secretary,
Helen Aratani, handed me a note reading:

"Call Lois Moran, Harvard Club. Important."

I asked Helen if it was the *real* Lois Moran.

"Who is Lois Moran?" Helen asked.

"Never mind," I said. "I'll find out. Get her on the phone,
please."

A moment or two later, Helen announced:

"Miss Moran on the line."

I picked up the telephone wondering if this were some kind of a gag.

"Is this *the* Lois Moran?"

"Well, I don't know about that, but my husband and I are in New York and I just wanted to call and thank you for remembering me on the 'Today' show some years back. I thought I'd let you know what did happen to Lois Moran."

Suddenly I was eager to meet the movie actress of my boyhood dreams.

"What are you doing for lunch?" I asked.

"Just a minute."

I heard her ask her husband.

"Is it all right, dear, if I have lunch with Frank Blair?"

I could hear his reply from off in the distance.

"Sure, I'll be busy. I think it would be nice."

Lois returned to me on the phone.

"Fine," she said. "Where'll we meet?"

"I'll pick you up at twelve at the Harvard Club. We can go to a place close by."

"Good, see you then."

I was all atwitter, like a kid on a first date.

I called Lil and told her what had happened and asked if she thought it would be all right.

"Fine," Lil said. "I think it would be great. Wish I could be there to see you."

"Cut it out," I said. "No teasing now. I'm nervous enough."

"Okay, have fun. See you when you get home."

We met in the lobby of the Harvard Club. I recognized her as soon as she entered, an attractive woman in her late forties.

"The same," I thought, as I went toward her.

"Frank?" she inquired, smiling.

"Yes, I'm Frank and you've got to be Lois."

"Yes, I'm Lois Moran, grown up and a lot older than the ingenue in the movies years ago."

"But still lovely," I said. "I've made reservations for us at The Cattleman just around the corner. We'll have lunch there if that's all right with you."

"Sure, anything you say."

We walked over to The Cattleman, a restaurant in the western frontier style, and went through the usual New York routine of standing in line to be seated. Fortunately, the *maître d'* recognized me.

"Your table is ready, Mr. Blair," he said.

I hoped "my date" was impressed. I slipped him a five-dollar bill.

We were ushered to the second floor, where there were individual dining rooms. We were separated from the outside world by a beaded, half-curtained doorway. I hadn't asked for it, but that five-dollar contribution to the *maître d'* had paid off. We had privacy.

When the waiter came I ordered a vodka martini on the rocks. Lois said she'd have the same. Beautiful, I thought, we like the same drinks.

We had a couple of martinis and we talked. I told her how much I had admired her, how I'd gotten a job as an usher in a theater just to see her more often.

She was flattered. She said she didn't know she had such loyal fans. She told me she had stayed in the movies only a few years and then had married. Her husband was a top executive with Pan American World Airways. They were happy.

Lois was amazed that I was the father of eight children. I showed her a few family pictures. (I just happened to have them with me.)

We had lunch and then a few more drinks and sat there

talking, until four o'clock in the afternoon, when, reluctantly, I think, we decided we had to leave.

We walked the block or so to the Harvard Club, arm in arm. I left her at the door and caught the next train for Stamford. Fortunately, there was a bar car on the train. I went directly to it, and before the conductor announced, "Stamford—next stop," I had had two more martinis and relived every moment of my rendezvous with Lois Moran.

When I got home Lil asked, "Have a good time with your old girlfriend?"

"Delightful," I replied, "and she isn't that old!"

That night while I was sleeping, Lil nudged me.

"Huh?"

"You're talking in your sleep again."

"Oh? What did I say?"

"You were saying something about, 'Two, right this way. Follow my flashlight, please! Two seats right on the aisle.'"

"Yes, I know. Sorry if I disturbed you. Good night."

I rolled over and, as I was dozing off, Lois Moran was suddenly there again on the silver screen, smiling back at me.

One of the great, exciting things that happened to me during the Morgan-Downs era was the chance to take part in the first commercial television program to be telecast live from Europe. We made communications history but, believe me, as it looked from behind the scenes, that show was not so much a milestone in television as an exercise in things zany.

The Early Bird communications satellite had been launched from Cape Kennedy on April 6, 1965. It was arranged that "Today" would make the first use of it on May 3 for a live commercial program to originate from London, Paris, Rome, and Amsterdam—all during the same two-hour period.

It was an incredibly complex undertaking. There were language barriers to overcome, a communications network to set up, studios to be organized and checked out, and a switching center to be manned at the headquarters of the European Broadcasting Union in Brussels.

Barbara Walters, who by now was doing on-camera reporting, was assigned to handle the Paris origination. Jack Lescoulie would come on the air from Amsterdam, the late Aline Saarinen from Rome, and Hugh and I from London, the anchor point. My role would be the newscasts, the weather in Europe and the United States, and the sports news. As a gesture to the British, I would include the cricket scores. American newsfilm would be inserted from New York. It gave me a thrill simply to think I would be sitting in the BBC studios in London and cuing film from New York with the words, "for more on that we switch to New York." Paul Cunningham, as associate producer, was in charge.

In the planning stage, one seemingly insurmountable problem developed. We wanted to open the program with a short message from Pope Paul at the Vatican. Then we wanted to switch to Buckingham Palace for live coverage of the changing of the guard. But the changing-of-the-guard ceremony would begin precisely at noon London time, or seven New York time, which was just when we would be coming on the air with the papal message. It would not do to switch to the Palace with the changing of the guard already in progress. That would not be good television.

Paul and Al Morgan pleaded with the Palace and the Foreign Office to effect a one-time-only change in the schedule. Al wanted the guardsmen's ceremony to begin two minutes late. But to the British that was unthinkable. Starting the ceremony precisely at noon was part of a hallowed British tradition. A change in that revered schedule should be made merely to accommodate an American television show? Really, ol' boy! The only answer we could get was an adamant "No." The British would not bend—not even by thirty seconds—and that, we were told, was final.

Then, by a strange quirk, Al met one of Her Majesty's guardsmen on the night before the big broadcast. Specifically, this chance encounter took place at the bar of a London pub. The guardsman had heard that the ceremony would be televised live to the United States. He was overwhelmed by the prospect. He had an aunt in Omaha, and she would be watching to see her nephew perform. She, too, the guardsman said, was utterly thrilled.

"Sorry," Al said, "but she won't be seeing you."

The guardsman was deflated.

Al shook his head sadly and went on:

"We're not going to do the changing of the guard."

He explained the problem. The timing would be wrong.

The guardsman stood there in silence for a moment, sipping his gin and orange juice with a contemplative look on his face. Then he smiled.

"Tell me," he said, "at precisely what time would you want the ceremony to start?"

"At two minutes and ten seconds after the hour."

"Keep it in, mate! Keep it in!"

He assured Al he could arrange everything.

At precisely noon the next day, London time (7 A.M. New York time), the NBC peacock flashed on the television screens all across America, and moments later Pope Paul appeared—and, back in Brussels, our chief director, Marvin Einhorn, shouted over the land lines to Rome what has got to be one of the classic lines in television history:

"Cue the Pope!" he said. "Cue the Pope!"

As the Pope began reading his message to America we saw

a strange event taking place on our closed-circuit TV monitors from Buckingham Palace, from the camera that Marvin would switch to when the Pope finished. There in front of the palace, Al Morgan's friend the guardsman committed an unpardonable sin just at the moment the changing ceremony was to begin. He dropped his rifle.

It took his superior officer approximately two minutes to chew him out, which he did, as we sat there, watching.

Then, when the Pope finished, we switched to the camera trained on Buckingham Palace. By now it was two minutes and ten seconds past the hour—and it was at the precise moment of the switch that the delayed changing-of-the-guard ceremony finally began. It was superb television.

There was another memorable moment in that historic telecast when we switched to Barbara Walters, who was with Yves Montand on a balcony overlooking Paris. We saw Barbara and Yves all right, but the French technicians had not opened their microphones.

"*Ouvrez le microphone!*" Marvin shouted from the control room atop the Palace of Justice in Brussels. "*Ouvrez le microphone* and *keep* the goddam *microphone* open!"

Yes, television is a nervous-making industry, and a live television show is particularly nervous making in the early-morning hours when so many people—producers, talent, technicians—are likely to be more prone to error. In the matter of nerves, I think I was luckier than many others. In a sense I had grown up on the air. A live microphone had been a part of my daily life since my teen years in Charleston. Television no longer held any terrors for me, not because of any great and admirable qualities on my part. I had long ago developed the self-confidence to deal with almost any situation that might arise when we were on the air. I am sure the tension was there inside me, and I am sure tension was one of the reasons why I reached so often for my martinis and bloody marys, but somehow I managed to keep control of myself and hide my irritations in my relationships with other people. I had also learned something about the art of survival in the television jungle. The trick, I thought, was to understand the other fellow's position and be willing to compromise on almost anything except a principle. There is an old saying in television—maybe it's heard in other industries, too: "Take your money and smile on the way to the bank." That's what we used to say to people who were upset about small and inconsequential things. The meaning, of course, was that salaries were good and life wasn't too bad and quarrels about petty things were not really worthwhile. That's all very easy to say, but for people who bear the enormous responsibility of producing a multimillion-dollar television show—ten hours of live television every week—and for people who have to be in front of the cameras and perform, it was an axiom that was not easy to follow year in and year out. Personality clashes on "Today" were almost inevitable. I think it was a personality clash, perhaps involving Al Morgan, that led to Jack Lescoulie's dénouement as a member of the "Today" cast.

The show was in the Virgin Islands. I was not there. I had stayed in New York to insert live newscasts into the segment taped in the Caribbean. The crew had finished taping, and the weekend was coming up. Jack wanted to stop in Puerto Rico on the way home, but he had run out of ready cash. That was not particularly unusual, but what followed, I felt, was most unusual. I heard about it in detail when all concerned returned to New York.

Jack asked our unit manager, Tom Sternberg, for a three-hundred-dollar cash advance.

It's one of the jobs of a unit manager to control the money. Sternberg, who was not overly popular with his coworkers, was known on the show as a man who counted pennies.

He told Lescoulie there was no money available for him.

What followed, in that suite in Blue Beard's Hotel on St. Thomas, was a first-class brouhaha.

"Get some money if you don't have it!" Jack said.

"I can't."

"What?"

Jack's voice was rising along with his temper. As everyone on the show knew, a unit manager rarely ran out of cash, and if he did, he could always cable for it.

As Jack stared at Sternberg in disbelief, Sternberg turned to a show editor, Leonard Leddington.

"Leonard," he said, reaching into his pocket and pulling out a thick roll of bills, "how much of an advance was it that you wanted? I can let you have a couple of hundred."

Jack stalked out of the room.

He tracked down Morgan and laid down an ultimatum:

He (Jack) would be back in New York and ready to go on the show the following Monday morning. But if Sternberg was on the set—if Sternberg was still assigned to "Today"—he (Jack) would walk out.

Morgan nodded.

The cast and crew flew home over the weekend. On Monday morning Jack walked into the studio at his usual time, six in the morning. And Sternberg was there.

Jack turned around and walked out.

He couldn't have known it, but he had made his final appearance on the "Today" show.

Morgan consulted with his superiors; a decision was reached to stand pat. Sternberg was not to be ousted, and apparently a further and more ominous decision was made, because when Jack Lescoulie's agent telephoned to try to resolve the issue, he got an unexpected reception.

He was told that Lescoulie, by stalking off the set, had

broken his contract, and NBC was not interested in renegotiation of any nature.

That ended Jack's "Today" career.

Next, tension developed between Al Morgan and Hugh Downs. I was appalled. I liked them both very much. But there was something between them, something more than a personality clash that would pass. Both kept themselves under control. The ill will between them was not highly visible. But we knew it was there, and I think it affected the morale of all of us, because both Al and Hugh were personally popular.

A story went the rounds: Hugh or his agent had gone to Bill McAndrew as president of NBC News and demanded that Al be replaced as the "Today" producer. As the story went, Bill replied:

"Don't tempt me, because if it comes to a choice between my producer and my talent—no way!"

But soon thereafter, Bill died. As I write that, I can feel the tears welling in my eyes. Bill was a man who helped to shape television and television news, but more than that, he was my dear friend. He died after slipping in his bathtub, suffering internal injuries. After his death his deputy, Reuven Frank, took over, and I am not sure that Reuven had quite the power in NBC that Bill had had.

With Reuven in the saddle, Hugh's contract came up for renewal, not only for the "Today" show, but also for the exceedingly prosperous daytime show "Concentration," of which he was still the host. Hugh's starring role on two highly successful shows gave him tremendous clout. Shortly after Hugh's contract-renewal negotiations were concluded, Al left as producer of "Today."

XXI

I THOUGHT STUART SCHULBERG was precisely the right man for the job in those changing times. With much of the country in revolt against the Vietnam War and with new values developing at every level of our society, Americans were focusing more and more on the news. Perhaps for the first time since the "Today" show's inception, the mood of the country was right for a more news-oriented program, although it would not do to liven the show too much. We were still catering to a sometimes harried early-morning audience with an essentially short attention span. But more emphasis on news seemed in order, and Stuart was a dedicated journalist. In addition, he was a talented filmmaker with a show-biz background. He had spent much of his childhood in Hollywood. His father, B. P. Schulberg, was president of Paramount Pictures in its early days. His mother, Ad Schulberg, was one of the country's best-known talent agents, representing a stable of top stars. Later she became a top-level literary agent. Stuart's brother was Budd Schulberg, the best-selling novelist. Theirs was a fascinating family of Jewish intellectuals. Stuart himself was a hard-drinking, hard-living man, short in stature, with hair that turned gray on his new job and a waistline that bulged. He had produced feature pictures in Hollywood and documentaries for the Marshall Plan organization in Europe, and before joining "Today" he had been an award-winning NBC News producer in Washington, handling among other things a weekly David Brinkley report. Stuart was a sports fan, and under his direction our sports coverage improved materially. Joe Garagiola—witty, personable, exuding an earthy charm—became a regular member of the cast, at Stuart's insistence.

In his own field, Stuart was as accomplished as his brother Budd, although Budd of course was better known. That was in the nature of things, and it was fodder for one of Joe Garagiola's funnier bits of horseplay.

Joe stood up in front of the rest of us at the show's twentieth-anniversary party. He waved a piece of paper in the air and said he had something to read to us all. His eyes twinkling, he claimed that what he would read was a telegram sent by Robert Sarnoff from his remote office as president of RCA, the NBC parent company.

"Congratulations. But who is this *Stuart* Schulberg? I had understood the job was going to Budd. Anyway, whoever he is, the show seems to be going all right."

One of Stuart's major moves as producer was to hire Bill Monroe as "Today's" Washington editor. Bill at the time was the NBC news director in Washington. When he took over, "Today" began getting a steady run of important news-making interviews with major figures in Congress and the Administration. Later Bill resigned to become moderator and executive producer of "Meet the Press."

Stuart also began giving Barbara Walters a somewhat larger role in the program, accelerating the trend started by Al Morgan. She handled more of our news-making interviews in the New York studio. Sometimes it appeared to me that she was edging out Hugh Downs. Hugh had bought a retirement home in Carefree, Arizona, and I know he was yearning to get out of the rat race. He had made his money, and the hours were beginning to get to him. If it concerned him that Barbara Walters seemed to be capturing more of the headlines, he never showed it.

Hugh finally stepped down in the fall of 1971, and Frank McGee was brought in to replace him. That was another move reflecting the show's growing commitment to serious journalism. Frank was a hard-hitting journalist who for years had covered the top of the news both as a reporter and as an anchorman. He would have a successful reign as "Today's" host, and through it all he would refuse to let himself be overwhelmed by Barbara, whose ambitions were visibly growing.

But in spite of it all, and in spite of an increasingly painful illness, Frank McGee kept Barbara in her place on the "Today" set. Her prestige was high and, as we later learned, she was already maneuvering for a further step up, but she had not yet achieved the status of "Today's" cohost. It was still Frank who opened each half hour of the program, except in unusual circumstances, and Frank made sure that Barbara remained in a secondary role. The show was his life.

I don't know what drove Frank, but something did, and it made him one of the greats of broadcast journalism. He lived his job. He had few other interests, apart from a few martinis in the evenings while he tried to relax. His work absorbed him and—who knows?—very possibly it was the job and the tension it generated that finally overcame him.

No one could have been more aware than he of the responsibility that falls to a newsman reporting to millions of people. Frank struggled endlessly for objectivity and fairness, and he had a fetish for accuracy in even the most minute detail. He would have a guilt feeling about misreporting the color of a man's eyes. His language had to be simple and precise, but I never heard him "talk down" to anyone, on camera or off. He hated pretense and he hated muddled thinking, and his intolerance of "journalese" was legendary. The writer who handed him a script with a cliché was in instant trouble. It was not uncommon to see Frank hurrying to a typewriter at six-thirty in the morning to rewrite an entire segment of the show.

Despite his all-consuming drive and dedication, he had unexpected touches of warmth—a red rose and a card, for example, for every woman in the "Today" office on St. Valentine's Day, or a spur-of-the-moment invitation to lunch and a martini for a writer who seemed momentarily depressed.

Frank fell ill early in 1973, and soon after his illness was diagnosed—it was cancer—he knew he was dying. But he carried on, and months passed before he told anyone on the show. I myself first began to worry about him only because of a small incident on the set.

Frank and Barbara and Joe broadcast from a desk that was on a raised platform. The platform was perhaps a foot above the floor level. When Frank finished the show one morning in the spring of 1974, he stepped to the edge of the platform and then stopped suddenly, grimacing. It was clear that he was in severe pain. He had to call to a stagehand to help him make the step down.

His absences from the show—the short-term absences lasting only a day or so while he was in the hospital for treatment—became more frequent, and all of us on the show felt growing concern.

What we did not realize, and Frank did, was that his medication was dangerously lowering his resistance to other disease.

On April 17, 1974, he went into a New York hospital for

more treatment, and while there he came down with a common cold.

That afternoon, from his hospital bed, he telephoned a friend on "Today" and for the first time his voice showed emotion and, finally, fear. His cold had turned to pneumonia.

"This is it," he said, and he sobbed just once. "I'm not going to make it this time. I'm not going to live through the night."

He died around five-thirty the next morning. We were told about it just before the clock turned seven to signal the start of the show. There were misty eyes in the studio, and for many of us there was a hard struggle for composure. One hard-bitten newsman made a feeble attempt at newsroom humor. His face was working when he said:

"Good man, Frank! He remembered to die on our time."

"On our time" was our way of saying that a news event had occurred at such a time that we would report it first, before the evening news programs. Frank's death was the lead story of my news report that morning.

Before he was buried there was a memorial meeting—it could hardly be called a service—for his family and NBC colleagues. It was held in a funeral home on upper Madison Avenue in New York. The auditorium was packed, and people stood in the aisles and outside the doors. A few of Frank's friends made speeches that were deliberately short and free of corn, free of the maudlin tone that Frank would have deplored.

Julian Goodman presided, not because he was at the top of NBC as chairman of the board, but because he and Frank had long been friends. When the last of the scheduled speeches had been made, Julian stood at the podium and looked out over the audience of mourners. His glance fell on

Frank's sixteen-year-old son, Mike, who was seated in a front row.

"What say, Mike?" he asked. "Want to say something?"

Young Mike got up slowly and made his way to the podium. When he spoke his voice shook. He spoke of his love and in so doing he uttered two sentences that I can never forget.

"I didn't know my father very well," he said. "He was always too busy."

Frank gave the job everything he had.

After Frank died, we went through a long list of potential replacements. A number of fine newsmen were brought in for short trial periods as guest hosts, in what amounted to on-air auditions. We tried such people as Tom Brokaw, Garrick Utley, Floyd Kalber, Ray Scherer, and Tom Snyder. Each had his strong points, but none was eager to do commercials, which remained an important part of the job. Finally, the nod went to another strong contender, Jim Hartz, the anchorman of the local evening-news program on NBC's flagship station in New York, WNBC. Jim had had ten years with the company as an anchorman and reporter. He had covered everything from the moon landings to Middle East wars. He agreed to do commercials. Jim felt, and I always had, that there was something artificial about the barrier dividing anchormen and commercial announcers.

When Jim joined us, he was more relaxed about the job than Frank McGee had been. Jim refused to let his work dominate his life. He had an adoring wife, three beautiful children, and a home life he loved. He enjoyed the job, but he had watched Frank McGee and others immerse themselves in journalism and leave themselves little time or energy for other things. He told his friends he would not make the same mistake.

Jim's boyish grin and his warm, friendly personality brought something fresh and new to the show. I liked his work. I thought his easygoing manner was just right for early-morning television. However, the brass was not in full accord. Dick Wald, as president of NBC News, once told him to sit up and show more drive when he was on the air, and stop sitting there in front of the cameras with his chin in his hand. Dick said he was too relaxed and not sufficiently aggressive. Jim answered that this was his style; he thought an interviewer should ask the questions and let the interviewee do the talking without interruptions. He refused to change. He was not an interviewer in the Barbara Walters style, nor was he willing to interrupt Barbara herself and take over the lead in any two-way exchange between them if doing so would suggest bad manners. In a sense, Jim was too much of a gentleman.

If Barbara was consciously competing with Jim, she was in a far stronger position than she had ever been before, because long before the death of Frank McGee, she and her agent had had a clause written into her contract specifying that, if Frank finally left the program for whatever reason, she would be elevated to the status of cohost. Thus, when Jim joined her, they alternated with each other—in accordance with the terms of a binding contract—in doing the show openings. If Jim opened the show at seven o'clock, Barbara would open it at eight. If Barbara introduced the program at seven-thirty, Jim would do so at eight-thirty. The arrangement was all but engraven in stone, and to violate it would mean to violate a contractual agreement. Furthermore, the interview assignments had to be fairly divided. Thus Barbara became the first woman cohost of the "Today" program, and her reputation took on even more luster. But some of us who knew her well wondered if even now her ambition was satisfied.

At about the time she achieved cohost status, Al Morgan brought out a new novel, and when I read it I thought he must have had a crystal ball. The cover of the book bore this blurb:

"She was glamorous and sexy, the queen of the morning show, but she wanted the spot at the top, to compete against Severeid and Cronkite as television's first . . . ANCHOR-WOMAN."

The cover of *Anchorwoman* bore an artist's sketch of a woman with a microphone in hand, and that woman bore an amazing resemblance to Barbara.

I didn't know much about Barbara when she first joined the show as a writer. She was another in the list of staffers who might come and go. However, in her early days on "Today," two things distinguished her: ambition, and her skill on the written assignment.

The title "writer" is really a misnomer on the "Today" staff. A writer on "Today" is really a producer. He or she produces a segment of the show, organizes and supervises filming and taping, oversees the film and tape editing, and with the help of talented people in the Scenic Arts Department of NBC decides what the set will look like, and with help from other artists organizes static visual material, such as still photographs, sketches and graphs, and writes the script. Copies go to the director, the associate directors, the audio engineer, the man who flashes still material on the screen. The on-air man or woman may deviate from the script, of course, although that may be impractical if it's a complicated production. The script itself will include the word cues that tell the director to roll film or call up other visual material. If it's an interview, the writer also writes questions. The on-air personality may substitute, of course, but if he or she is not thoroughly backgrounded in the subject to be discussed, the writer's questions will suffice.

Barbara was unusually skilled in each phase of the "Today" writer's job, and apart from her native talent and dedication, her personal background was helpful. As the daughter of Lou Walters, who operated New York's Latin Quarter, an entertainment restaurant featuring, as we used to say, booze and broads, she had grown up on the fringe of show business. She had done well at Sarah Lawrence College (some of her fellow students there later said she had few friends, tended to keep to herself, and sometimes appeared morose). After graduation she had gone from secretary in an ad agency to public relations and writing assignments for WRCA, WPIX, and WCBS in New York. At CBS she had been a writer for the "Morning" show when it was trying unsuccessfully to compete with "Today." Hers was the story of a young woman on the way up, and in her first months on "Today" it became clear to us all that she would not be content for long with a writer's job. She wanted much more.

Several months after she joined us, Shad Northshield, then the producer, sent her to Paris to cover the Dior and Maxime fashion shows. On her return, after she had edited her film and written her script, Shad asked her to go on camera and voice the script instead of Robin Bain, the "Today" woman of that time. I was assigned to introduce Barbara to the viewers and to interview her briefly at the close of her segment. She was to go on the air on August 29, 1961—her first on-air assignment.

But her ambition was stronger than her fear. An on-camera job was now clearly her goal and, in talking with her, I felt that very little would stand in her way, certainly not her own apprehension. I did what I could to reassure her. I told her I was confident she would do well.

In fact, she did. If her nervousness persisted after we went on the air, it was hidden well. Her hands were steady and there was no quake in her voice. She spoke with confidence. She had a slight lisp and she had some difficulty in pronouncing her r's, but she had stage presence. When the show was over I told Shad Northshield that if he ever needed a substitute "Today" hostess, he had one right there in our own shop.

Barbara wanted to move into that role, but her day hadn't come yet. She continued to get on-air assignments, but the assignments were well spaced.

A turning point in her career came when Mrs. Jacqueline Kennedy as First Lady made a trip to India in March of 1962. Barbara was assigned to cover the story, which was rich in color and human interest as well as political meaning, and she did the job very well.

Barbara was earning her success by virtue of hard work, long hours, and an unusual talent, and she was also the beneficiary of circumstances. In the first place, we were feeling the need for a real woman journalist. There were very few of them in electronic journalism in those times, and the regular " 'Today' girls"—as we called them before it became a sexist phrase—were show-biz people rather than newswomen. Barbara, on the other hand, was right there on our staff, not only as a woman, but also as a competent one. In September of 1964, she became a regular on the cast. She replaced Maureen O'Sullivan, the motion-picture actress, who had not been able to hack it in live television—a beautiful and charming woman who was at home making a movie but not geared for live shows.

By way of background, Barbara also benefited, I think, by

the rift between Al Morgan and Hugh Downs. As time passed, it seemed to the rest of us on the show, Al began giving Barbara more and more of the on-camera work. Hugh seemed complacent about that. He carried on in his easy, relaxed manner, always the nice guy, while Barbara put the tough, probing questions that often made headlines.

Years later, defending Barbara against the charge that she was pushy and overly aggressive, Al said:

"Barbara was just filling the vacuum created by Hugh Downs, who was the laziest man in television."

Hugh, Al said, rarely did his homework, while Barbara never approached an interview without study to get herself thoroughly grounded in the subject to be discussed.

However, there was still something less than total confidence at NBC in her ability to handle the really major interviews with top government people. I myself played a small role in the machinations that helped to eliminate that lack of confidence in the upper echelons of the network.

Soon after Hubert Humphrey took office as Vice President, Barbara lined up an interview with Mrs. Humphrey. It turned out to be an interesting interview, and after it was filmed, Barbara capitalized on the good will it created by asking for an interview with the Vice President himself. Perhaps unexpectedly, her bid was accepted.

Both Al Morgan and Don Meaney, who was then the vice president of NBC News responsible for "Today," felt that Barbara lacked the stature and experience to handle such an interview alone. They wanted to send Edwin Newman or a Washington-based correspondent along with her. My news editor, Leonard Leddington, heard about that and told me about it. He said that if an established, recognized correspondent went along, the interview would lose some of its impact. I shared his view. I felt that we would have something fresh and different if a bright young woman did the interview alone.

Leonard and I presented the argument to Morgan and Meaney and, although they were somewhat uneasy about it, we won our point. Barbara went to Washington alone. The interview went extremely well.

After that, there was less concern at NBC about giving Barbara major interview assignments of a serious nature.

It seemed to me, too, that her questions began to get tougher, and also more personal. Sometimes she asked the questions one would expect from a cheap, tabloid reporter.

When Maurice Chevalier appeared on "Today" at the age of seventy-four, she asked him about his sex life.

She asked Ingrid Bergman what it's like for great beauties to grow old.

To Truman Capote she put the question: "Were you made fun of as a child because you were different?"

Only rarely did her interviewees snap back at her.

However, when she asked novelist Laurence Durrell how he liked finding himself rich, he turned on her and asked sharply: "Have you been leafing through my checkbook?"

But if she was pointed and perhaps unduly personal with some interviewees, it seemed to me she was sugary with others, especially those in positions of power. She sometimes held back, refusing to put the hard questions.

"But she gets people who won't sit with a scowling Dan Rather or a very persistent John Chancellor," Stuart Schulberg once said. "I'd rather have seven tenths of an interview than none."

If her occasionally sugary approach contrasted with her often barbed questions, there were similar paradoxes in her relationships with the rest of us.

Barbara could be caustic with a clumsy film editor or a lazy writer, but at the same time she could be tender and gentle with "Today" people who were in trouble. When "Today" writer Doreen Chu fell ill while in Iran covering the twenty-five hundredth anniversary of the Persian monarchy, it was Barbara who helped nurse her back to health, while at the same time doing much of her work.

It was never commonly known, but during the last months of Frank McGee's life she and he would not speak to each other, except, of course, on camera.

"He was another one who couldn't stand for success for a woman," she was later quoted as saying.

That, I thought, was below the belt, because Frank never expressed to me or anyone else, to my knowledge, the nature of his feelings for Barbara. He never criticized her on camera.

In our last years together on the show I found myself alternately admiring her and disliking her techniques.

In my twenty-three years on "Today" I had met a lot of famous people—heads of state, prominent scientists and scholars, politicians, authors, celebrities from the show-business and sports worlds—but it was Barbara who really got to know them and who was successful in persuading the most prominent and controversial to appear on the program when others had failed.

When she made the switch from the "Today" program to ABC in 1976, to co-anchor the evening news with Harry Reasoner, I read with keen interest all the comments made, and all the criticisms that were heaped upon her. With many of the critical points I concurred—but some left me feeling just a bit outraged.

Walter Cronkite was quoted in *Newsweek* as saying that when he heard the news of Barbara's switch he experienced the sickening sensation that all efforts to hold TV news aloof from show business had failed.

Comments like that left me fuming. I wondered if Walter Cronkite really considered TV news totally free of a show-biz tinge. I wondered if Walter thought he did not change his own tone when he went from a serious news story to something light and funny, in order to communicate more effectively, and if he did not think that in so doing he was using a show-biz technique. I wondered if he really thought that television news is not shot through with show-biz techniques, most of which improve the quality of communicating, but some of which are adopted strictly for audience appeal. In editing film, wouldn't Walter or his staff automatically choose the most compelling scenes? In my opinion television, like radio, is in fact part show business, and there's no way to get away from it. It's the nature of the medium. No TV newsperson is going to appear on camera poorly dressed or with hair askew. When those beady little red lights come on, on the cameras, we all put our best foot forward.

Comments like Walter's conveyed the notion somehow that Barbara was not a TV journalist. Her grounding had been thorough, her writing abilities surely had been evident to all in her book *How to Talk with Practically Anybody About Practically Anything,* her questions—however controversial—had produced countless hard news stories, and her experiences had been rich. She had interviewed Presidents Johnson and Nixon, Secretary of State Henry Kissinger, Egyptian President Sadat, Israeli Prime Minister Golda Meir, Dean Rusk, Prince Philip of Britain . . . the list seems almost endless.

Whether Barbara has been abrasive and abusive and bordered on rudeness is another matter. Certainly I never liked to hear her interrupting guests in the middle of an answer, and I once said something to that effect in reply to a questioner after making a speech in Jacksonville, Florida. My reply, unhappily, was blown out of proportion. Barbara had said something very much along the same lines in "Herself" in answer to a question put to her by a columnist.

"I'm abrasive, aggressive, and ambitious," she said, "and for a woman this is considered unfeminine."

To another interviewer she said:

"I'm an aggressive interviewer, but that's the job I had to do."

Yes, Barbara did her job as she saw it.

XXII

I DON'T REALLY REMEMBER when I lost control of myself, nor can I find any underlying reason for my behavior. There was no excuse for it. I had a good job, had earned some respect for the work I was doing. I had no marital or family problems. I had just about everything a man could desire in this life. Nevertheless, I created misery for my family and friends and for myself.

Now that I've been able to correct the problem, I don't even like to look back on it, and certainly I don't like to have to write about it, but since we are being frank about things, it has to be told.

Somehow I was no longer a social drinker. I was compulsive. Maybe I'd been in the same job too long or the daily routine and upside-down schedule was getting to me, or maybe I was suffering from some inner anxiety over the news with crisis piled upon crisis that I had to report each morning, but whatever it was, the problem had persisted and escalated beyond my ability to grapple with it. I felt compelled to have that crutch, and each morning when nine o'clock rolled around and the show was over I'd go at once to Hurley's Bar to have bloody marys, or sometimes martinis, depending on the mood I was in. Some mornings I'd have breakfast there, but most mornings the thought of food was repulsive to me and I'd drink instead of eat.

I consoled myself with the thought that the major part of my work—broadcasting the news—was over, and, except for the daily office work I tried to put in each morning, I was free of responsibility.

Then walking the thirteen blocks home in the early afternoon I'd usually stop off at the English Grill in Rockefeller Center or the Barberry Room in the Berkshire Hotel for a few more belts. I'd always meet the same group of guys at the bars I frequented. I thought I was having a good time and unwinding. I didn't have sense enough to perceive what was really happening to me and what I was doing to my wife and family. I know Lil was concerned about me. She tried in vain to talk some sense into my head, but I could always invent some excuse for my actions.

Two or three times a week, at the request of the Sales Department, I would have to attend a luncheon for a "Today" client or advertising representatives. It's what we used to call "waltzing the sponsor around." On such occasions it was easy to justify the several martinis I'd consume.

I began to realize that I was addicted to the drug—alcohol —and that I'd have to do something about it if I were to survive. Occasionally I'd go to St. Patrick's Cathedral on my way home and pray for help, and usually on those days I'd go directly home and bypass the bars en route. I'd feel very proud of my achievement.

I tried giving up the hard stuff and switched to beer, but it wasn't too long before I invented some excuse to have a martini, and it started all over again. Why Lil tolerated me I don't know; I assume she felt sorry for me and hoped and prayed that I'd overcome my handicap, and it was a handicap.

I always felt lousy, and it seemed that the only thing that would make me feel better was to have a drink. When the alarm clock would go off each morning I felt like chucking the whole thing, just rolling over and going back to sleep, but I never did that, no matter how badly I felt.

I was compulsive in other ways, too; I felt compelled to get up and get dressed and get to the studios, even though there were days when I'd have been better off to have stayed in bed.

I don't know, for the life of me, why I couldn't see what was happening to me, and do something about it. There were enough signs I should have recognized. Even though I wasn't eating as I should have, I was gaining weight and began to look older than I should have for my age. When I'd look in the mirror while shaving in those early-morning hours what I saw was "The Picture of Dorian Gray."

I went through that torment for about four years, until one day I made a decision, the most important decision I'd guess I ever made in my life. I think the decision was partially made for me, but I like to take credit for it as I look back on it.

I decided that the only way to solve my problem, save my marriage, and retain the respect of my family and friends was to change my environment and create a whole new life. So I decided to bring it to a halt and get out of the syndrome I was caught up in, to leave the "Today" show and get out of New York and try to put my life together again, not only to save myself, but also to protect those I loved and who loved me.

I made it known that I planned to retire from the rat race, although retiring to a do-nothing existence was not what I had in mind. It's not easy to write an autobiography and to be honest about oneself. I've learned more about myself in writing these many pages than I would have in going through psychoanalysis.

In a way my decision to leave "Today" was made for me. To get down to essentials, the first move was made by NBC.

It was in November of 1974 that Stuart Schulberg told me Dick Wald wanted to have lunch with me at the Gloucester House on East Fiftieth Street that same day, if I was free. I told him I had no commitments and I would be there. I thought no more about it. I had no idea why the president of NBC News would want to see me.

Schulberg and Wald arrived together at the Gloucester House. I thought Schulberg's presence was unusual, and I began to wonder just what this was all about.

The conversation over lunch was cordial. We talked about many things, including the new ABC entry, "Good Morning, America."

Then Dick came to the point.

"You've been thinking about retiring from the show, I understand," he said.

"Yes," I said, "I've been giving it a lot of thought and about concluded I've gotten into a rut, and I've been considering striking out on my own. I've got a few ideas I'd like to try."

Stuart didn't say a word; in fact, he didn't say much during the entire meeting.

"We'd like you to make a decision. We feel that you're beginning to slow down."

There was an element of shock in what he had just said, and I replied:

"I don't agree with your assessment of my work, but I would agree that after twenty-three years the routine is getting to me."

"You don't have to make up your mind right this minute, but we would like to know your plans so that we can make some other arrangements," Dick said.

"I think I can give you my decision right now," I replied. "I've been thinking about it for some time and I think I'd like to throw in the sponge as far as the 'Today' show is concerned.

"Oh, there's one thing more," I said. "March 15 when my contract is up is about four months away, and I'm scheduled for my usual Christmas vacation. What do we do about that?"

"You should take it, you've earned it," Dick replied. He added, "That would be a good time to make the announcement of your leaving, if you agree. Do you want to do it or do you want us to announce it?"

"I'd prefer that NBC did it," I replied. "I think it will sound better that way."

"We're going to give you one helluva farewell party," Dick said.

"Thanks."

"I think it's well deserved," he said. "You've worked hard for it for a long time."

"Thanks."

We continued to talk and it was concluded that I would retire from the show on March 14, 1975.

Dick said, "Well, now that we've got that settled I think I'd like to have a bloody mary."

Stuart joined him, and I ordered a martini. Dick seemed like a man with a load off his mind. We finished our drinks, shook hands, and they headed back to the RCA Building and I headed in the opposite direction toward my apartment at 400 East Fifty-sixth Street. I felt lighter than air, as if a great weight had been lifted off my shoulders.

Lil was away visiting Theresa and her family in West Palm Beach. I telephoned her as soon as I got to our apartment and broke the news.

"I hope you know what you're doing," Lil said.

"Yes, I'm pretty sure, and I just know everything is going to work out fine. I feel very much relieved already. I think we can make a whole new life for ourselves, and I assure you you'll never regret it."

And as it turned out it was one of the best things I've ever done for my family and myself.

We left for vacation at our Florida condominium after I did the show on Friday, December 19, and the announcement that I was retiring was released to the press that morning. All the wire services carried the story, and just about every newspaper in the country carried it, as well as John Chancellor on "NBC Nightly News" and Walter Cronkite on "CBS Evening News."

When I was getting ready to write this book I talked it over at length with Lil, who I suppose knows more about me than anyone else in the world, including myself. I asked her if there was anything she would have changed during our long life together.

There was a long pause, and then Lil replied:

"I just wish you hadn't spent so much time in Hurley's and Toots Shor's. I wish you hadn't gotten caught up in that trap the way a lot of other people have. I don't see there's anything wrong in coming home and having a few cocktails or going out to a party, but when it comes to . . . when it takes possession of you to the point where you miss watching the children grow up and deny them the privilege of seeing you with the fine mind you have. You took it away for a number of years."

She paused again and I waited. Finally, Lil said:

"Those are days and years that can't be relived."

I stopped drinking a few weeks after I left the "Today" show. But when I begin to feel proud of myself, I think back to my lost hours at the bar in Hurley's or Toots Shor's—the hours that add up to years. Lost years. Then comes my struggle to rationalize. I survived. I played a deadly game there in Rockefeller Center, and the stakes were high. People around me came and went with the changing whims in the executive suites. Careers were made and broken with a nod or the stroke of a pen. But somehow I survived. I wish dearly that I had done more with my time, that I had made more effective use of the influence I had to create a better, more informative news program, but on the other hand, I did survive, and, whatever the pressures, I did not, for so much as a moment, relax in the effort to tell the truth, unvarnished and without bias.

I have to genuflect to the memory of Edward R. Murrow, who said:

"It's a great time to be alive."

Yes, indeed, and I'm happy that God allowed me to survive it.

My good friend Freddie Cole, brother of Nat Cole, appears here on Hilton Head Island several times each year, and whenever I walk into the club where he's playing and he sees me he sings one of my favorite songs: "Yesterday Is Gone Tomorrow!"

Isn't that true?

So Let's Be Frank About It!

That's enough about yesterday and "Today," and, as Lowell Thomas would say, "SO LONG UNTIL TOMORROW!"